The Critical Link 4

Benjamins Translation Library

The Benjamins Translation Library aims to stimulate research and training in translation and interpreting studies. The Library provides a forum for a variety of approaches (which may sometimes be conflicting) in a socio-cultural, historical, theoretical, applied and pedagogical context. The Library includes scholarly works, reference works, post-graduate text books and readers in the English language.

EST Subseries

The European Society for Translation Studies (EST) Subseries is a publication channel within the Library to optimize EST's function as a forum for the translation and interpreting research community. It promotes new trends in research, gives more visibility to young scholars' work, publicizes new research methods, makes available documents from EST, and reissues classical works in translation studies which do not exist in English or which are now out of print.

Volume 70

The Critical Link 4: Professionalisation of interpreting in the community
Edited by Cecilia Wadensjö, Birgitta Englund Dimitrova
and Anna-Lena Nilsson

The Critical Link 4

Professionalisation of interpreting
in the community

Selected papers from the 4th International Conference on
Interpreting in Legal, Health and Social Service Settings,
Stockholm, Sweden, 20-23 May 2004

Edited by

Cecilia Wadensjö

Linköping University

Birgitta Englund Dimitrova

Anna-Lena Nilsson

Stockholm University

John Benjamins Publishing Company

Amsterdam / Philadelphia

Library of Congress Cataloging-in-Publication Data

International Conference on Interpreting in Legal, Health and Social Service
        Settings (4th : 2004 : Stockholm, Sweden)
The critical link 4 : professionalisation of interpreting in the community :
selected papers from the 4th International Conference on Interpreting in Legal,
Health and Social Service Settings, Stockholm, Sweden, 20-23 May 2004 / edited
by Cecilia Wadensjö, Birgitta Englund Dimitrova and Anna-Lena Nilsson.
        p.   cm. (Benjamins Translation Library, ISSN 0929–7316 ; v. 70. EST
subseries)
        Includes bibliographical references and index.
        1. Translating and interpreting--Congresses. I. Wadensjö, Cecilia,
        1954- II. Englund Dimitrova, Birgitta, 1946- III. Nilsson, Anna-Lena. IV.
        Title.

        P306.I448 2004
418'.02--dc22   2007060743
ISBN 978 90 272 1678 6 (Hb; alk. paper)

John Benjamins Publishing Co. · P.O. Box 36224 · 1020 ME Amsterdam · The Netherlands
John Benjamins North America · P.O. Box 27519 · Philadelphia PA 19118-0519 · USA

Table of contents

Acknowledgments   IX

Foreword: Interpreting professions, professionalisation, and
professionalism   1
    Cecilia Wadensjö

Part I. Critical linking up

Critical linking up: Kinship and convergence in interpreting studies   11
    Franz Pöchhacker

Part II. Interpreters on duty in interaction: Studies of micro dynamics

The interpreter in multi-party medical encounters   27
    Amalia Amato

Interpreting in asylum hearings: Issues of saving face   39
    Sonja Pöllabauer

Conversational dynamics as an instructional resource in interpreter-
mediated technical settings   53
    Birgit Apfelbaum

A data driven analysis of telephone interpreting   65 𝗑
    Brett Allen Rosenberg

Part III. Interpreters in the community: Studies of macro dynamics

Interpreter-mediated police interviews: Working
as a professional team   79
    Isabelle A. Perez and Christine W. L. Wilson

Community interpreting in Poland   95
  Małgorzata Tryuk

Alternative futures for a National Institute of Translation: A case
study from Malaysia   107
  Roger T. Bell

The interpreter's 'third client': Interpreters, professionalism
and interpreting agencies   121
  Uldis Ozolins

Part IV. Developing local standards

The Swedish system of authorizing interpreters   135
  Leena Idh

Establishment, maintenance and development of a national register   139
  Ann Corsellis, Jan Cambridge, Nicky Glegg and Sarah Robson

From Aequitas to Aequalitas: Establishing standards in legal
interpreting and translation in the European Union   151
  *Erik Hertog, Ann Corsellis, Kirsten Wolch Rasmussen,
  Yolanda van den Bosch, Evert-Jan van der Vlis and
  Heleen Keijzer-Lambooy*

The California Standards for Healthcare Interpreters: Ethical principles,
protocols and guidance on roles and intervention   167
  *Claudia V. Angelelli, Niels Agger-Gupta, Carola E. Green and
  Linda Okahara*

Part V. Professional ideology: Food for thought

Professionalisation of interpreting *with* the community: Refining
the model   181
  Graham H. Turner

"Why bother?": Institutionalization, interpreter decisions,
and power relations   193
  Stephanie Jo Kent

The interpreter as advocate: Malaysian court interpreting
as a case in point   205
   Zubaidah Ibrahim

Professionalisation of interpreters: The case of mental health care   215
   Abdelhak Elghezouani

Professional stocks of interactional knowledge in the
interpreter's profession   227
   Satu Leinonen

Aristotelian ethics and modern professional interpreting   241
   Patrick Kermit

**Part VI. Improving and assessing professional skills: Training
initiatives and programmes**

Formative assessment: Using peer and self-assessment
in interpreter training   253
   Yvonne Fowler

Interpreter internship program: Forging employer-community
partnerships   263
   Sheila Johnston

On-line and between the lines: The internet and glossary production
for public service interpreters   273
   Jane Straker

Interpreter training from scratch   283
   Beppie van den Bogaerde

From helpers to professionals: Training of community
interpreters in Sweden   297
   Helge Niska

Index   311

Acknowledgments

Critical Link was founded in 1992 in Canada, as a network with the aim of organizing the first international conference on community interpreting. This conference was held at Geneva Park, Toronto, Canada, in 1995, and the proceedings were published in Carr, Roberts, Dufour and Steyn (1997). It was followed by another two international conferences, which also took place in Canada: in 1998 in Vancouver, with the theme "Standards and Ethics in Community Interpreting: Recent Developments", and in 2001 in Montreal, with the theme "Interpreting in the Community: the Complexity of the Profession". The proceedings of those conferences were published in Roberts, Carr, Abraham and Dufour (2000) and Brunette, Bastin, Hemlin and Clarke (2003), respectively.

After the three conferences in Canada, it was decided to "go overseas" for the next event, and Stockholm, Sweden, was selected as host for the fourth conference, which took place in May 2004. We took on the challenge with great enthusiasm and are proud to present another selection of papers produced within the Critical Link framework. Our choice of theme was "Professionalisation of Interpreting in the Community", a timely issue in the young profession that is community interpreting.

The Stockholm conference and the editing of the proceedings were made possible by generous grants from: The Granholm foundation, Stockholm University; Linköping University; The Stockholm-Uppsala Research Program "Translation and Interpreting – a Meeting between Languages and Cultures", funded by the Bank of Sweden Tercentenary Foundation; The Swedish Research Council; The Institute for Interpretation and Translation Studies, Stockholm University; The Department of Linguistics, Stockholm University; The Memorial foundation of Marcus and Amalia Wallenberg; The City of Stockholm. We gratefully acknowledge their support.

Stockholm and Linköping in September 2006
Birgitta Englund Dimitrova,   *Cecilia Wadensjö*
Anna-Lena Nilsson   Linköping University
Stockholm University

References

Brunette, L., Bastin, G., Hemlin, I. & Clarke, H. (eds.). 2003. *The Critical Link 3: Interpreters in the Community. Selected papers from the Third International Conference on Interpreting in Legal, Health and Social Service Settings, Montréal, Canada, 22–26 May, 2001.* Amsterdam/Philadelphia: Benjamins.

Carr, S., Roberts, R., Dufour, A. & Steyn, D. (eds.). 1997. *The Critical Link: Interpreters in the Community. Papers from the first international conference on interpreting in legal, health, and social service settings (Geneva Park, Canada, June 1–4, 1995).* Amsterdam/Philadelphia: Benjamins.

Roberts, R., Carr, S., Abraham, D. & Dufour, A. (eds.). 2000. *The Critical Link 2: Interpreters in the Community. Selected papers from the Second International Conference on Interpreting in legal, health and social service settings, Vancouver, BC, Canada, 19–23 May, 1998.* Amsterdam/Philadelphia: Benjamins.

Foreword

Interpreting professions, professionalisation, and professionalism

Cecilia Wadensjö

The Critical Link conference, from the very beginning at Geneva Park, Canada, in 1995, was meant to signify both the interpreter as a critical link between people not sharing a common language, and the conference itself, as a critical meeting point for people working with interpreting in the community. As the exchange of ideas is carried further, new kinds of links are developing. The series of Critical Link publications is one of these. The present volume is a selection of papers presented at the fourth Critical Link conference, at Stockholm University, Sweden, in 2004. The overall theme of this conference was "professionalisation of interpreting in the community", meaning interpreting performed in legal, health and social service settings.

What does it mean to be professional?

Being professional can mean a variety of different things. In everyday language, professionalism might signify shared feelings of pride and responsibility for the everyday activities performed in and by working teams. Also, when referring to workers of various trades, people tend to evaluate their skills, knowledge, efficiency, precision etc., by praising their professionalism – 'These people are real 'pros'!'

In everyday talk, professionalism is an attractive concept, and most of the time it is positive to be viewed as a professional. An exception would be when it comes to sports, where amateurism traditionally is (or at least was) estimated higher than professionalism. Amateurism as related to interpreting can mean both 'not-for-payment' performed interpreting services and interpreting providers having no professional training for the task. This can still characterise communication in institutional settings, which the organisers of the Critical Link conferences like to think of as a shared and professional field, where people have to deal with a certain problem but do not share a language in which this can be achieved. However, as could be seen, for instance in the corpus of work selected from these conferences, things have changed in this respect in many countries. Quite obviously, people working with interpreting in various spheres of society and various parts of the world are now involved in a process of professionalisation. This implies a range of individual and collective efforts, including struggles to achieve a certain social status, suggestions to define standards of best practice, to control access to professional knowledge – theoretical models and practical skills – and to control education and work opportunities.

Researchers have performed studies of the social base of professionalism, as well as the role of professionalisation in the overall development of society, using various analytical tools and points of departure. For instance, in Parson's (1964) classical definition, a professional (in contrast to a non-professional) has three characteristics: (1) emotional neutrality – all the professional's clients are treated equally ("universalism"), (2) the professional's services are provided for the collective good and are restricted to the factual task ("functional specificity") and (3) the individual gains professionalism through personal training ("achieved competence") and not through heritage. Included in Parsons' definition of professionalism is also an idea of the importance of ethical norms for the maintenance of proper conduct. His definition fits quite well with the role of interpreter, one would think, as it is broadly understood among all categories of interpreters, and those they work with.

Parson's and other 'essentialist' approaches, establishing criteria to distinguish professionals from non-professionals, dominated studies of professionalisation from the 1930s to the 1970s. However, the approach was criticised, for instance by Magali Sarfatti-Larsson (1977), who instead took as a point of departure that professionalisation processes were part of struggles between conflicting interests of groups and societies. The focus on the very process of professionalisation became a new orientation, dominating from the 1970s and onwards. Central issues dealt with in this field of research are, for instance, the role of theory for the development of a profession, the relation between a profession and the (welfare) state, and professionalisation and higher education. Some researchers use the development of professions to highlight social change more generally, whereas others focus specifically on processes of institutionalisation and on institutional order.

The orderliness that can be observed within institutions differs, tied as it is to the specific ideologies and rationalities each institution develops. As reported in the edited volume *Talk, Work and Institutional Order* (Sarangi & Roberts 1999), there is a long tradition in discourse-based sociolinguistic and sociological studies of professional communication, focusing on ideological processes at work in various institutional settings and on micro-level interaction in workplaces. In the present volume, there are some such studies represented. However, the volume's theoretical and methodological scope involves much more than discourse studies.

Indeed, the field of interpreting is partly developed in and by ongoing conflicts, not only concerning what defines professionalism, but also about issues of control over resources and social status. Conflicts of interest can be traced between various groups of interpreters, between interpreters and the professionals they assist, between interpreters and lay people, as well as between interpreters and the institutions in which they work. As Davidson (2000) states in his study of medical interpreting in a U.S. hospital, the interpreter is often placed low in the internal professional hierarchy, if placed at all. Davidson's investigation is based on data collected in 1996. Both the practice and the academic field of interpreting have undergone changes since then, some of which the present volume will bear witness to.

The multitude of more or less overlapping synonyms such as community, community-based, liaison, public service, sign-language, court, conference and dialogue interpreting, can partly be explained by conflicting ways of conceptualising and thinking of the activity, about the actors involved and their status in terms of professionalism. As will be seen in the volume at hand, the terminology is no more standardised than it was before. However, I am inclined to think that this is not a problem. Partly, this variety reflects practical and theoretical traditions in different countries and communities. Bringing together people representing these, the book provides a platform for understanding others' views of what is acknowledged as a shared field of interest. This can in itself be seen as an achievement. Also, different terms to signify various types of interpreting are motivated by the need to technically define them, in order to establish them as objects of research. With the expansion of Translation studies generally – something that indeed must be regarded as a positive development – the number of sub-areas will probably grow, and with this the number of empirical sub-fields and also the need for specialised terminologies.

The themes of this book

The present volume sheds light on the professionalisation of interpreters, working in distinctive institutional environments, from a variety of angles. The book is organised into six sections, based on thematic, theoretical and methodological considerations. Interpreting studies – no less than Translation studies generally – is interdisciplinary in character (cf. Snell-Hornby 1988; Toury 1995; Pöch-hacker 2004). The articles represent a spectrum of approaches, from fine-grained linguistic analyses of talk and social space, to wider accounts of overarching social order and reflections on ideological issues. The book draws attention to regulations and issues of control, from within interpreters' professional associations and from within national and international organizations. The introductory chapter – placed in a section of its own – thematises the variety of paradigms represented in the field of Interpreting studies.

Part I. Critical linking up

Franz Pöchhacker, who delivered the first keynote lecture at the Stockholm conference, also introduces the volume. Looking for kinship and convergence in the recently emerged discipline of Interpreting studies, he reflects on the potentials of current research on community based interpreting. Relating community interpreting to the wider field of Translation studies he also discusses the role of research on interpreting in the process of interpreters' professionalisation.

Part II. Interpreters on duty in interaction: Studies of micro dynamics

The second part comprises four contributions, dealing with the micro dynamics of interpreter-mediated interaction. Looking at naturally occurring interpreter-mediated encounters, the authors show that interpreters on duty – more or less professionally trained – play out a variety of professional identities.

Amalia Amato, using data collected in an Italian rehabilitation institute, investigates the interpreters' share of all talk in multi-party encounters, and how it relates to the respective primary participants' discourse. The picture that emerges from her study is that the interpreters tended, first and foremost, to be oriented towards pleasing the doctor. Moreover, at times they seemed to be privileging their own rapport with the doctor, before the conversational link between the doctor and the primary participants', a child patient and his or her two parents. *Sonja Pöllabauer* observes, in her transcripts of asylum hearings recorded in Austria, a similar orientation of the interpreter towards the person in charge, in this case, the asylum officer. Showing how this occurs in interaction, she particularly focuses on the complexities of face saving in this kind of interpreter-mediated, institutional encounters. *Birgit Apfelbaum* uses samples from a videotaped, German-French technical interpreter training session and analyses how setting-specific tasks such as negotiating technical terms are interactionally achieved. She also provides arguments for why, in interpreter training, focusing on the task of managing discourse can improve role performance in real life interpreting.

Telephone interpreting is a growing area business wise. In the literature, however, it has hardly been attended to at all. The varied image of this activity drawn in *Brett Allen Rosenberg*'s contribution to the volume, based on his own experience as professional interpreter in the U.S.A., should be useful for further studies of this empirical field.

Part III. Interpreting in the community: Studies of macro dynamics

Part three includes four articles adopting macro sociological perspectives, dealing with matters of control and organisation of interpreting services in society. The paper by *Isabelle Perez* and *Christine Wilson* reports on the authors' long experience in training Scottish police officers in working with and through interpreters. Pointing at initial problems and opposing expectations, they suggest how these can be overcome. In conclusion, Perez and Wilson propose an extensive Guide to Interpreting for professionalising the integration of interpreting into police settings and activities, emphasising the need of mutual understanding and respect between interpreters and police officers for their respective requirements and obligations. *Malgorzata Tryuk*'s article speaks about the emergence of an interpreting profession and with that a new professional identity of interpreters in Poland. It reports on a questionnaire study, conducted among sworn translators, active as interpreters in a variety of Polish institutions. *Roger Bell* describes the current, formal, regulating status of the Malaysia National Institute of Translation and discusses its prospected future(s). *Uldis Ozolins* sheds light on how aspects of professionalism are connected to the organisation of interpreting agencies, using the development in Australia as a case in point. His paper links to several issues brought up in the fourth section.

Part IV. Developing local standards

In Sweden, state authorization of interpreters was introduced in 1976. Section four starts with *Leena Idh*'s brief outlining of how the Swedish state-financed system is organised. The certifying body, The Swedish Legal, Financial and Administrative Services Agency, publishes lists of currently accredited interpreters. (Authorization is valid for five years and then has to be renewed.) These lists are available to the public, but not in the same elaborate way as the system described in the second contribution of Part IV, written by *Ann Corsellis, Jan Cambridge, Nicky Glegg* and *Sarah Robson*. Their paper explains how a UK National Register was developed, established and is now maintained. The National Register of

Public Service Interpreters (NRPSI Ltd) is a not-for-profit organisation, owned subsidiary of the Institute of Linguists in London.

An important purpose of national registers is to make accredited interpreter skills more easily accessible countrywide. National certifying bodies also fill a function when it comes to setting national professional standards. The third contribution to this section reports on three projects, arranged for the purpose of establishing multi-national standards, more precisely European standards in legal interpreting and translation practices. Two of the projects were financed by a EU partnership programme named after Hugo Grotius (groundbreaking natural rights theorist of the late 16th and early 17th centuries). The third one, designed as a follow up, is funded by another partnership programme – Agis. Dealing with legal interpreting and translation as a specific and integrated activity, the report introduces a 'new' category – the professional sub-group of legal interpreters and translators (LITs). The contribution is co-authored by *Erik Hertog, Ann Corsellis, Kirsten Wolch Rasmussen, Yolanda van den Bosch, Evert-Jan van der Vlis* and *Heleen Keijzer-Lambooy,* each representing a EU member state, more precisely Belgium, the United Kingdom, Denmark, Spain, the Netherlands and the Czech Republic.

The fourth section concludes with a collaborative effort targeting standards in medical interpreting specifically. *Claudia Angelelli, Niels Agger-Gupta, Carola Green* and *Linda Okahara* present the California Standards for Healthcare Interpreters and describe the process of development and validation of these professional principles, which have been in use since 2002. The authors represent The California Healthcare Interpreting Association (CHIA), a membership-based non-profit organisation established in 1998, including interpreters, trainers, managers, clinicians, administrators, researchers and university faculty.

Part V. Professional ideology: Food for thought

The fifth section consists of six papers discussing professionalism and professionalisation of interpreting from ideological and philosophical standpoints. In the first contribution, *Graham Turner*, building on his own and others' previous research, outlines a model of interpreting as collaborative activity between practicing interpreters and those using their services. This involves refining and explaining the notion of 'a cycle of empowerment'.

Coming next is U.S. based *Stephanie Jo Kent, who* problematizes interpreters' impartiality, using her experience from interpreting between American Sign Language and English. The principle of impartiality is also focused on in *Zubaidah Ibrahim*'s paper, drawing on the current Malaysian justice situation. *Abdelhak*

Elghezouani draws on his professional experience from bilingual mental health care and suggests linking interpreters' professional status to their involvement in and qualification for this particular institutional setting. *Satu Leinonen* scrutinises the code of professional ethics for court interpreters in Finland, raising questions about what it specifies and what is left open to further specification when it comes to defining the constitution of interpreters' professional knowledge. In the last paper of section five, *Patrick Kermit* investigates how Aristotelian reasoning can help sort out the question of interpreters' impartiality and other key issues in current debates about interpreters' professionalism.

Part VI. Improving and assessing professional skills: Training initiatives and programmes

The single topic that figured by far most frequently in the abstracts at the Stockholm Critical Link conference was interpreter training. This also became a major theme in the final programme, and it surfaces in many papers not specifically focusing on teaching and schooling. Arguably, education is the main path through which people achieve specialist knowledge and hence can claim professional authority.

If previous sections make inquiries about the nature of professional identity and professional skills, the last one rather takes for granted that there is (or should be) a shared view on these points and suggests ways for individual (candidate) interpreters to assess and improve professional knowledge. In the introductory article, *Yvonne Fowler* shares her experiences of educational practice in the UK, more precisely of peer assessment, self-assessment and evaluation, and their significance in interpreter training. *Sheila Johnston* of the Canadian Hearing Society describes the initial outcome of a pilot internship programme for student interpreters, also placing emphasis on self-analysis. Building upon her experience in teaching terminology courses for interpreters and translators, *Jane Straker* gives advice about how to work with glossary production using the Internet. *Beppie van den Bogaerde*, in her contribution gives a concrete example of how to build up a Bachelor Programme in Interpreting. The languages in this case were two – Dutch and *Nederlandes Gebarentaal* (NGT), the sign language commonly used in the Netherlands, but the demands and challenges inbuilt in the task are hardly unique. In many countries there is a shortage of interpreters with certain language combinations and educators may be forced to accept students with low proficiency in one of the working languages. *Helge Niska*, finally, briefly describes the Swedish community interpreting scene. In the professionalisation process, *training* of interpreters and *training* of interpreter trainers has played and plays a key role.

In conclusion

In conclusion, as Bowen *et al.* (1995) have shown through numerous examples, interpreters of the past, working for states, missionaries, colonisers and explorers "served not only as witnesses but as participants in the unfolding of history" (*ibid.* 245). Reasonably, interpreters of today, also those working in more everyday, community-based settings, have had and will have a certain impact in the making of modern history. The role of these interpreters, and the significance of their professional qualification, for instance in processes of segregation, integration and assimilation, largely remain unexplored. Nevertheless, little by little, a shared body of knowledge about interpreters and about professionalism in interpreting is building up. This volume is meant to be a contribution to this process.

References

Davidson, B. 2000. The interpreter as institutional gatekeeper: The social-linguistic role of interpreters in Spanish-English medical discourse, in *Journal of Sociolinguistics* 4/3, 2000, 379–405.

Bowen, M., Bowen, D., Kaufmann, F., & I. Kurz 1995. Interpreters and the making of history, in Delisle, J. & Woodsworth, J. (eds.) *Translators through History.* Amsterdam/Philadelphia: John Benjamins, UNESCO Publishing, 245–273.

Parsons, T. 1964. Professions, in *International Encyclopaedia of the Social Sciences,* No 12.

Pöchhacker, F. 2004. *Introducing Interpreting Studies.* London/New York: Routledge.

Sarangi, S. & Roberts, C. 1999. (eds.) *Talk, Work and Institutional Order – Discourse in Medical, Mediation and Management Settings.* Berlin/New York: Mouton de Gruyter.

Sarfatti-Larsson, M. 1977. *The Rise of Professionalism: A sociological analysis.* Berkeley: University of California Press.

Snell-Hornby, M. 1988. *Translation studies: An integrated Approach,* Amsterdam/Philadelphia: John Benjamins.

Toury, G. 1995. *Descriptive Translation Studies – and Beyond.* Amsterdam/Philadelphia: John Benjamins.

PART I

Critical linking up

Critical linking up

Kinship and convergence in interpreting studies

Franz Pöchhacker
University of Vienna, Austria

This paper broadly reflects on the identity and status of community-based interpreting as a field of practice and academic study. With a focus on research and its role in the process of professionalization, it explores the kinship among the various domains of interpreting from a historical, conceptual and socio-academic point of view. Based on a review of the recently emerged discipline of interpreting studies in terms of different paradigms, an analysis of common ground and interrelations is undertaken for interpreting studies as part of the wider field of translation studies and for community interpreting as such. The picture that emerges from this analysis shows the dialogic interactionist approach developed mainly for research on community interpreting as a distinct paradigm which offers great potential for a synergistic relationship with other theoretical and methodological approaches in interpreting studies.

Introduction

In an effort to situate community interpreting as a field of practice and research within the domain of interpreting studies, I would like to explore the idea of 'linking up' in several dimensions, including professional pathways, models, and paradigms. My underlying assumption is clearly that the evolution of a profession implies systematic reflection and academic pursuit, so that 'profession' and 'research' are complementary ('linked up'), and a paper focusing on research should be relevant to the theme of professionalization.

Another basic assumption here is that interpreting is a form of translation, in the wider sense, and that interpreting studies as a discipline, though open to a variety of interdisciplinary approaches, has a place in the broader field of translation studies. The kinship between the two will not be dealt with here for lack of space; an extensive discussion can be found in Schäffner (2004).

More fundamental to my argument than the conceptual relation between 'interpreting' and 'translation' are the distinctions applied to the concept of interpreting as such. Throughout most of history, interpreting was simply interpreting, with little need for subcategorization. In the twentieth century, however, when consecutive interpreting with notes and simultaneous interpreting from a booth became prominent, the distinction was generally made with reference to the temporal mode of realization, i.e. consecutive versus simultaneous interpreting. The setting – international organizations and conferences – was a given, and not an issue. With the emergence of new settings and professional domains since the late twentieth century, the traditional mode-based distinction has become less effective, and I suggest that the more relevant criterion may be the social sphere of interaction in which interpreting takes place. In other words, interpreting would be distinguished mainly by institutional settings, to foreground, for instance, healthcare interpreting, legal interpreting, media interpreting or, to revive an old term, parliamentary interpreting.

More generally, I have proposed a view of interpreting as a conceptual continuum, with two broad distinctions: first, between inter-national and intra-social, or 'community-based' settings; and, second, with regard to the format of interaction – prototypically, multilateral conferencing vs. face-to-face dialogue. Drawing on these two conceptual dimensions allows for much middle ground, including conference-like events in the community (especially involving Deaf people) or dialogue interpreting in diplomacy, hence the overlap of the two ellipses in Figure 1.

There are of course many other relevant criteria by which to characterize this bipolar distinction, the more important ones being interactant role (institutional representative vs. individual) and power relations. A more delicate distinction is that between more versus less professional forms of interpreting. Clearly,

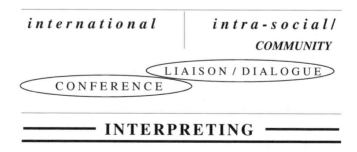

Figure 1. Conceptual spectrum of interpreting

what is considered professional or not depends on specific social, political and economic realities; while these are vital issues that we have to contend with, the point is that the label 'professional' is not necessarily tied to a particular area on the conceptual spectrum. Descriptively, of course, we can say that professionalization, however defined, is not as far advanced in one domain of interpreting as in another. We normally hear this with reference to community-based interpreting vis-à-vis simultaneous interpreting at international conferences. That is why I would like to cite an example from history, which points to a 450-year heritage of professional interpreting in the community.

Professional pathways

A key component in the process of professionalization are legal provisions governing the exercise of a task. In sixteenth-century Spain, such regulation by supreme authority was in fact applied consistently to interpreters involved in the Spanish Crown's administration of its American colonies. The compilation of colonial legislation (*Recopilación* 1791) includes a total of fourteen laws regulating the work of the interpreters needed for legal and administrative dealings with the indigenous population. This legislation, in the form of ordinances by Governors and laws of the King of Spain, provides, inter alia,

– that the interpreters for the Indian language(s) shall have the necessary capacities and qualities and shall be paid from the funds of the Court;
– that the interpreters shall not accept or ask for presents or gifts of any sort from the Indians or any other party;
– that the interpreters shall not hold private meetings with Indian clients;
– that the interpreters shall not act as advocates for the Indians;
– that interpreters sent to an assignment away from their domicile shall receive a per diem.

These provisions relate to important aspects of professional ethics; but it is even more striking to read what Governor Antonio de Mendoza, the Viceroy and Governor of 'New Spain' had stipulated in the early sixteenth century for the interpreters' standards of performance: Interpreters had to be duly sworn to perform their task 'well and faithfully', expressing the matter before them 'clearly and frankly', 'without hiding or adding anything', 'without acting in favor of any of the parties', and 'without deriving any profit from their task other than the pay due to them' (cf. Mendoza 1548: xxxi).

Without doubt, both international conference interpreters, who pioneered their code of ethics in the 1950s, and sign language interpreters in the US, who drafted theirs in the 1960s, can look with pride to these precedents of regulation in the interest of their clients and of the profession. The fact is, however, that the sixteenth-century provisions were developed, though not by the interpreters themselves, expressly for interpreting in the community, which thus boasts some deep professional roots. While my concept of interpreting does not permit me to say that community interpreting is "the oldest 'type' of interpreting in the world" (Roberts 1997:7), the example of the old Spanish codes, however problematic for their context of colonial power and domination, shows that interpreters in the community have an impressive ancestry.

For most of the twentieth century, of course, the professionalization of interpreting happened in the sphere of international organizations and conferences. Sign language interpreting in the US and community-based spoken-language interpreting in immigration countries such as Australia, Sweden and the UK made considerable strides in the 1970s, but the various domains were clearly moving along separate pathways, with hardly an intersection in sight. The most remarkable exception was the 1977 NATO Symposium in Venice (Gerver & Sinaiko 1978), which featured international conference as well as sign language interpreting, with at least some reference to liaison interpreting and interactional issues like role and power.

It was only in the course of the 1980s that interpreters in different domains began to take greater notice of one another. Several meetings and publications (e.g. Longley 1984; McIntire 1984) reflect considerable involvement by members of the conference interpreting community in initiatives for the professionalization, and especially training, of interpreters in community-based settings. Such involvement may seem obvious, and probably was, but it also has some obvious limits. Training methods for skills such as note-taking and sight translation, which are well-established for would-be conference interpreters, would seem useful for community interpreters as well, to the extent that interpreting is viewed mainly as a language-based processing task. However, the more we foreground the institutional and behavioral aspects of mediated interaction, the greater the likelihood that expertise in conference interpreting will prove insufficient for the actual training needs of interpreters in the community. This raises a fundamental question in our search for kinship, namely, to what extent is there shared ground in the way we conceive of interpreting? Is there a common model that can underpin our approach(es) to training as well as research?

Models

Defining a 'model' as a 'way of seeing', a way of representing a phenomenon by identifying its component parts and the relations holding among them, there seems indeed to be a consensus that interpreting can best be modeled as consisting of three parts – as a tripartite and often a 'triangular' structure. This would suggest an impressive degree of agreement. However, there is a fundamental difference regarding the nature of the three components. This results from two different ways of thinking about interpreting – as a mental process or as a social process of interaction. In the former case, the triangle reflects the major cognitive processing stages; in the latter it represents the three main parties involved in the interaction. With processing stages and interaction roles as the respective focal points, we can thus speak of a duality of tripartite models: processing models on the one hand, and interaction models on the other. The most famous example of a triangular processing model of interpreting is undoubtedly the one by Seleskovitch, developed further by such authors as García-Landa (1981) and Laplace (1994); an original version of the tripartite interaction model is probably Anderson's (1976) type-case model of the three-party constellation, a particularly detailed elaboration of which is offered by Bélanger (2003).

These different ways of seeing and modelling the phenomenon go some way toward explaining the existence of more than a single research tradition in interpreting studies. But a shared model is only part of the common ground required in a research community. A set of basic assumptions, values and standard methods also need to be shared by the members of a scientific community for there to be what Thomas Kuhn (1962) defined as a 'paradigm' – a 'worldview' which shapes a researcher's way of 'doing science'. In what follows, I would like to use the notion of paradigm for a brief sketch of some five decades of research on interpreting, aiming to show the emergence and convergence of various strands.

Paradigms

With a few interesting exceptions, research on interpreting began in the 1960s, when psychologists took an interest in the spectacular skill of simultaneous interpreting. Working within their own paradigm(s), they studied interpreting, by way of experiments, as a form of language processing rather than as a professional service. The latter aspect was more prominent in the writings of conference interpreters, chief among them Danica Seleskovitch. As early as 1962, Seleskovitch published an article in which she described the professional activity of conference interpreting and also offered a tentative explanation of the underlying cognitive process – her famous three-stage model based on language-independent 'sense' (Seleskovitch 1962: 16). At around the same time, Otto Kade (1963), in what was then East Germany, published a paper on note-taking in consecutive interpreting in which he hypothesized six processing stages, including the processing of conceptual content. Both Kade and Seleskovitch published a significant monograph in 1968; and yet, there was no 'linking up' between these French and (East) German pioneers. On the contrary, Kade's association with the so-called Leipzig School of Translation Studies, which set the study of translation and interpreting in the disciplinary framework of linguistics and searched for equivalence relations between language systems, proved as divisive as the physical barrier of the Iron Curtain. To Seleskovitch, linguistic transfer rules – as implemented at the time for machine translation – were diametrically opposed to her idea of interpreting as a process of making sense based on the interpreter's knowledge of the world and of the situational context of interaction.

It was this focus on the authentic context of interaction that made Seleskovitch equally skeptical of psychological experiments on interpreting in the laboratory, as epitomized at the time by Henri Barik's (1969) pioneering PhD research. While it is true that Barik's study suffered from serious problems of experimental design, the work of his fellow psychologist David Gerver (1971) clearly demonstrated that useful insights were to be gained for the professional practice of interpreting from controlled experimenting. In his 1971 PhD thesis, Gerver defined interpreting as "a fairly complex form of human information processing involving the reception, storage, transformation, and transmission of verbal information" (Gerver 1971: viii). This idea of interpreting as a complex information processing skill encountered a favorable environment in the 1970s, when the interdiscipline of cognitive science emerged as a promising new super-paradigm for the study of language processing and other cognitive functions. Nevertheless, for the time being, the study of interpreting remained in the hands of professional conference interpreters, led by Seleskovitch, who managed to launch a doctoral studies program at the University of Paris in 1974. In this habitat flourished a unique paradigm, based on Seleskovitch's 'interpretive theory' (IT) and on the observation of authentic professional performance rather than experiments in a laboratory. The 'IT paradigm' of the so-called Paris School worked as a paradigm would: for more than a decade, it was the dominant theoretical and methodological approach to the study – and teaching – of conference interpreting.

In the early 1980s, however, a group of conference interpreters, including Daniel Gile, Jennifer Mackintosh, Barbara Moser-Mercer and Catherine Stenzl, called for a more (self-)critical, scientifically oriented approach to research. The 1986 Symposium at the University of Trieste (Gran & Dodds 1989) turned into a milestone event at which the 'new breed' openly questioned the certainties of the Paris School and called for a revival of empirical, and often experimental, research in cooperation with other disciplines. With a focus on interpreting as cognitive processing (CP) in the tradition of Gerver, the 'CP paradigm' proved open to interdisciplinary approaches from the broad domains of psychology and, to a lesser extent, linguistics. More specifically, cognitive neuropsychology served as a framework for studying the lateralization of linguistic functions in the brain, giving rise to a neurolinguistic (NL) paradigm of interpreting research (e.g. Fabbro et al. 1990).

On the other hand, the process-oriented conception of text linguistics, as developed in particular by Robert de Beaugrande (1980) based on advances in cognitive science, helped direct attention to the interpreter's textual product. The idea of interpreting as text production was shared by a group of translation scholars who, in the course of the 1980s, (re-)conceptualized translation (and interpreting) as a 'purposeful' activity, aimed not at the 'equivalent reproduction' of a source text but at producing a 'target text' designed to fulfil its function in the target-cultural environment. Translation, on this account, was not a linguistic transfer but a process straddling two cultural systems which required the active mediation of meaning to suit target-cultural needs. Spearheaded by Hans Vermeer at the University of Heidelberg, the German functionalist theory of translation, or skopos theory, proved largely compatible with the decidedly descriptive approach to the target-oriented study of translation as promoted in particular by Gideon Toury (1995). Although neither version of the target-text-oriented translation-theoretical (TT) approach has gained a high profile in interpreting research, the studies that have been carried out (e.g. Shlesinger 1989; Pöchhacker 1994) seem distinct enough to warrant the identification of a 'TT paradigm' of interpreting research.

This sketch of the evolution of research paradigms – IT, CP, NL and TT – brings us up to the mid-1990s. And yet, viewed from a Critical Link perspective, all of this could be brushed aside as 'pre-historical', as predating the full emergence of community interpreting on the international scene at the first Critical Link conference in 1995 (Carr et al. 1997). There, innovative approaches to the study of interpreting as interaction came to fruition within a newly emerging community of professionals. Most consequentially, Cecilia Wadensjö's (1998) view of interpreting as managing discourse in a triadic relationship, with a focus on interactivity rather than monologic text production, shaped a new paradigm. Centered on dialogic discourse and interaction (DI), this 'DI paradigm' drew mainly on concepts and methods from such fields as sociolinguistics, conversation analysis and social psychology. As evident from the important contribution of sign language interpreting researchers such as Cynthia Roy (2000), the DI paradigm proved well suited to spoken- as well as signed-language interpreting. Indeed, it is one of the strengths of the Critical Link community that it links up the concerns of community-based interpreters in either modality.

While there is no room here for a more detailed discussion (see Pöchhacker 2004, Ch. 4), Figure 2 offers an intuitive visualization to characterize the position of the various paradigms in the disciplinary space extending between the realm of professional practice and training, on the one hand, and established scientific disciplines, on the other. The original IT paradigm is shown mainly in the realm of professional practice and training. Extending from it with more scientific aspirations is the CP paradigm, with the NL paradigm as its most specialized scientific outgrowth. The TT paradigm is depicted at the base, rather autonomously from established scientific disciplines. Most importantly for the purpose of this discussion, the DI paradigm is shown as a link, both between the professional and scientific spheres, and between the CP and TT paradigms of the discipline. As indicated at either side of its elliptic shape, the DI paradigm is sourced from both professional practice and scientific disciplines, with some of its representatives, like Holly Mikkelson, coming from the profession and others, like Ian Mason, working from a disciplinary base in the language-related sciences.

The map of paradigms shown as Figure 2 suggests considerable overlap, and I would like to discuss in more detail what these areas of convergence in interpreting studies might be.

Convergence?

Over and above some basic conceptual and methodological common ground, there are many areas of shared concern for interpreting researchers across domains and paradigms. I will focus on a few broad areas of interface with regard to settings, modes and topics.

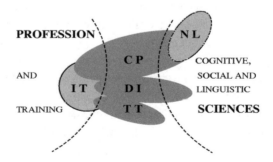

Figure 2. Cluster of paradigms in interpreting studies

Among interpreting **settings**, the courtroom has a central position in several ways. Whereas the formality of the proceedings and the use of specialized terminology make courtroom proceedings similar to a conference-like setting, the involvement of a defendant participating in the interaction on his/her own behalf, usually speaking a minority language, is a defining characteristic of community-based interpreting. Moreover, the use of simultaneous interpreting, if only in the whispering mode, is common (at least in some jurisdictions), thus making the courtroom interpreter's skills base comparable to that of the conference interpreter.

A similar point of interface among interpreting settings are the media, and recent literature includes fine illustrations of the fact that this territory is shared by simultaneous conference interpreters, signed-language interpreters and spoken-language dialogue interpreters alike. More obviously still, bilateral talks in the fields of diplomacy and trade have long been regarded as the professional turf of interpreters with high-level training in conference interpreting, even though such talks typically imply the format of face-to-face dialogue interpreting, presumably with a good portion of discourse management and mediation. There have been some gripping anecdotal accounts, but very little research, as this type of situation is highly delicate and thus very 'messy' to study in the field. Here, case studies of dialogue interpreting in no less delicate community-based settings could serve as a model for dialogue interpreting researchers in the international sphere.

Another central area of interface for research is the simultaneous **mode**, which has been predominant in the literature for decades. The fact that trained signed-language interpreters typically, though not exclusively, work in the simultaneous mode, and that spoken-language community interpreters also use this mode, e.g. for expert witness testimony in court or in therapeutic discourse, makes the simultaneous mode a significant shared concern rather than – as is sometimes claimed – a distinctive feature that sets international conference interpreting apart.

With regard to **topics**, finally, I would like to foreground three broader themes on which researchers from various domains might converge.

The first one, the role of 'psycho-social factors', was actually pointed out by none other than David Gerver, who followed up his definition of interpreting as a complex form of human information processing (quoted earlier) with the statement: "Furthermore, linguistic, motivational, situational, and a host of other factors cannot be ignored" (Gerver 1976:167). Speaking of "a host of other factors" clearly offers a lot of leeway, but even "motivational" and "situational" should be sufficient to make a strong case for a socio-linguistic orientation, in the broadest sense, which highlights the interacting parties' goals and intentions, backgrounds and relationships. This is highly compatible with Cecilia Wadensjö's

([1993]/2002: 368) "plea for a micro-sociological turn in studies of interpreting" and is no less germane to function- and norm-oriented translation-theoretical approaches.

Another theme of convergence is 'discourse', which is closely associated with a (broadly construed) socio-linguistic orientation. Historically, the work of Gumperz and Hymes (1972), for instance, can be shown to inform much of Vermeer's thinking on mediated interaction across cultures, and is of course central to the DI paradigm. The work of Hatim and Mason (1990) has successfully tapped the rich field of discourse for translation and interpreting studies, reaffirming approaches such as Beaugrande and Dressler's (1981) text linguistics and Hallidayan (1978) discourse grammar as valuable underpinnings.

Since the 1970s, the notion of discourse, and discourse studies, has undergone such a breathtaking expansion that it is now all-encompassing and synonymous with the study of language and communication (and much more). The fact that studying discourse may now mean anything from the assignment of anaphoric reference to the analysis of racist speeches can make the notion rather unwieldy; on the other hand, it is a welcome common denominator for the study of the 'cognitive processing of discourse' and 'discourse management in interaction', and can indeed serve to soften the distinction between the two.

This is precisely what is at the heart of the third theme of convergence, which we might label 'cognition in communication'. The key representative of this approach to the study of interpreting, which draws mainly on cognitive linguistics, speech act theory and relevance theory, is Robin Setton (1999). Setton's "cognitive-pragmatic analysis" complements basic tenets of the IT paradigm with a thorough application of linguistic frameworks in cognitive science, but his work is congenial with the DI paradigm as well. So far, Setton's empirical analyses have been based on transcriptions of monologic conference discourse and simultaneous interpretations, but his conceptual framework seems well suited also for dialogic discourse. Rather than quantifying textual features, Setton's interest lies in a qualitative second-by-second micro-analysis of communicative discourse processing, anchored in an input- as well as knowledge-driven mental representation. The interface with Wadensjö's "micro-sociological analysis" of discourse is rather evident, so the three themes of convergence in interpreting theory that I am suggesting here are closely interrelated.

In line with the tradition of triangular modeling, one could depict the three areas of convergence in a tripartite structure (Fig. 3).

These themes, I suggest, are likely to drive convergence in interpreting theory across the various paradigms of the discipline – if we accept the notion of distinct paradigms to begin with. After all, in Kuhn's (1962) original account, paradigms were conceived as mutually incompatible. Considering the growing acceptance

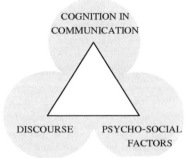

Figure 3. Themes of convergence

of multiple perspectives and methodological pluralism in our field, it seems reasonable to hope for a blurring of boundaries between paradigms, and thus for an increasingly coherent disciplinary space.

Conclusion

In conclusion, I hope to have shown that there are multiple manifestations of kinship in interpreting studies, and that dividing the field into separate paradigms purely on the basis of professional domains would not be helpful for interpreting research as a whole, as it would obscure productive links and interrelations. What I have called the DI paradigm, centered on the analysis of discourse in interaction, holds great potential as a sphere of convergence for various theoretical and methodological approaches and can indeed play a critical linking role in the evolution of interpreting studies as a discipline.

References

Anderson, R. B. W. 1976. "Perspectives on the role of interpreter." In *Translation: Applications and Research*, R. W. Brislin (ed.), 208–228. New York: Gardner Press.

Barik, H. C. 1969. *A Study of Simultaneous Interpretation*, doctoral dissertation, University of North Carolina, Chapel Hill.

Beaugrande, R. de. 1980. *Text, Discourse and Process*. London: Longman.

Beaugrande, R.-A. de & Dressler, W. U. 1981. *Introduction to Text Linguistics*, London: Longman.

Bélanger, D.-C. 2003. "Les différentes figures d'interaction en interprétation de dialogue." In *The Critical Link 3: Interpreters in the Community*, L. Brunette, G. Bastin, I. Hemlin & H. Clarke (eds), 51–66. Amsterdam/Philadelphia: John Benjamins.

Carr, S. E., Roberts, R., Dufour, A. & Steyn, D. (eds). 1997. *The Critical Link: Interpreters in the Community. Papers from the First International Conference on Interpreting in Legal, Health, and Social Service Settings (Geneva Park, Canada, June 1–4, 1995)*. Amsterdam/Philadelphia: John Benjamins.

Fabbro, F., Gran, L., Basso, G. & Bava, A. 1990. "Cerebral lateralization in simultaneous interpretation." *Brain and Language* 39: 69–89.

García-Landa, M. 1981. "La 'théorie du sens', théorie de la traduction et base de son enseignement." In *L'enseignement de l'interprétation et de la traduction: de la théorie à la pédagogie*, J. Delisle (ed.), 113–132. Ottawa: University of Ottawa Press.

Gerver, D. 1971. *Aspects of Simultaneous Interpretation and Human Information Processing*, D. Phil. thesis, Oxford University.

Gerver, D. 1976. "Empirical studies of simultaneous interpretation: A review and a model." In *Translation: Applications and Research*, R. W. Brislin (ed.), 165–207. New York: Gardner Press.

Gerver, D. & Sinaiko, H. W. (eds). 1978. *Language Interpretation and Communication. Proceedings of the NATO Symposium, Venice, Italy, September 26–October 1, 1977*. New York/London: Plenum Press.

Gran, L. & Dodds, J. (eds). 1989. *The Theoretical and Practical Aspects of Teaching Conference Interpretation*. Udine: Campanotto.

Gumperz, J. J. & Hymes, D. 1972. *Directions in Sociolinguistics*. New York: Holt, Rinehart and Winston.

Halliday, M. A. K. 1978. *Language as Social Semiotic*. London: Edward Arnold.

Hatim, B. & Mason, I. 1990. *Discourse and the Translator*. London: Longman.

Kade, O. 1963. "Der Dolmetschvorgang und die Notation." *Fremdsprachen* 7 (1): 12–20.

Kuhn, T. S. 1962. *The Structure of Scientific Revolutions*. Chicago: The University of Chicago Press.

Laplace, C. 1994. *Théorie du langage et théorie de la traduction. Les concepts-clefs de trois auteurs: Kade (Leipzig), Coseriu (Tübingen), Seleskovitch (Paris)*. Paris: Didier Érudition.

Longley, P. 1984. "What is a community interpreter?" *The Incorporated Linguist* 23 (3): 178–181.

McIntire, M. L. (ed.). 1984. *New Dialogues in Interpreter Education. Proceedings of the Fourth National Conference of Interpreter Trainers Convention*. Silver Spring, MD: RID Publications.

Mendoza, A. de. 1548. *Ordenanzas y copilación de leyes*. Mexico: Juan Pablos.

Pöchhacker, F. 1994. *Simultandolmetschen als komplexes Handeln*. Tübingen: Gunter Narr.

Pöchhacker, F. 2004. *Introducing Interpreting Studies*. London/New York: Routledge.

Recopilación. 1791. *Recopilación de Leyes de los Reynos de las Indias (…)*, Tomo Primero. Quarta Impresión. Madrid: Viuda de Joaquín Ibarra.

Roberts, R. P. 1997. "Community interpreting today and tomorrow." In *The Critical Link: Interpreters in the Community*, S. E. Carr, R. Roberts, A. Dufour & D. Steyn (eds), 7–26. Amsterdam/Philadelphia: John Benjamins.

Roy, C. B. 2000. *Interpreting as a Discourse Process*. Oxford: Oxford University Press.

Schäffner, C. (ed.). 2004. *Translation Research and Interpreting Research: Traditions, Gaps and Synergies*. Clevedon: Multilingual Matters.

Seleskovitch, D. 1962. "L'interprétation de conférence." *Babel* 8 (1): 13–18.

Setton, R. 1999. *Simultaneous Interpretation: A Cognitive-Pragmatic Analysis*. Amsterdam/Philadelphia: John Benjamins.

Shlesinger, M. 1989. *Simultaneous Interpretation as a Factor in Effecting Shifts in the Position of Texts on the Oral-Literate Continuum*, MA thesis, Tel Aviv University.

Toury, G. 1995. *Descriptive Translation Studies and Beyond*. Amsterdam/Philadelphia: John Benjamins.

Wadensjö, C. [1993]/2002. "The double role of a dialogue interpreter." In *The Interpreting Studies Reader*, F. Pöchhacker & M. Shlesinger (eds), 355–370. London/New York: Routledge.

Wadensjö, C. 1998. *Interpreting as Interaction*. London/New York: Longman.

PART II

Interpreters on duty in interaction

Studies of micro dynamics

The interpreter in multi-party medical encounters

Amalia Amato
University of Bologna, Italy

This paper presents the analysis of three interpreter-mediated medical en-counters. The aim of this study is to see whether the interpreter prioritises one participant or one conversational axis when working in a multi-party encoun-ter and whether a common participation model is adopted by the interpreters at work. The two categories of zero renditions and non-renditions as defined by Wadensjö (1998) were used to gain an insight about what the interpreters choose not to render and what conversational initiatives are autonomously undertaken by the interpreters. The main findings of this analysis are briefly discussed and illustrated by examples.

Introduction

Interpreters are not simply animators (Goffman 1981) – they do not merely re-peat in another language every single utterance by each participant. On the one hand they may not translate something said by a primary participant, thereby controlling access to the floor or the mutual power of primary participants. On the other hand they may undertake conversational initiatives and play the role of turn-taking coordinators (Roy 2000, Wadensjö 1998), mediators of divergence (Fogazzaro & Gavioli 2004), and primary participants speaking for themselves (Straniero Sergio 1999). This study looks at interaction in multi-party medical en-counters in order to see whether the interpreter's use of these strategies prioritises one participant or one conversational axis. It thus focuses on what the interpreter chooses to render and produce upon his/her own initiative rather than on how the primary participants' utterances are rendered in the other language.

The data presented comes from three encounters lasting from 14 to 30 min-utes each, for a total of about one hour and ten minutes overall. These encounters were held at a rehabilitation institute for brain-injured children in Italy where Italian and American doctors work together to rehabilitate French, German and

Italian children and communicate with patients and their families through an interpreter. The encounters are analysed for zero renditions, "originals that are left untranslated" (Wadensjö 1998: 108) to see whether or not the interpreter privileges particular participants' contributions, and for non-renditions (utterances produced by the interpreter on his/her autonomous initiative Wadensjö 1998: 108) to see whether a common participation model is adopted by interpreters in terms of behaviour/attitude towards primary participants.

Data

The three encounters presented here are part of a larger set (about four hours) which were videotaped and transcribed according to conversational analysis conventions (Sacks, Schegloff & Jefferson 1974/1978).[1] They were selected as the object of this study because they have certain situational and conversational features in common.

All three encounters are re-visits to check the appropriateness of the dietary and drug regime followed by the patient. The number and type of participants are the same in each: an Italian child and his/her Italian parents, an American doctor, and an interpreter. The same doctor is present in each encounter, but the interpreter is different. All the participants know the rehabilitation programme well, either because they have worked with the institute before (this is the case of the doctor and the interpreters) or because they have been following the rehabilitation programme for some time (the patients and their parents). All the primary participants have had previous experience of communicating through an interpreter in similar interactions, and the child's parents and the interpreter are familiar with the medical jargon used by the doctor. The encounters all take place in the same office and use the same languages – English and Italian. In each encounter the mother, with the help of the interpreter, fills in a form listing the drugs and diet regime to be followed.

All three encounters contain a great deal of overlapping talk, with extensive monolingual turn sequences between the interpreter and the doctor or the interpreter and one or both parents (as also found in the encounters analysed by Davidson 2002).

---

1.   Transcription conventions used in the examples: (.) less than one second; [ ] simultaneous or overlapping talk; ? questioning intonation (rising tone) = latching; e: or e::: lengthened vowel sound; (1) one-second pause (a different number indicates the duration of the silent pause); / abandoned utterance; **boldface** emphasis or loudness; °   ° uttered quietly or as an aside; xxx inaudibile.

The interpreters are all female: one has a degree in translation and the other two have certificates from a post-secondary education school of conference interpreting.[2] All have worked for this institute before and one of them (active in encounter 1) is a full time in-house interpreter and an American native speaker. The other two are free-lance interpreters, Italian native speakers and appear in encounters 2 and 3.

A quantitative analysis of the encounters

The three encounters will be briefly presented in terms of number of turns, amount of overlapping talk and amount of parallel conversations. A turn is treated as a stretch of talk by a speaker (whether a primary participant or the interpreter) beginning where s/he starts talking and finishing where s/he leaves the floor to another speaker: they may include pauses and may partially or totally overlap with other turns. Parallel conversations are exchanges between two or more speakers that occur simultaneously on different floors.

As shown in Table 1, encounter 1 is the shortest of the three. The primary participant who produces most turns is the doctor, while the distribution of turns by the mother and the father is almost equal, suggesting that neither one dominates the scene. This is confirmed by a close observation of the encounter, where there are no verbal or non-verbal signs of disagreement between the parents. The difference between the total number of turns by primary participants and by the interpreter is quite small. (This does not mean that this interpreter translates all that was said by the primary participants: this interpreter volunteered a large number of autonomous turns, as the analysis of non-renditions in the section on non-renditions below shows).

Encounter 2 (Table 1) is twice as long as encounter 1, with a great deal of overlapping talk. The mother is the most "productive" speaker, followed by the doctor, while the father plays a less active role and the child, who has a language difficulty, makes no verbal contribution. Unlike encounter 1 the mother and father disagree at times, expressing different views when answering questions asked by the doctor. The number of the interpreter's turns is much smaller than the total of primary participants' turns, suggesting that the latter were often not translated. In fact this encounter contains many direct exchanges between the doctor and the mother,

---

2. It is worth while noting that until 2001 there was no graduate course in Italy to train students to become community interpreters or court interpreters. There were only two graduate courses in interpreting (in Trieste and Forlì) to train conference interpreters. Our recent university reform has introduced a three-year graduate course in linguistic mediation specifically devoted to teaching interpreting in face-to-face interaction (commercial, medical, legal).

who understands some English, and who produces a large number of continuers and backchannels that the interpreter does not render, probably because she feels that they are directly accessible without translation.

Encounter 3 has rather more turns per minute than the others. The patient is a very active and restless little girl who constantly calls and shouts to her parents. The father has the task of "entertaining" her and he makes her read, draw and even blow up a balloon, addressing over three-quarters of his turns directly to her (106 out of 137). This generates many overlaps as the doctor continues to talk to the mother through the interpreter in parallel conversation and the father tries to listen as much as he can. As the interpreter does not translate the conversations between the child and the parents, there is a large difference between the total number of turns by primary participants and by the interpreter.

Zero renditions

All turns produced by primary participants that were not translated for the benefit of others were counted as zero renditions (Table 2).

In all the encounters, the doctor is the "most translated" participant. In encounter 3 the interpreter, working in very difficult acoustic conditions, kept the communication channel between the doctor, the mother and herself open by considering overlaps and parallel conversations between the child and her father as background noise (she never stopped to ask the child to be quiet).

To provide further indications concerning the translation approach adopted by the interpreters, the addressee and type of action corresponding to each zero rendition were analysed.

Main findings from the analysis of zero renditions

The main approaches adopted by the interpreters were the same in all the encounters (see examples below).

1. The doctor is the most "translated" participant not only in proportion of turns but also in terms of content. The only turns by the doctor not rendered by interpreters are backchannels, continuers, direct exchanges with the interpreter (example 2), direct exchanges in English with the mother (example 4), failed attempts to take the floor, and four reinforcement turns where the doctor restates what he had said in the previous turn.
2. Parents' turns addressed to the child are never translated (example 3).

Table 1. Distribution of turns

| Encounter | Duration | Primary participants | | | | | Interpreter | Total | Turns/minute |
		Doctor	Mother	Father	Child	Total			
1	14'29"	82	37	36	1	156	138	294	20.3
2	29'44"	154	184	51	0	389	203	592	20.0
3	26'39"	120	87	137	142	486	136	622	23.3
Total	70'53"	356	308	224	143	1031	477	1508	21.3

Table 2. Zero renditions by interpreters of primary participants' turns

Encounter	Duration	Doctor	Mother	Father	Child	Total
1	14'29"	12 (14.6%)	20 (54.1%)	18 (50.0%)	0 (0 %)	50 (17.0%)
2	29'44"	50 (32.5%)	118 (64.1%)	33 (64.7%)	–	201 (40.0%)
3	26'39"	16 (13.3%)	73 (83.9%)	120 (87.6%)	142 (100%)	351 (56.4%)
Total	<170'53">	78 (21.9%)	211 (68.5%)	171 (76.3%)	142 (99.3%)	602 (39.9%)

3. Comments or assessments pertaining to compliance with prescriptions are not translated unless they contain open disagreement (example 1).
4. Exchanges between parents are often not rendered or only partially presented to the doctor by the interpreter (example 2).
5. Parents' backchannels, continuers and short Yes/No answers, whether in English or in Italian, are generally not rendered (example 2).

Example (1) Encounter 2
Here the interpreter decides not to render a parental assessment concerning compliance with a medical prescription. (D=Doctor, M=Mother, F=Father, C=Child, I=Interpreter).

D = and our liquid balance should be just about the same (.)
　　　[about five] =
M [cinquanta ml]
　　[fifty ml]
D　　　　　　　　　　 = five to six hundred millilitres =
I = quindi cinquecento seicento　　　sempre　 il bilancio dei liquidi
　　　so　　five hundred six hundred the same liquid balance
(.)
M OK (2) °cinquecento ml ° una dose aggiuntiva cento ° =
　　OK (2) ° five hundred ml ° one additional dose one hundred° =
I = cento
　　one hundred
(.)
M e: e: infatti noi lo facciamo bere poco alla volta (3) quello che beve
　　e: e: in fact we have him drink a little quantity at a time (3) what he drinks
(4)

This sequence opens with the doctor's indication about the liquid balance. After the interpreter's rendition the mother checks that she has understood the dosage correctly by repeating it while she is writing it down. Then the interpreter repeats the dosage to confirm that what the mother is writing down is correct. This mother/interpreter exchange is not translated back to the doctor, probably because the interpreter feels that once the doctor's message has been conveyed, her function is successfully accomplished.

In her final turn, the mother produces an assessment about the doctor's indication that is not rendered by the interpreter. Robinson (2001) finds that assessment/evaluation turns are often produced by patients as vehicles for requests or to negotiate doctors' prescriptions or instructions. Consequently the decision by the interpreter not to render these turns perhaps constitutes a diminishment of the patient's power, denying the mother the possibility to negotiate the indication. The mother stresses the effort made by both parents to achieve the liquid balance: "e: e: infatti noi lo facciamo bere poco alla volta" (*we have him drink a little quantity at a time*). She then waits for three seconds, and when the interpreter does not translate it she repeats the same concept, this time underlining the discomfort for the child being only allowed to drink a limited quantity of liquids "quello che beve" (*what he drinks*). This turn is not rendered, perhaps because it does not contain open disagreement and is understood by the interpreter as an acceptance. Again it would seem that the main concern of the interpreter is to make sure that the doctor's indications and prescriptions are understood.

Example (2) Encounter 2
In this example the mother and father express different opinions.

D do you think Samuele that we can gain (.) one or two kilos
   (.) in the next few months ?
(.)
M [eh forse]
   [eh may be]
I [Samuele] pensi che   nei prossimi mesi   potrai ingrassare
   [Samuele] do you think that in the next few months you can put on
   uno o due chili ?
   one kilo or two ?
(2)
F sì eh
   yes eh
(1)
M è un po' difficile
   it's a bit difficult
(.)
F mangiare [deve magiare tanto]
   eating   [he has to eat a lot]
M   [si muo /] si muove tanto
           [he mo /] he moves a lot
(.)
I mummy is saying is going to be difficult because he moves a lot
D because ?
(.)
I he moves a lot =
D = yes
(.)

This is the only case in these encounters where the interpreter renders a turn addressed to the child. But although formally addressed to the linguistically-disabled Samuele, the doctor's request is substantially directed to the parents, who all the participants know will have to reply on his behalf as well as to take note of the instruction and ensure that Samuele complies.

The mother replies in overlap, without waiting for the interpreter to finish translating. The interpreter ignores the reply, however, thereby denying the mother access to the floor. When the interpreter finishes translating the doctor's question, the father gives a positive answer, while the mother repeats her expression of doubt and the interpreter decides to present this exchange to the doctor by voicing only the mother's position. Thereby she avoids reporting a divergence between parents that she perhaps considers private.

A final point to note is the zero rendition of the doctor's request to repeat ("because?") followed by the interpreter's answer and then by a backchannel by the doctor. This is perhaps considered by the interpreter as a direct exchange between her and the doctor that does not contain new information requiring translation for the parents.

Non-renditions

Turns containing expressions that are not renditions of primary participants' turns but are autonomously produced by the interpreter were categorised as turns with non-renditions. Applying this category is very helpful in identifying the conversational initiatives undertaken by the interpreter and consequently in understanding the level of active participation by the interpreter in the interaction.

The addressees of all non-renditions were either the doctor or the mother. This could be due to the fact that the mother is the one who fills in the form containing the doctor's instructions. The interpreters may have felt that their main task was to make sure that prescriptions were correctly and accurately understood and taken note of. Most non-renditions are requests for clarification or repetition and offer to help the mother (for instance providing indications about where to write down a dosage or about how to correctly take note of a dietary prescription).

Besides these three main types of non-renditions there are a number containing topic initiation, negotiation of prescriptions and restrictions to prescriptions which are produced by the interpreters autonomously (as illustrated in examples 3 and 4 below).

The interpreter in encounter 1 (Table 3) is highly active in terms of autonomous production. This could be due to the fact that she is a permanent in-house interpreter who has been working for this institute for many years and feels part

Table 3. Interpreter turns with non-renditions

Encounter	Interpreter turns	Interpreter turns with non-renditions
1	138	42 (30.4%)
2	203	11 (5.4%)
3	136	6 (4.4%)
Total	477	59 (12.4%)

of a team with the medical staff (when observing the encounter one gets the impression that at times she is conducting it).

Main findings from the analysis of non-renditions

No common model of participation for the three interpreters emerges from the analysis of non-renditions. Their behaviour varies from highly active and more patient-oriented as in encounter 1 to less active towards the patient as in encounters 2 and 3.

The examples below show that the interpreters play an active role in the interaction but their attitudes towards both the patients and the doctor differs. In example 3 the interpreter negotiates with the doctor an advantage for the patient, while in example 4 a dietary restriction prescribed by the doctor to the child is treated differently by the interpreter who produces an expression of exaggeration (perceived as such since it is followed by laughter), which contributes to the conversational *rapport*.

Example (3) Encounter 1
I = OK of course he would like cheese you know this / they have
      eliminated all milk and milk products [xxx]
D   [I I will] give him cheese
      (.) I will put in cheese =
I = ha detto si può dare un po' di formaggio (.) I mean special time
      could it be [cheese on] /
      he said you can give him a little cheese (.) I mean special time
      could it be [cheese on] /
D   [any time] may be a couple of times a week =
I = parmigiano on the pasta =
D = sure =
I = ha detto sì un paio di volte alla settimana si può dare il formaggio
      = *he said yes a couple of times a week you can give him cheese*
      (.) magari il parmigiano sulla [pasta]

> *(.) preferably parmesan on the [pasta]*
> F   [sentito] ? =
>   *[did you hear] ? = (addressed to the child)*
> M = sentito ?
>   *= did you hear ? (addressed to the child)*
> (.)
> F   un poco di formaggio ogni tanto *(addressed to the child)*
>   *a little cheese every now and then*
> (.)
> I   and (.) gelato magari si può dare ice cream eh:::m una volta? once
>   at what time ? =
>   *and (.) ice cream maybe you can give him ice cream eh:::m once*
>   *a week? once at what time?=*
> D = once a week
> (.)
> I   una volta a settimana anche gelato
>   *once a week ice cream too*
> (.)

This sequence opens with the interpreter's rendition of a turn by the mother, who has expressed her child's wish to have cheese and ice cream introduced in his diet. The doctor agrees to introduce cheese and the interpreter translates the doctor's turn back to the parents introducing a restrictive expression "un po' " (*a little*). She then initiates an exchange with the doctor where she negotiates first the time – "I mean special time could it be cheese on" – and then in her next turn, the way in which to introduce cheese in the child's diet: "parmigiano on the pasta". She then reports the whole sequence to the parents as a decision made by the doctor: "ha detto sì" (*he said yes*). The following turns by the mother and father to the child are not translated, probably because they are perceived by the interpreter as a private family exchange of happiness. In the next turn by the interpreter she initiates a new request to the doctor and a new topic (ice cream) and translates her request to the parents. She is not only negotiating on behalf of the patient, as it were, but she is also putting a constraint on the doctor who has to give a yes or no answer. She also suggests the dose of ice cream: "once at what time?". In short this interpreter is making sure that the patient's wish to eat dairy products, which had previously only been expressed in general terms, does not go unheard: she insists on getting precise dietary indications for the family to follow.

Example (4) Encounter 3
Here the same topic is at issue: the possibility to introduce dairy products into the patient's diet. The doctor has already told the parents that cheese is allowed and the mother is now enquiring what type of cheese.

(.)
D   OK =
M   = mozzarella
D   mozzarella [(1) bene]
M   [ah ah] (laughter of satisfaction)
(1)
M   parmigiano ?
(.)
D   sure (.) sì
        sure (.) yes
(1)
I   [poco]
      [a little]
M   [un po] co poco [poco]
      [a litt] le a little [a little]
F   [poco] (.) poco però ah ? poco =
                              [a little] (.) but really little though ah? =
                                              (addressing the child)
I   = e anche [poco per voi]
        and also [for you a little]
M   [eh ehe] (approving laughter)

The first part of this sequence contains a direct doctor/mother exchange while in the second the interpreter produces non-renditions, which propose stricter limits than the doctor's prescription. Although the orientation of the interpreter here may seem opposite to that in the previous example (where the interpreter negotiated an "advantage" for the patient), the non-rendition here is clearly exaggerated, as the mother's recipient laughter indicates, and is primarily designed to contribute to conversational *rapport*.

Conclusions

The multi-party medical encounters presented here were analysed to see whether the interpreters prioritised one participant or one conversational axis. The distribution of turns by speaker shows that in all encounters the sum of turns produced by primary participants was smaller than the total number of turns by the interpreters. Analysis of zero renditions showed that all interpreters privileged the doctor as participant and the doctor/mother conversational axis in their translation function, and that specific kinds of zero rendition were recurrent in all the encounters. In contrast, the analysis of conversational initiatives undertaken autonomously by interpreters (non-renditions) showed that the attitude of interpreters towards the primary participants ranged from highly active and patient-oriented to less active towards the patient. This suggests that a good number of discretionary decisions by interpreters may come into play in medical settings, in relation to the management of the interaction and the construction of satisfactory interpersonal *rapport* (as in the last example). Further research work and comparative studies with data from countries which have developed professional health interpreting standards may help in the development of training methods to provide a more uniform quality of service.

References

Davidson, B. 2002. "A model for the construction of conversational common ground in interpreted discourse". *Journal of Pragmatics* 34: 1273–1300.

Metzger, M. 1999. *Sign Interpreting – Deconstructing the Myth of Neutrality.* Washington DC: Galludet University Press.

Fogazzaro, E. & Gavioli, L. 2004. "L'interprete come mediatore, riflessioni sul ruolo dell'interprete in una trattativa d'affari". In *Linguistica e interpretazione*, Bersani Berselli, G., Mack, G. & Zorzi, D. (eds), 169–191. Bologna: Clueb.

Goffman, E. 1981. *Forms of Talk.* Philadelphia: University of Pennsylvania Press.

Robinson, J. 2001. "Asymmetry in action: Sequential resources in the negotiation of a prescription request". *Text 21–1/2:* 19–54.

Roy, C. 2000. *Interpreting as a discourse process.* New York & Oxford: Oxford University Press.

Sacks, H., Schegloff, E. & Jefferson, G. 1974/1978. "A simplest systematics for the organisation of turn taking for conversation". *Language 50:* 696–735.

Straniero Sergio, F. 1999. "The Interpreter on the (Talk) Show". *The Translator*, vol. 5, n° 2: 303–326.

Wadensjö, C. 1998. *Interpreting as Interaction*, London & New York: Longman.

Interpreting in asylum hearings

Issues of saving face

Sonja Pöllabauer
Karl-Franzens University, Graz, Austria

The study presented in this paper investigates the role of interpreters in asylum hearings in Austria. It is based on transcripts of authentic asylum hearings which were recorded at the Federal Asylum Office in Graz, Austria, and transcribed and analysed using a discourse analytical approach.

In Austria, interpreters in asylum interviews are often faced with conflicting role expectations. Some aspects of the interpreters' attempts to save their own and/or the other participants' face will be discussed in this article.

Introduction

This paper will present some of the results of a research project (Pöllabauer 2003), which focused on interpreting in asylum hearings. The study is based on transcripts of authentic asylum hearings which were recorded at the Federal Asylum Office in Graz (Austria), and transcribed and analysed using a discourse analytical approach (Fairclough 1993, 1995). Some aspects of the interpreters' attempts to save their own and/or the other participants' face will be discussed in this paper. The general aim of the study was to investigate the role of interpreters in asylum interviews and identify specific factors influencing the speakers' behaviour. Special attention was paid to role conflicts, discrepant role expectations, the asymmetrical power distribution in asylum hearings and the validity of existing (traditional) norm systems.

The results of the study prove that interpreters are not "invisible" intermediaries in interpreter-mediated asylum hearings (see Pöllabauer 2003: 331ff.). They very often openly intervene (with the officers' permission), abbreviate, paraphrase and "filter" the participants' (mainly the asylum-seekers') utterances and, sometimes, even tend to judge the relevance and usefulness of statements voiced by the asylum-seekers. With respect to issues of face, evidence from the study suggests that interpreters seem to feel obliged to save their own face and mark the source of misunderstandings or threats to their own and/or other participants' face, in order to avoid any blame for communication breakdown. Before discussing some of these aspects in detail, a brief overview of the fragile and delicate communication situation of interpreter-mediated asylum hearings will be outlined, as issues of power and asymmetry tend to have a considerable influence on the participants' "face-wants" (Brown & Levinson 1978/1987: 13).

Asylum hearings: Asymmetrical interactions

Asylum hearings are not police interrogations per se. Asylum-seekers are not defendants or detainees – the right to seek asylum is guaranteed by the Universal Declaration of Human Rights and the Geneva Convention Relating to the Status of Refugees, adopted by the United Nations in 1951, as well as the Protocol to the Convention, adopted by the General Assembly of the United Nations in 1967. The fundamental aim of asylum interviews is, however, similar to that of police interrogations, the identification of objective, material facts, i.e. the "truth", with regard to the asylum-seekers' claims (also see Pöllabauer & Schumacher 2004: 20). To some, asylum hearings are also considered as "rituals" which do not primarily aim at establishing the "truth", but also attempt to justify (negative) decisions taken by the officers: "Interviews are an arbitrary and political tool" (Monnier 1995: 322).

Asylum hearings are highly asymmetrical interactive situations: the asylum-seekers' basic linguistic resources, acquired (and internalised) in their home countries, do not necessarily prove to be useful in the host country's institutional settings, such as the context of asylum hearings. The participants' socio-cultural and institutional background knowledge differs considerably: the content and purpose of the hearings, i.e. which questions are addressed to the asylum-seekers and how their answers will subsequently be judged, are not equally apprehensible to all participants (see also Scheffer 2001: 41). This asymmetrical distribution of linguistic resources can also be noticed in the structuring of the discourse and the arrangement of turn-taking. Asylum-seekers are required to provide logical, (chronologically) coherent, and 'true' statements. The highly standardised 'question-answer' structure of asylum interviews generally requires asylum-seekers to provide answers to questions which were initiated by the officers and does not leave much scope for them to independently initiate questions or present their claims in a less regulated manner (see also Blommaert 2001: 414f.). The officers, in their function as institutional representatives, control turn-taking, have the exclusive right to initiate questions and can also decide whether the asylum-seekers' answers are adequate for the purpose of the hearing. Asylum interviews may also be characterised as gate-keeping encounters (Erickson & Schultz 1982), in which

representatives of the institution have the right to grant or withhold certain services or assistance to the clients.

Interpreters have a vital influence on the outcome of these interactions, which
are characterized by power asymmetry and structural imbalance. Some authors
claim that interpreters have to act as "cultural mediators" or "intercultural agents"
(Barsky 1996: 45f.), who (metaphorically) help to bridge the linguistic and cultural
barriers between the unequal participants in asylum hearings. On the other hand,
interpreters are also often required to perform their translation job as "neutral"
and impartial "language converters", who should provide a literal (word-to-word)
translation and not attempt to "interpret" the meaning of utterances ("translate"
but not "interpret") (see Morris 1995: 30f.). Several studies prove, however, that
interpreters are not neutral "language converters", but often assume the role of
equal third parties in the interaction, who also seem to be aware of their own
or the other participants' face-wants (see Knapp 1986; Wadensjö 1998; Mason &
Stewart 2001). This paper attempts to analyse how interpreters deal with issues of
saving (their own or other participants') face.

Face-saving strategies

The need to save one's own or other participants' face (by using different politeness strategies[1]) is an important aspect of monolingual as well as interpreter-mediated interactions. Based on Goffman's concept of face (Goffman 1967), Brown
and Levinson suggest in their "politeness theory" that every individual attempts
to maintain a certain "public self-image that every member wants to claim for
himself", also called "face" (Brown & Levinson 1978/1987: 61). This notion of face
consists of two aspects: a personal *positive* and *negative face* (ibid.). The notion of
"negative face" includes an individual's wish "to be unimpeded in one's actions"
(ibid.), i.e. to have freedom of action and freedom from imposition (see ibid.); the
notion of "positive face" consists of the desire "to be approved of" (ibid.): "This is
the bare bones of a notion of face which (we argue) is universal, but which in any
particular society we would expect to be the subject of much cultural elaboration"
(ibid.: 13).

Certain face-threatening acts (FTAs) may endanger the other's positive or
negative image ("face"). Rational interactants in face-to-face situations will either
seek to avoid such face-threatening acts or employ certain face-saving strategies

---

1.   Politeness is regarded by Brown and Levinson as a flouting of Grice's (Grice 1975: 45ff.) "co-
operative principles" of talk: "Politeness is then a major source of deviation from such rational efficiency, and is communicated precisely by that deviation" (Brown & Levinson 1978/1987: 95).

to minimize the threat (Brown & Levinson 1978/1987:68) – unless, of course, they intentionally initiate the FTA to achieve the highest possible effect (ibid.:59f.).

For asylum hearings, it may be assumed that all the primary participants (asylum-seekers, officers, interpreters) attempt to maintain their own as well as the other interactants' personal positive and negative face. Presupposing, however, that the officers' major conversational aim is to identify and establish "objective" facts, it may be concluded that it will not always be possible for them to save the asylum-seekers' face. The officers are primarily interested in "believable", coherent statements. Due to the personal, sometimes highly intimate, and potentially face-threatening nature of such information, however, collecting such facts will not always be feasible without initiating a threat to the asylum-seekers' face. Certain questions addressed to the asylum-seekers by the officers, or certain acts they have to perform, which they probably regard as an obligatory component of their institutional and normative role (Goffman 1961:93), may automatically pose a threat to the asylum-seeker's positive or negative image. Questions or interrogation strategies, for instance, which are necessary to the officers for determining the relevance of the asylum-seekers' claims, may be regarded as inadequate or even taboo in the asylum-seekers' culture and, thus, will threaten the asylum-seekers' positive image. Similarly, certain acts or behaviour, such as searching the asylum-seekers' personal belongings or taking them into police custody for the duration of the asylum procedure – a common practice in Austria and many other European countries and heavily criticised by human rights organisations – will threaten the asylum-seekers' negative face. On the other hand, particular behaviour by the asylum-seekers, which may even be culturally determined, may be a potential threat to the officers' positive image.

It may also be assumed that the interpreters will attempt to protect their own "professional" face as neutral and impartial language experts and co-ordinators of discourse as demonstrated in similar studies (cf. e.g. Wadensjö 1998:77–179). The primary parties will normally expect interpreters to translate and not to side with one of the other speakers. It will probably be regarded as a threat to the interpreters' face when one of the other interactants questions their ability to translate and/or their impartiality.

On the basis of these theoretical assumptions, issues of face and the interpreters' strategies for dealing with FTAs in asylum hearings will now be discussed.

Corpus

The corpus of the project includes audio recordings of 20 asylum hearings, recorded between October 1, 2000 and July 5, 2001 at the Federal Asylum Office in Graz. The average length of the hearings was 62.3 minutes. The total length of all recordings is 20 hours and 46 minutes. The longest interview lasted nearly three hours (175.34 minutes) and the shortest hearing was 19.05 minutes. The corpus only includes hearings with English-speaking asylum-seekers. The interpreters translate from English into German and vice versa.

Three different officers (B1, B2 and B3), all of them male, and three different interpreters (D1, D2 and D3), all of them female, took part in the hearings. B1 was responsible for fifteen interviews, B2 for three, and B3 for two. D1 interpreted in eight interviews, D2 in ten and D3 in two, (interpreters D1 and D2 were professional interpreters, whereas D3 had no official training, but ample experience as an interpreter in asylum settings). In total, nineteen different asylum-seekers (five of them women and fifteen men) from four different countries (Nigeria, Sierra Leone, Liberia, and Sudan) were interviewed.

Some results and discussion

Threats to the asylum-seekers' face

Knapp suggests that interpreters – he refers to so-called "natural interpreters", i.e. interpreters with no professional training in interpreting, although we presume that this behaviour may also be true of professional interpreters – tend to let an FTA pass, if they regard themselves and the representatives of the institution to be "superior" to the other interactants (see Knapp 1986: 16f.). In the following example, the officer initiates a direct on-record FTA (Brown & Levinson 1978/1987: 68f.), which is addressed to the asylum-seeker.

Excerpt 1 (BAG1:300–302)[2, 3]

```
+---------------------------------------------------
¦B1[                                    You want a copy?
¦AW[                          ((Signs record))
¦D1[ Can you add your full name.                   Okay.
300 +---------------------------------------------------------


+----------------------------------------------------
¦B1[                      Very simple, you have to say yes
¦D1[ Do you want a copy of this statement? . Hm?      Yes or
301 +---------------------------------------------------------


+----------------------------------------------------
¦B1[ or no.
¦AW+        Yes.
¦  +       ((Quietly))                 ((Takes personal belongings))
¦D1[   no?           This is yours.           Sie haben da jetzt
                                              Here you have
302 +---------------------------------------------------------
```

In line 300, the (male) asylum-seeker signs the record of the interview, after the interpreter has translated the (German) record into English on-sight, and confirms with his signature that he agrees with the content of the record. In the same line, the interpreter presumably indicates with "okay" that the asylum-seeker has signed the record in the correct form (full signature, not only initials) and at the correct place (at the bottom of each page). Almost simultaneously, the officer asks the asylum-seeker in English if he would like to have a copy of the record. In line 301, the interpreter simply repeats the officer's English question – a strategy interpreters often adopt if the officers, for whatever reason, switch to English. The asylum-seeker does not instantly react to the officer's or even the interpreter's question. The officer's comment in line 301 ("Very simple, you have to say yes or

---

2. The audio recordings were transcribed using the HIAT transcription system (see Ehlich 1993). Transcription conventions:

.   short silence (less than 3 seconds)
.. longer silence (more than 3 seconds)
/   false starts
underlining   Emphasis
((xxx))   non verbal features or explanatory comments
(xxx)   inaudible passage
CAPITALS   anonymous information (names, place names etc.).

3. The information given in brackets refers to the name of the respective transcript (e.g. BAG1) and the lines of the excerpt (e.g. 114–118). B [Beamte] = Officer, D [Dolmetscher] = Interpreter (the numbers 1–3 stand for the respective officers or interpreters), AW [Asylwerber] = Asylum seeker, SK [Schreibkraft] = Typist, GV [Gesetzlicher Vertreter] = Legal Representative, VP [Vertrauensperson] = person of confidence; for German text passages, an English translation (in italics) is provided in the line below the German text..

no.") may be regarded as an on-record FTA, which clearly endangers the asylum-seeker's positive face. The ironic "very simple", on the one hand, condescendingly implies that the asylum-seeker obviously failed to comply with an apparently "simple" request, possibly insinuating that the officer has a poor opinion of the asylum-seeker's intellectual capabilities, and, on the other hand, also demonstrates the officer's superiority by signalling that the asylum-seeker's range of possible answers is limited to "yes" or "no". The interpreter relays the FTA without initiating a face-saving act and insists on an answer: "Yes or no?" By leaving out the ironic "very simple question", she may have attempted to mitigate the FTA.

In the next example, the interpreter seems to be more aware of the face-threatening nature of a comment addressed to the asylum-seeker by the officer and obviously attempts to indicate the authorship of the comment.

Excerpt 2 (BAG3:315-322)

```
    +----------------------------------------------------
    ¦B1[       Also ich habe den Eindruck, dass seine Daten hier
              Well, I get the impression that his data here
    ¦D1[ legen.
         submit.
315 +----------------------------------------------------------------


    +-------------------------------------------------
    ¦B1[ offensichtlich/ oder dass dieser Zettel offensichtlich
         obviously /    or that this paper obviously
316 +----------------------------------------------------------------


    +-------------------------------------------------
    ¦B1[ Lernzwecken dient.
         serves learning purposes.
    ¦D1[   The officer has the impression that this paper serves
317 +----------------------------------------------------------------


    +-------------------------------------------------
    ¦AW[                                          Hm?
    ¦D1[ you as a sort of help with particulars to study.   The
318 +----------------------------------------------------------------


    +-------------------------------------------------
    ¦D1[ paper, this is the officer's impression, the paper con-
319 +----------------------------------------------------------------


    +-------------------------------------------------
    ¦D1[ tains information, and you need the paper so to learn
320 +----------------------------------------------------------------


    +-------------------------------------------------
    ¦AW[ No. I throw it away because of this one. I wanted to
    ¦D1[ it.
321 +----------------------------------------------------------------


    +-------------------------------------------------
    ¦AW[ write it so that if I come here I will submit it. If I
322 +----------------------------------------------------------------
```

The general situation and atmosphere in this transcript is very delicate and awkward for the asylum-seeker. Accidentally, on his way to work in the morning, the officer had found a piece of paper on the pavement in front of the asylum office. All the personal data, as well as the history of persecution of that respective asylum-seeker, who was to be interviewed by the officer some minutes later, was written down on that piece of paper. In this transcript excerpt, the officer bluntly informs the asylum-seeker that he suspects him of having learned the facts on the paper by heart. By commenting in line 317 "… this paper obviously serves learning purposes", he implies that the facts on the paper may not be the asylum-seeker's genuine data, but a "fake" story which the asylum-seeker has learned by heart in order to improve his chances of being granted asylum.

In her translation, the interpreter performs a deictic change from the first person singular in the officer's accusation ("Well, *I* get the impression…") to the third person singular ("*The officer* has the impression…"). She, thus, clearly indicates that the officer is the author of the statement and makes it clear for the asylum-seeker that *the officer*, but not necessarily she herself, does not believe him. It remains unclear whether her complicated paraphrasing of "Lernzwecke" ("…a sort of help with particulars to study") and the rise in register she performs ("particulars" instead of "personal data") is understandable to the asylum-seeker.

In the next example, the interpreter again leaves out a comment which might pose a threat to the asylum-seeker's positive face.

Excerpt 3 (BAG15:57-58)

```
+-----------------------------------------------------
¦B1[ Wohin is er gefahren? Er soll keine Geschichten
     Where did he go to? He is not supposed to tell
¦AW[                              I don't know. I just
¦D2[ Just tell me, where did you go?
57 +----------------------------------------------------
```

```
+---------------------------------------------------
¦B1[ erzählen, er soll mir sagen, wohin.
     stories, he is supposed to tell me where he went.
¦AW[ enter the ship. But I know the ship is coming from
58 +--------------------------------------------------
```

She filters out the officer's blank request to be brief ("He is not supposed to tell stories."). From the officer's comment, it is obvious that the asylum-seeker's answer does not yet comply with the institutionally imposed requirement of presenting a plausible, logical and believable claim. He is not able to present an adequate "other" (Barsky 1995: 82f.).

By opting to leave out the rather impolite and face-threatening "He is not supposed to tell stories" and choosing a more neutral translation the interpreter, on the one hand, may want to protect the asylum-seeker's face who does not realise that his face is in danger. On the other hand, she may also intend to protect her own position as a professional "go-between" who does not side with any party. This instance of talk could also serve as an example of discourse control: By leaving out the officer's comment she may also attempt to sustain a positive communicative atmosphere and keep the talk "going".

Threats to the officers' face

The officer's face is seldom threatened by the asylum-seekers or interpreters. In some transcripts, we find examples in which asylum-seekers (intentionally or unintentionally) initiate comments which might be viewed as offensive by the officers. For instance, an asylum-seeker may request a correction of the record. Such requests might be judged as a FTA by the officer as the production and wording of the record is the responsibility of the officer alone (and possibly the typist) and any hints to potentially faulty passages might be taken as a challenge to his professionalism. (The responsibility for what the record says will in the end be ascribed to the asylum-seeker.)

In excerpt 4 the asylum-seeker is asked whether there is a river in his home town.[4]

Excerpt 4 (BAG4:362-364)

```
    +---------------------------------------------------
    |B1[ große Fluss in ORT1?
         big river in VILLAGE1?
    |AW[                                          Mhm.
    |D1[                     Okay, and this big river,  what is it
362 +---------------------------------------------------------------

    +---------------------------------------------------
    |AW[        The name?      I tell you I don't know the name o
    |D1[ called?        Ahm.
363 +---------------------------------------------------------

    +---------------------------------------------
    |B1[                                ((4s)) Als politisch
                                               As a political
    |AW[ the river.
    |D1[            Den Namen weiß ich nicht.
                   I don't know the name.
364 +---------------------------------------------------------
```

In line 363, the asylum-seeker expressly (and slightly impatiently) underlines that he has already explained that he did not know the name of the river ("I tell you I

4. Asylum-seekers are sometimes asked questions about geographic or other facts about their home country or home town to prove the credibility of their testimony (see also Scheffer 2001:139ff. about such "credibility tests").

don't know the name o[f] the river."). In asylum hearings, like in other similar institutional contexts, the right to initiate questions lies with the officer, whereas the asylum-seekers are requested to provide "logical" answers and refrain from initiating new questions or personal comments. An impatient or impolite answer ("I tell you I don't know the name o[f] the river.") might lead to a charged atmosphere and threaten the officer's face as institutional representative. The interpreter, however, leaves out the blunt comment ("I tell you, ...") and simply translates: "I don't know the name." Here again, she opts for a strictly neutral and matter-of-fact rendition. This example may again be viewed as an example of the interpreter's effort to protect her position as an impartial mediator between the two parties and as co-ordinator of discourse.

The asylum-seeker's comment might, of course, also have been addressed to the interpreter. Instead of translating, the interpreter just replied directly ("Ahm") to his previous request for clarification, "The name?". Another reading of this passage might also imply that the asylum-seeker simply wanted to underline that he really and honestly ("I tell you...") did not know the name of said river.

Threats to the interpreters' face

In the next excerpt, the interpreter's face is threatened by a request for correction and clarification which is initiated by the officer.

Excerpt 5 (BAG2:659-664)

```
+-----------------------------------------------
¦B1[ also?
     well?
¦AW[                                    Mhm.
¦D1[      So, what ahm do you supposing . in case/ supposing,
659 +-----------------------------------------------

+-----------------------------------------------
¦D1[ suppose you . supposing you go back or they send you
660 +-----------------------------------------------

+-----------------------------------------------
¦B1[                             Na, na.        Was befürch-
                                No, no.        What does she
¦D1[ back to Nigeria, what do you think would happen to you?
661 +-----------------------------------------------

+-----------------------------------------------
¦B1[ tet sie? Was hätte sie/ was hätte ihr gedroht, wenn sie
     fear? What would shen/ in which way would she have been
¦D1[                                        Ah, des net.
                                           Ah, not that.
662 +-----------------------------------------------
```

```
+-----------------------------------------------------
¦B1[ dort geblieben wäre?
     threatened if she had stayed there?
¦D1[                          Aha, wenn sie dort geblieben
                              Aha, if she had stayed there.
663 +---------------------------------------------------------------


+------------------------------------------------
¦D1[ wäre. So if you had not left your country, what do you
664 +---------------------------------------------------------------
```

The (female) asylum-seeker had explained that riots had started in her home village after the Islamic *Sharia* was introduced. The officer wants to know what might have happened to her if she had stayed in her country, his wording, however, seems rather unclear and does not exactly specify the temporal (or geographical) context of his question: "What is she afraid of?" In line 659, the interpreter starts to translate the officer's question. The series of false starts and subsequent restarts and repetitions signal that she seems to have problems integrating "suppose" in her translation. In line 661, she is interrupted by the officer ("No, no.") who seems to have followed her translations, and signals to her that she obviously misunderstood the question. The officer's interruption can be viewed as a FTA which poses a threat to the interpreter's positive face, i.e. her translation competence. After the officer paraphrases his question in line 662 ("… what would have happened to her if she had stayed there?"), the interpreter indicates that she has now located the source of the misunderstanding, and she comments in line 662: "Ah, not that." In another subsequent remark ("Ah, if she had stayed there."), she signals to the officer that she now understands the purpose of his question. She does not directly blame the officer for the misunderstanding, yet her comment might imply that she transfers responsibility for the problem to the officer. After these two brief comments, she then renders the officer's question into English.

In some instances, asylum-seekers also directly threaten the interpreters' face.

Excerpt 6 (BAG2:317-320)

```
+---------------------------------------------------
¦AW[                                    No.
¦D1[ bels? You understand rebels? Rebels?     . Hm, you know
317 +---------------------------------------------------------------


+---------------------------------------------------
¦AW[                      Rebel?      I don't know what you
¦D1[ what rebels means?      Yea.
318 +---------------------------------------------------------------


+-------------------------------------------------
¦AW[ talk. I don't understand your English, Miss.
¦D1[                                    Ich verstehe Ihr
                                        I don't understand
319 +---------------------------------------------------------------
```

```
+----------------------------------------------------
¦B1[                                                  Eine
                                                      A
¦D1[ Englisch nicht, ich weiß nicht, was rebels sind.
     your English, I don't know what rebels are.
320 +----------------------------------------------------
```

In this excerpt, the asylum-seeker obviously does not understand the word "rebel" used by the interpreter. The interpreter's original question was: "[Are you member] to a group of extremists?" When the asylum-seeker does not understand the term "extremists", the interpreter paraphrases it by using "rebels". The asylum-seeker, however, does not understand "rebels" either, which leads to the misunderstanding (or even communication breakdown) in the transcript above. When the interpreter attempts to clarify the source of the misunderstanding in line 318 ("You don't know what rebels means?"), the asylum-seeker comments in line 318: "I don't know what you talk. I don't understand your English, Miss." The interpreter first relays the open FTA without initiating any face-savings acts ("I don't understand your English, ..."). In a second sentence, however, she then seems to blame the misunderstanding on the asylum-seeker's poor linguistic competence (English is not her mother tongue). This strategy can be observed in other transcripts, too: in the case of direct FTAs, which are addressed to them, the interpreters first provide a literal translation and then, if possible, indicate through additional comments, the participant who, in their opinion, is to blame for the communication breakdown.

Conclusion

The examples discussed show that interpreters seem to be entangled in an intricate and very complex web of face work. If possible, they apparently opt to protect the other participants' (positive or negative) face. For different reasons, however, they obviously do not always sustain that strategy but sometimes relay face-threats. Simultaneously, it is also important to them to protect their own face as competent linguistic experts and impartial mediators. In certain instances, they also seem to act as coordinators of talk in an attempt to keep the "talk going".

The transcripts in this paper also seem to confirm what has already been suggested in other similar discourse analytical studies (e.g. Wadenjö 1998), especially with respect to footing and face work. While the officers generally address the asylum-seekers in the third person singular ("When did *she* ...?"), the interpreters mostly seem to opt for addressing the asylum-seekers directly in the first person singular ("When did *you*...?"). If, however, the officers' face is threatened by utterances initiated by the asylum-seekers (or vice versa), the interpreters may effect a change of footing to protect their own positive face by transforming the message's deictic structures. They indicate the authorship of "offensive" questions/utterances and thus point out that the speaker who initiated the face-threat is responsible for the content.

The examples discussed in this article suggest that issues of face, loyalty and impartiality make interpreted asylum hearings very complex interactions in which the interpreters have to assume different roles and are exposed to diverse (sometimes conflicting) role expectations by the other participants.

References

Barsky, R. F. 1995. "The Construction of the Other and the Destruction of the Self: Efficacious Discursive Production in the Convention Refugee Hearing." In *Encountering the Other/s*, G. Brinker-Gabler (ed), 79–100. New York: SUNY.

Barsky, R. F. 1996. "The Interpreter as Intercultural Agent in Convention Refugee Hearings." *The Translator* 2/1, 45–63.

Blommaert, J. 2001. "Investigating narrative inequality: African asylum seekers' stories in Belgium." *Discourse & Society* 12/4, 413–449.

Brown, P. & Levinson, S. C. 1978/1987. *Politeness. Some universals in language usage* [Studies in Interactional Sociolinguistics 4]. Cambridge: Cambridge University Press.

Ehlich, K. 1993. "HIAT: A Transcription System for Discourse Data." In *Talking Data: Transcription and Coding in Discourse Research*, J. A. Edwards & M. D. Lampert (eds), 123–148. Hillsdale, NJ: Lawrence Erlbaum Associates.

Erickson, F. & Schultz, J. 1982. *The Counselor as a Gatekeeper: Social Interaction in Interviews*. New York: Academic Press.

Fairclough, N. 1993. *Discourse and Social Change*. Cambridge: Polity Press.

Fairclough, N. 1995. *Critical Discourse Analysis. The Critical Study of Language*. London: Longman.

Goffman, E. 1961. *Encounters. Two Studies in the Sociology of Interaction*. Indianapolis/New York: The Bobbs-Merrill Company.

Goffman, E. 1967. *Interaction rituals: Essays on face to face behavior*. Garden City, New York: Anchor Books.

Grice, H. P. 1975. "Logic and Conversation." In *Syntax and Semantics. Volume 3 Speech Acts*, P. Cole & J. L. Morgan (eds), 41–58. New York: Academic Press.

Knapp, K. 1986. *Sprachmitteln – Zur Erforschung des Dolmetschens im Alltag* [L.A.U.D.T. Series B 152]. Duisburg: Linguistic Agency University of Duisburg (previously Trier).

Mason, I. & Stewart, M. 2001. "Interactional Pragmatics, Face and the Dialogue Interpreter." In *Triadic Exchanges. Studies in Dialogue Interpreting*, I. Mason (ed), 51–70. Manchester, UK: St. Jerome.

Monnier, M.-A. 1995. "Field Report. The Hidden Part of Asylum Seekers' Interviews in Geneva, Switzerland: Some Observations about the Socio-Political Construction of Interviews between Gatekeepers and the Powerless." *Journal of Refugee Studies* 8/3, 305–325.

Morris, R. 1995. "The Moral Dilemmas of Court Interpreting." *The Translator* 1/1, 25–46.

Pöllabauer, S. 2003. *Translatorisches Handeln bei Asylanhörungen. Eine diskursanalytische Untersuchung.* Graz: Unpublished dissertation.

Pöllabauer, S. & Schumacher, S. 2004. "Kommunikationsprobleme und Neuerungsverbot im Asylverfahren." *Migralex* 01/2, 20–28.

Scheffer, T. 2001. *Asylgewährung. Eine ethnographische Verfahrensanalyse.* Stuttgart: Lucius & Lucius.

Wadensjö, C. 1998. *Interpreting as Interaction.* London/New York: Longman.

Conversational dynamics as an instructional resource in interpreter-mediated technical settings

Birgit Apfelbaum
Hochschule Harz, Germany

Knowledge about interactional patterns community interpreters are involved in is increasingly recognized as being of crucial importance for the successful management of dialogically organized settings. It has been argued that interpreters as well as primary parties systematically and necessarily co-orient toward communicative tasks such as signaling changes in footing, i.e. managing different ways of production or reception of utterances. Focusing on communicative skills concerning the coordination of talk seems to improve role performance not only in typical institutional settings community interpreters are involved in but also in a variety of related professional contexts such as international business negotiations or cross-cultural technical meetings. Samples from a videotaped German-French technical interpreting training session are analyzed in this paper as to how setting-specific tasks such as negotiating technical terms are interactionally achieved and how the conversational dynamics of repair activities can be used as an instructional resource in interpreter training more generally.

Role plays in interpreter training for (technical) translators

Most of the academic programs for (technical) translators in Germany and elsewhere offer additionally interpreting courses owing to the fact that translators may be called upon in their professional careers to also serve as interpreters. Training mainly consists of course work in which advanced level students perform (consecutive) interpreting tasks in dialogically organized role plays, with team teaching the generally preferred mode of instruction.

Experimental training courses have shown that two instructors from a different language and culture background and/or an instructor interacting with an (exchange) student serving as primary participants allow for a relatively authentic setting (cf. Schäffner 1995; Ko 1996; Apfelbaum 1997). The interactional patterns have a lot in common with those found in dialogically organized settings which community interpreters are typically involved in (cf. Apfelbaum 2004). Following the programmatic papers of Lang (1978) and Keith (1984) in this field, training and assessment (should) aim at "a greater awareness of the total interactional pattern of which the interpreter is a part" (Lang 1978: 242) and instructors (should) manage to simulate a "mediated conversation in which the role of the interpreter is that of a responsible organiser of the entire discourse, not merely a translator of individual texts" (Keith 1984: 313).

Assessment of students' performances should include "an assessment not just of their ability to process and reformulate relatively poorly formed texts but also their management of various interaction events related to footing, non-adjacency, turn-taking, intersubjectivity etc." (Keith 1984: 316).

When it comes to ways of conducting role plays in interpreter training classes for (technical) translators, error correction is often considered to be of crucial importance. From the perspective of language teaching it is recommended, however, not to interrupt the role play dialogue for error correction, but allow time for this purpose at the end of session and to make use of an audio or video recording (cf. Parnell 1989: 254).

While the majority of articles and papers devoted to the conception of role plays in interpreter training for (technical) translators are drawn from a rather broad range of teaching experience, some empirical studies have been done on the basis of transcripts of audio and/or video recordings involving student interpreters with limited foreign language fluency. The following problem areas have been identified by making use of descriptive approaches informed by discourse analysis, Conversation analysis (CA) and Interpretive Sociolinguistics:

a. strategies for coping with lack of background knowledge as a problem in foreign language and culture comprehension (cf. Schäffner 1995),
b. ways of initiating and managing successfully clarification sequences when comprehension problems concerning technical knowledge have to be dealt with (Apfelbaum 2004: Chapter 8.2.3) and
c. ways of making use of deictic references to artifacts when gaps have to be bridged or production problems have to be repaired in renditions of (technical) explanations into a foreign language (cf. Apfelbaum 2004: Chapter 8.2.4).

A look at the participants' contributions in terms of turn construction regularities (or *conversational dynamics*) helps to reconstruct components of communicative and interactive competences necessary for a functional task sharing between *all* participants involved (primary parties as well as interpreters). The analysis of transcribed video data shows how interactional patterns and changes in footing are systematically co-constructed with the interpreter by means of verbal and non-verbal synchronization.

Samples from a videotaped German-French technical interpreting training session in the field of mechanical engineering are analyzed in this paper as to how setting-specific tasks are interactionally achieved, such as negotiating technical terms that are of particular importance in sequences dealing with the explanation of corresponding concepts. It will be demonstrated how the conversational dynamics of repair activities can be used as an instructional resource in role plays: The students are not only given a chance to improve their (technical) second language proficiency but also learn at the same time how to gradually take responsibility for the coordination of talk and turn allocation. It will be argued that analyzing this dual function of such sequences and recognizing their regularities can therefore be useful in (the development of) training concepts in the field of technical interpreting as well as in related areas such as medical interpreting in the community. Such increased awareness should facilitate a more systematic development of components of communicative competence by focussing on interactive practice(s) dialogue interpreters have to be familiar with.

The drill scenario: An interpreter-mediated role play

Date of recording: 26.06.1997 (machine shop, University of Hildesheim, Germany).

The *drill scenario* is characterized by the following features:

a. the dialogically organized exchange (German-French) is assisted by an interpreter (cf. Wadensjö 1998);
b. the exchange takes place in a technical setting (as opposed to a conversational setting), more specifically, in the field of mechanical engineering;
c. the (female) German interpreter is engaged as a novice interpreter (vs. an expert interpreter)[1] with limited foreign language fluency in French (as opposed to a more bilingual-bicultural community interpreter in other settings).

---

1.   Moser-Mercer (1997:255) refers to a *novice* (interpreter) as to "someone who has little or no experience in a particular domain" and to an *expert* (interpreter) as to "someone who has attained a high level of performance in a given domain as a result of years of experience".

Figure 1. The drill scenario

Role-play participants

Werner D.: German mechanical engineering instructor; no knowledge of French
Michel F.: in the role of instructor from Mulhouse University, France; with a microphone in left hand and a glossary at his disposal during recording session
INT: female student enrolled in *business and technical interpreting program*; with a glossary at her disposal

Scenario
Michel F. wishes to be informed about machine tools students are introduced to in their technical training courses.

Context
The German instructor Werner D. has just finished explaining the basic parts of a drill and another student interpreter is about to take over. Werner D. intends to explain next now how tools are clamped and moved (*eingespannt und bewegt*):

(1) eingespannt und bewegt – clamped and moved[2]

```
     11  Michel F.                          [clears his
->       Werner D.       (…) jetzt=äh . müsste man . m:: .
                         (…) now=uhm . we would have to
```

2. *Transcription conventions:* The transcription of video data includes the notation of prosodic phenomena (such as intonation, stress, length of segments, tempo, rhythm and pauses) as well as nonverbal information (with a special focus on eye contact, gaze and gestures).

```
12   Michel F.          throat]
     Werner D.          besprechen. wie das Werkzeug bewegt/
                        talk about . how the tool is moved/
```

```
13   Werner D.          eingespannt und bewegt wird,
                        clamped and moved,
                        [looks briefly to INT]  [turns to Michel F.]
```

```
14   INT                          (...)
     Werner D.          [turns to INT]
```

Dealing with word and terminology search

As the video data show, participants in the *drill scenario* systematically focus on interactionally relevant word and terminology search, particularly when the interpreter student is rendering explanations into her foreign language. Such word and terminology search is dealt with often in connection with repair activities in which, following Keith (1984: 313), a change in footing occurs since the "macro-conversation", i.e. the rendition of Werner D.'s German explanations for Michel F.

Transcription symbols are based upon musical score notation:

Michel F.	un corps,	simultaneous or overlapping utterances
	a shaft	interlinear translation into English
INT	un c/	

Other transcription symbols:

/	(self-) interruption
. ...	short, intermediate and longer silences within one or between two utterances (relative length estimated)
&	'rush through'
' , -	rising, falling, level intonation (follow intonation contours)
in **ein**gespannt	stressed word or syllable
oui: co:rps	lengthened sound
nicht(t)	doubtful sound
jetzt=äh	blurred word contours
peut ≠ être	unusual absence of linking
(mhm, ?)	transcription uncertain
(........?)	incomprehensible segment
*mouvé	ungrammatical form
[*softly*] + [*approaches drill*] +	para- and/or non-linguistic events; "+" signals end of event

into French, is left momentarily for a "micro-conversation" with one of the primary parties (here: between INT and Michel F.).

The following excerpt (2) illustrates how INT manifests her difficulties in finding the right French terms for *eingespannt und bewegt* and how she initiates a change in footing.

(2) *mouvé...

```
-> 14   INT          mhm' . bon on va parler alors
                     uha' . well we will talk next then
                                         [turns little by little
        Werner D.    (...)
```

```
   15   INT          maintenant comment l'outil e:st . serré
                     about how the tool i:s . clamped
                     to Michel F.]                    [seeks
```

```
   16   Michel F.                                    non-
                                                     no-
        INT          et . euh . . mm . . *mouvé'       & bougé-
                     and . uhm . mm . . *mouvé*'       & moved-  (tr.)
                     eye contact with Michel F.]
        Werner D.                              [follows exchange
```

```
   17   Michel F.    déplacé'        oui- . se déplace, .
                     moved' (tr.)    yes- . moves, (intr.) .
        INT                      & déplacé:,
                                 & moved, (tr.)
        Werner D.    betw. M.F./INT]               [turns to
```

```
   18   Michel F.    hmhm- [Pause 3 sec]
                     uhuh- [3 sec pause]
        Werner D.    INT and Michel F.]
```

When INT starts rendering Werner D.'s explanation into French, hesitation phenomena (i.e. prosodic cues) co-occur with a change in gaze and eye contact (here: from Werner D. to Michel F.; in 15/16). INT, being uncertain, hesitates and then utters *mouvé* (in 16) with rising intonation, but her addressee does not ratify it (*non*; 16), initiating an attempt at self-repair (*bougé-*; in 16). Michel F., though, corrects her again (*déplacé*; 17) and INT repeats the term immediately with falling intonation (in 17). During this phase of word search Werner D. is not involved in the exchange and only after yet another, still more decontextualizing correction has been made by Michel F. (*se déplace*; in 17), he turns to INT and Michel F. After the following 3 sec pause Werner D. selects himself as next speaker for further explanations.

The next excerpt (3) shows that similar methods are used for signaling a switch in dominant activities when INT manifests difficulties to find the right term in French for *zylindrischer Schaft/cylindrical shaft*. She first makes a tentative suggestion (*queue cylindrique*; in 23/24), but then initiates an other-repair by addressing Michel F.:

(3) *un corps cylindrique – a cylindrical shaft*

-> 22	INT	(...) une partie des outils' ce sont des
		(...) some of the tools' are
	Werner D.	*[follows exchange between INT and Michel F.]*

23	Michel F.	
	INT	outils avec euh . euhm: . . une queue
		tools with uhm . uhm: . . a cylindrical
		[looks at her glossary]

24	Michel F.	[softly] un co:rps,
		a shaft,
	INT	cylindrique non-
		tail no-

25	Michel F.	un corps, + mhm'
		a shaft, + uha'
	INT	un c/ un corps . cylindrique'
		a sh/ a cylindrical . shaft'

26	Werner D.	diese Werkzeuge (...)
		these tools (...)
		[moves tool ...]

Michel F. supplies twice the correct term (*un co:rps, un corps;* in 24/25) which helps INT to complete the rendition she is working on (*un corps . cylindrique'*; in 25). Before Werner D. takes the next turn (in 26), Michel F. ratifies again the correct term for the class of drill tools Werner D. is going to demonstrate (*mhm'*; in 25).

Excerpt (4) shows how INT is looking for the correct French technical term for the German *Drei-Backen-Futter* (*three-jaw-chuck*) that Werner D. has introduced next in connection with the type of chuck which drill tools with a cylindrical shaft can be clamped into. INT knows the term for *Futter/chuck* (*mandrin*), but the French equivalent for the modifier *Backe(n) / jaw(s)* presents a problem:

(4) *un mandrin à trois mors – a three-jaw-chuck*

-> 28	INT	oui euh . ces outils euh avec le corps yes uhm . these tools uhm with the .
	Werner D.	*[clamps the tool]*

29	INT	cylindrique sont euh . serrés dans un cylindrical shaft are uh . clamped in a
30	Michel F.	oui- mors' yes- jaws'
	INT	mandrin à trois euh . mors' . . chuck with three uh . jaws' . .
31	Michel F.	*[softly]* oui . trois mors . je crois + . . yes . three jaws . I think + . . *[turns away from INT and checks with his*

32	Michel F.	*glossary]*

	Werner D.	*[softly]* das kann (…)
		          I can't (…)
		         [looks for tool]

INT is given again the opportunity to find the French equivalent for *Drei-Backen-Futter*, but then interacts with Michel F. who supplies the correct term (*mors'*) that INT ratifies immediately (in 30). Michel F. also checks his glossary and comments on it (in 31) – signaling thereby a more decontextualized treatment of the lexical item in question. Only at this point Werner D. takes over the turn to demonstrate the next type of chuck which is called *Schnellspannfutter* (*quick-change-chuck*) in German.

When INT starts her rendition (see excerpt 5), she first tries to paraphrase the unknown term (in 37/38) and then ratifies the correct term given by Michel F. (*un mandrin rapide*; in 38/39).

(5) *un mandrin rapide – a quick-change-chuck*

37	INT	ça c'est un mandrin à trois mors qui peut this is a three-jaw-chuck that can *[turns to Michel F.; points at drill]*
	Werner D.	*[points to object behind camera, walks to it]*
38	Michel F.	ah- un mandrin oh- a quick-change-
	INT	≠ être serré euh vite' be clamped uh fast'

39	Michel F.	rapide,	(mhm,?)
		chuck,	(uha,?)
	INT		un mandrin rapide'
			a quick-change-chuck'
	Werner D.		*[approaches drill slowly]*

40	Michel F.	& version rapide' et	[softly] ah oui,
		& quick version' and	oh yes,
	Werner D.		(...)

Just as in excerpt (3) and (4), INT ratifies the technical term supplied by Michel F. with rising intonation which may have been understood by the French partici-pant as a cue for further word search (*version rapide*'; in 40). And this, in turn, may have been understood by Werner D. as a turn taking signal, since he starts a new turn, but then stops again, being out of turn, so to speak.

Conversational dynamics as an instructional resource

Changes in footing – ranging from translation activities to word and terminology search and vice versa – are accomplished in the analyzed excerpts by collaborative turn construction and interactional achievement of repair activities (including ratifications that can not always be distinguished from corrections). Prosodic cues like length of pause and intonation contours are interactionally synchronized with syntactic and nonverbal cues, all signaling changes in (dominant) activities.

As far as training aspects in the field of community interpreting and related areas are concerned, this conversational dynamics might be made use of as an instructional resource by increasing awareness of the dual function of repair ac-tivities for interpreting instructor(s) and interpreter student(s):

a. It should be understood that repair activities involving the native addressee of a rendition can help to improve second language proficiency, as long as word or terminology search is not completely decontextualized as it some-times happens in phases of grammatical error correction. Especially when changes in footing are self-initiated by the student interpreter(s), when they are successfully managed and when the macro-exchanges are not lost track of (here: between the German technical instructor and his French addressee), instructors can make use of the potentially ambiguous function of expanded ratification, i.e. by signaling general understanding of explanations given by the student interpreter but introducing and teaching "naturally" a (more) adequate terminology at the same time.

b. Awareness of regularities of error correction in explanatory sequences may also be increased by analyzing together the audio and/or video recording at the end of a training session, adopting, then, a retrospective and more cognitive approach.

c. As additional activity, role-play recordings can be compared with model explanatory sequences found in (recordings of) authentic settings. Research on authentic settings involving (more) experienced interpreters has shown that terminology search and repair activities are also an integral part of their job (cf. Apfelbaum 2004; Meyer 2004). Students thus will not only be shown that repair activities lead potentially to a more balanced linguistic competence in both working languages, but students might also understand that they need to be given gradually more responsibility for the coordination of talk and turn allocation, since this will be taken for granted as a professional skill by primary parties in all sort of (technical) business and community settings.

References

Apfelbaum, B. 1997. "Zur Rolle der Diskursanalyse in der Ausbildung von Gesprächsdolmetern." In *Translationsdidaktik. Grundfragen der Übersetzungswissenschaft*, E. Fleisch-mann, W. Kutz & P. A. Schmitt (eds), 268–275. Tübingen: Narr.

Apfelbaum, B. 2004. *Gesprächsdynamik in Dolmetsch-Interaktionen. Eine empirische Untersuchung von Situationen internationaler Fachkommunikation unter besonderer Berücksichtigung der Arbeitssprachen Deutsch, Englisch, Französisch und Spanisch.* Radolfzell: Verlag für Gesprächsforschung.

Keith, H. A. 1984. "Liaison interpreting – an exercise in linguistic interaction." In *Die Theorie des Übersetzens und ihr Aufschlußwert für die Übersetzungs- und Dolmetschdidaktik*, W. Wilss & G. Thome (eds), 308–317. Tübingen: Narr.

Ko, Leong. 1996. "Teaching dialogue interpreting." In *Teaching Translation and Interpreting 3. Papers from the third language international conference Elsinore, Denmark 9–11 June 1995*, C. Dollerup & V. Appel (eds), 119–127. Amsterdam: John Benjamins.

Lang, R. 1978. "Behavioral aspects of liaison interpreters in Papua New Guinea. Some preliminary observations." In *Language interpretation and communication*, D. Gerver & H. W. Sinaiko (eds), 231–244. New York/London: Plenum Press.

Meyer, B. 2004. *Dolmetschen im medizinischen Aufklärungsgespräch. Eine diskursanalytische Untersuchung zur Arzt-Patienten-Kommunikation im mehrsprachigen Krankenhaus.* Münster: Waxmann.

Moser-Mercer, B. 1997. "The expert-novice paradigm in interpreting research." In *Translationsdidaktik. Grundfragen der Übersetzungswissenschaft*, E. Fleischmann, W. Kutz & P. A. Schmitt (eds), 255–261. Tübingen: Narr.

Parnell, A. 1989. "Liaison Interpreting as a Language Teaching Technique." In *The theoretical and practical aspects of teaching conference interpretation*, L. Gran & J. Dodds (eds), 253–256. Udine: Campanotto.

Roy, C. B. 2000. *Interpreting as a Discourse Process*. New York/Oxford: University Press.

Schäffner, C. 1995. "Establishing common ground in bilateral interpreting." In *Topics in interpreting research*, J. Tommola (ed.), 91–107. Turku: University of Turku. Centre for Translation and Interpreting.

Wadensjö, C. 1998. *Interpreting as Interaction*. London: Edison Wesley Longman.

A data driven analysis
of telephone interpreting

Brett Allen Rosenberg
Virginia Commonwealth University, U.S.A.

The telephone is quickly becoming the predominant medium through which interpreting services are delivered. However, aside from some initial descriptive works (Wadensjö 1999; Niska 1998), objective empirical analysis of this kind of interpreting is conspicuous by its absence in the literature. Over a two-year period I collected data on the features of some 1876 interpreter-mediated telephone calls. The analysis of this data shows that these calls are far more complex than as suggested in earlier studies. Three main subcategories are analysed herein: telephone interpreting or, three-way telephone conversation, speakerphone interpreting, remote interpretation of a face-to-face encounter, and finally, telephone passing, a face-to-face encounter where the telephone is passed from one party to another.

Introduction

Telephone interpreting is growing at such a pace that it is beginning to displace the use of in situ interpreters in some medical and legal contexts. Telephone interpreting offers certain undeniable advantages, namely, easy access to interpreting services, even in remote areas, and relatively low cost. These benefits motivate those who utilize these services and the administrators who allocate funds for them to be rather enthusiastic about these developments. However, court interpreters have generally been ambivalent when not openly hostile towards the advancement of telephone interpreting (Vidal 1998; Mintz 1998). In spite of some initial descriptive works (Wadensjö 1999; Niska 1998; Oviatt & Cohen 1992), it is surprising then, that such a limited amount of empirical research has been undertaken that describes the linguistic characteristics of this particular mode of interpreting. This paper offers an initial quantitative taxonomy of the types of communicative configurations that occurred in a corpus collected over a two-year period in which I myself worked as a telephone interpreter. It was discovered that these interactions are indeed unique, not because of linguistic differences between telephone and face-to-face communication, rather that many of the most salient characteristics in interpreted-mediated telephone communication are the product of the complexity of the situational, extra-linguistic factors that intervene as a result of the expanding access to the interpreter. Further comparative research is needed in order to quantify the frequency of occurrence of certain errors in interpreter-mediated conversations in face-to-face interactions and interpreted telephone communication.

Professionalisation of community interpreting

A lot has already been written about professionalizing the work of community interpreters (Mikkelson 1995; Roberts 1994; inter alia). There is no doubt a need to improve training for interpreters and for those who utilize their services in community settings. However, in order to do this it is necessary that we adequately understand what it is we are training people for. In other words, there is a need for an accurate, realistic description of the types of linguistic encounters an interpreter is likely to find during a typical day's work, in order to better prepare them to deal with all the complexities of this kind of interpreting. Unfortunately, much of what has been written about telephone interpreting is from interpreters who are fearful of this change in their profession and thus portray it as entirely negative, or from telephone interpreting company representatives, who, unsurprisingly, are entirely positive.

> A sound theoretical base is necessary, not only for testing and training community interpreters, but also for the development of the profession. Theory must, however, be supported by data, not only norms or beliefs (Niska 1998).

As we shall see, of the 1876 telephone-interpreting events studied here, very few fall entirely into the classic idealized model of interpreted interaction. Future interpreters need to be prepared to deal with the new reality of the remote working environment. Furthermore, those who manage telephone-interpreting companies can benefit from this research to find ways to maximize the efficacy and accuracy of their interpreters' work.

Previous research

Empirical research on public service interpreting has only recently begun to appear and is based on relatively small samples of data. Amongst the few existing examples of empirical research there are even fewer that have been carried out on interpreter-mediated telephone discourse in public services settings. Two notable exceptions are Oviatt & Cohen (1992) and Wadensjö (1999) whose empirical re-search on interpreter mediated telephone conversations have shed some light onto some of the particular linguistic characteristics of these speech events. Oviatt & Cohen, as summarized in Niska (1998), arrived at some interesting conclusions when comparing interpreter-mediated calls (by one experienced Japanese-Eng-lish interpreter) with non-interpreted telephone conversations. Two of the most important conclusions from my standpoint are:

Contrary to normal practice, telephone interpreters tended to refer to the parties in third person; the first person "I" was reserved for self-referral; requests for confirmation amounted to 31.5% of total words in interpreted calls, compared to 23.5% in non-interpreted calls (Niska 1998).

These results show that interpreter-mediated telephone conversations do not follow the idealized, conduit model of interpreting, but rather the interpreter is an active participant in the conversation as is the case in many community settings.

For her part, Wadensjö compared two interpreted events involving the same participants in a police setting, one over the phone and another face-to-face. Her basic findings were that the tele-interpreted call lacked the fluency and coordina-tion present in the face-to-face setting.

I find two things lacking in the prior research:

Both studies are based on a very small sample of data.

Both seem to assume that all telephone-interpreted calls are basically alike and that their particular problems arise as a result of some supposed inherent linguistic differences with face-to-face speech events.

There are indeed differences between these two modes of communication; however, as Hopper (1992) states, these two forms of discourse remain more alike than different. The most obvious of these differences is the total lack of visual contact. The lack of visual contact with the interlocutors is indeed a disadvantage at times, but it also offers certain advantages (greater patient privacy, less dis-tractions for the interpreter). Furthermore, with present advances in technology, what Niska (1998) refers to as videophony, or transmission of a facial image in conjunction with a telephone call, this difference could well disappear in the near future. Another often mentioned difference with the telephone as a medium for interpreting is the supposed overall poor sound quality. While noise is indeed a problem in many interviews, inaudible discourse as a result of people screaming and all talking at once, telephones ringing, etc. are part and parcel of all com-munity interpreters' work environment. I discovered this harsh reality during my seven years experience as an on site medical interpreter in clinics and hospitals in Texas.

After two years experience working as a telephone interpreter, I believe that some vital information is being missed in the existing research in this area due to the small sample sizes used as the basis for the research. In what follows, a brief description of the corpus and how it was collected is followed by a discussion of some of the distinct communicative configurations and their effect on interpreting efficacy and accuracy, and finally some conclusions and suggestions for further research.

Data collection

Over a two-year period, in which I worked as a part-time Spanish/English telephone interpreter out of my home, I kept logs indicating the total number of calls per month for 14 of the 24 months. The information in these logs includes the length in minutes of each individual call and the nature of the conversation, medical or commercial, (broadly construed). As you will have noticed, legal interpreting is conspicuous by its absence. This is not an oversight, but rather the result of the reality of collecting "real" data in a real setting. The company for which I worked during this period of time does not offer tele-court interpreting. Furthermore, there are special technical requirements for court telephone interpreting, i.e. special phones that enable simultaneous interpreting. All the data described herein was consecutively interpreted. A record was also kept of the communicative configuration of the calls. Three main categories emerged from the initial analysis:

- Interpreted telephone conversations, all three parties were on the phone together but in different places, in other words a three-way telephone conversation,
- Face-to-face conversations interpreted through the use of a speakerphone.
- The primary participants were face to face, but the telephone was passed back and forth (either because there was no speaker phone or no one knew how to operate it), this will be referred to as telephone passing.

Although the data I collected was from my own work, this is not totally unheard of in translation and interpreting studies. In fact, one of the most promising new approaches to the study of translation are the think-aloud protocols (TAPs). These are transcriptions of "verbalizations" of thoughts, which subjects are instructed to produce while carrying out a translation task. Much in the same vein, as I interpreted the telephone conversations, I did what could be called the "note-taking protocols", in other words, I wrote down my thoughts that occurred during my work as an interpreter.

Results

Over the 14-month period a total of 1876 calls were interpreted. The average number of calls per month came to 134. The total length of these interpreted-mediated telephone conversations was 15,571 minutes or 258 hours and 6 minutes. The length of the average call was 8.27 minutes.

By rounding off the percentages, of these 1876 calls 1188 or roughly 63.4% of the total number of interpreter-medicated calls are classified as medical, these include telephone nurse triage/advice calls, emergency room consultations, interviews with employees of the hospital financial offices, private physicians offices, preoperative consultations with surgeons and anaesthesiologist, and calls directed to the phone of recently hospitalised patient's rooms.

The second largest group are the commercial calls, which comprised roughly 33.9% of the corpus, or some 637 calls. The vast majority of these calls were making hotel reservations, customer service calls for people inquiring about insurance coverage or product warranties, banks pursuing payment of loans and mortgages. These calls were almost entirely three way telephone conversations save 5 examples of arbitration between employees done by their plant manager.

The smallest category, I shall refer to as the totally failed calls, for lack of a better name. These are calls in which either the Spanish-speaking client had already hung up by the time I was placed on the line, or the company representative had left the Spanish-Speaking client on hold and I was transferred onto the line with no representative of the company, which usually resulted in a great deal of

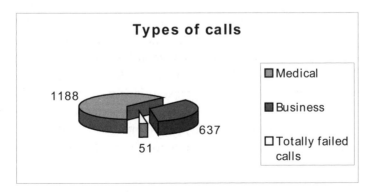

Figure 1. Types of calls

confusion. These calls generally required a lengthy explanation on the part of the interpreter about why the client could not be helped with their needs, and for my part, I had to explain that I was just a subcontracted interpreter without access to the necessary information. In other words, this category is comprised totally of dyadic conversations either in English or Spanish, and no interpreting takes place. Thankfully these calls only made up about 2.7% of the total amount of calls or about 51 calls, which, as one can imagine, tended to be quite short in duration.

In what follows I will offer a detailed account of the different categories and subcategories of interpreted speech events as they occurred in the above-mentioned corpus. This is a preliminary pilot study that could serve as the basis for future research of these types of interpreted events.

Basic structure of calls

All of the calls begin with an initial dyadic interaction (or in some case 2 dyadic interactions) before the interpreting has even begun.

Telephone:	Ring, ring…
Interpreter (I):	Hello
Company Operator (CO):	Hello, this is X (name of operator) from Y (name of interpreting company), I have a call for you from Z (name of Client (C1[1]), number 12345.
I:	Thanks
CO:	[to –> (C1) (C2?)] Hello, I have Spanish interpreter number 54321 on the line.
CO:	[to I] Go ahead, client is on the line.
I:	Hi, this is interpreter 54321 on the line…

From this point forward the communication can take various forms. Some C1's will begin to address the client in first person without so much as greeting the interpreter, or even less common, briefing the interpreter as to the nature of the call. In this corpus, the physicians tended to be more considerate in this regard and often gave a brief summary of their patient's case before starting the triadic interview. Most commercial calls started almost immediately with a brief statement like "the client is on the line, go ahead" as if the interpreter was already supposed to know what to say before C1 gave anything to interpret. Another common scenario is a nurse who asks the interpreter to ask the patient a series of questions,

---

1.   C1 refers to the English speaker, C2 will be the Spanish-speaking client since it is almost always C1 who call the company asking for assistance.

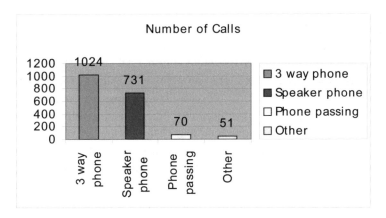

Figure 2. Number of calls

but the interpreter is forced to inquire if the C2 can hear him/her (is C2 on the line, am I on a speaker phone or worse yet, they are going to pass the phone). These dyadic-triadic shifts are common to community interpreting settings; in my previous research (Rosenberg 2001) of community interpreting I referred to many of these original interpreter utterances (or *non-renditions* using Wadensjö's (1998: 108) terminology) and the omitted utterances (or *zero renditions*) of C1 and C2 as the result of the complexity of community interpreting settings. These are utterances that simply are not directed from C1 to C2. (For example, doctor to nurse or other physician, nurse to interpreter, or a patient or customer talking to a family member or friend.) Many times these utterances that are not interpreted are not "errors" as such, but are simply part and parcel of the etiquette of community interpreting. For example, when a nurse says to the interpreter "I am going to put you on speaker phone, OK?" or if the nurse asks the interpreter to stay on the line until the physician arrives after doing his/her initial assessment of the patient. I will refer to all such episodes as *dyadic-triadic shifts* in the conversations. Problems only result from these shifts when, due to the interpreter's inability to see C1 and C2, s/he is unable to determine if a previous utterance was dyadic or an unheard triadic one. Another common problem that led to non-renditions was the poor audio quality. At times it was impossible to hear an utterance directed from C1 to C2 or vice-versa and I had to ask for repetitions.

In the following section the three main communicative configurations are described as they occurred in the corpus and their effect on the efficacy and ac-curacy of the interpretation from the interpreter's perspective will be discussed.

Interpreter-mediated telephone conversations (TWT)

Virtually all of the interpreter-mediated commercial calls were three-way telephone conversations, save for 5 conversations witha supervisor who arbitrated conflicts among employees in his office, utilizing a speakerphone. About a third of all the medical calls were also three-way interpreter-mediated telephone conversations. This means that out of a total of 1876 calls logged, roughly 55% (1024 calls) of the corpus was made up of interpreter-mediated three-way telephone calls. These are also by far the least problematic as one can well imagine, given that all interlocutors (C1, C2 and Int) were on an equal footing. There was no visual contact with any of the callers. Perhaps the only caveat I would add to this is what Hopper (1992) refers to as *caller hegemony*. That is to say, that the person placing the call has the advantages over the other interlocutors in that as the conversation begins, it is the caller not the answerers who know the objectives of the call. The interpreter is especially excluded, since C1 ostensibly works for some kind of business or medical institution and can contextualize the call, at least in general, and C2, usually, has some concrete matter that has motivated the call. Nearly all the TFC (totally failed calls) were to be interpreted telephone conversations. In spite of these minor problems, in general I found these calls to be superior to the other two categories in terms of sound quality, and the facility with which one could coordinate the three party speech.

Interpreter-mediated face-to-face conversations with speakerphones

Around 39% (731) of the total interpreter-mediated calls in the corpus were conducted, at least in part, through the use of speakerphones (SPI). Speakerphones caused the greatest number of problems with regards to sound quality. This was either as a result of poor placement of the phone (to far from C1 or C2) or if the phone was too close to a source of noise (television, radio, crying baby). In addition there were certain technical shortcomings with some of these phones in that one could not hear and speak at the same time. This limitation made it impossible for the interpreter to hear some of the back-channelling discourse markers and one-syllable answers to yes and no questions, if C1 or C2 did not speak loud enough or spoke too soon after the question was rendered. Another problem with the use of speakerphones is that physicians tended to address patients more often in first person. Though this might seem a positive development, it creates confusion if there has not been an adequate briefing of the interpreter beforehand. For example, on one occasion, the physician started the conversation right off with "I believe I've seen *you* before" (directed to C2). However, that "*you*" is problematic for languages like Spanish which grammatically mark such words for gender, formality, and number. The best possible rendering of this utterance given the context could have been: *Creo que **te/lo/la/los/las** he atendido antes.*

Given that I could not see C2, I settled for a "*Creo que ya nos hemos conocido*" (literally: I believe we have already met, which avoided the above-mentioned options). One final problem worthy of mention here are disconnects. Often times, after the interview has already started, someone unplugs or accidentally hangs the phone up and cuts off the communication abruptly. Unfortunately, I did not keep a log of the number of occurrences of these phenomena.

Telephone passing

Telephone passing is by far the most problematic of the three configurations, although it only accounted for a little over 3.7% (70 calls) of the total number. Typically these interactions were the result of the nurse or physician not being able to operate the speakerphone option on the telephone, or these were calls transferred directly into patient's rooms where the phones were not equipped with a speaker. The problems derived principally from the fact that this is not really a triadic communicative event, but rather two parallel conversations in which the interpreter is being used as an emissary. The worst cases are those where the health care provider would give me a long list of questions to ask the patient and then pass the phone to them. Many of the patients had no idea, to start with, who they were speaking to; secondly, they would often answer some of the questions with rather long narratives or ask questions about the questions which made it extremely difficult to take notes. On a number of occasions the practitioner removed the phone from the patient before I could finish obtaining answers to all the questions.

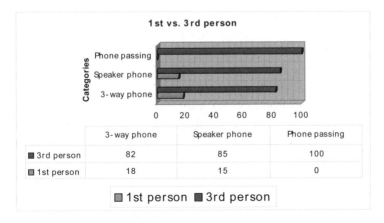

	3-way phone	Speaker phone	Phone passing
■ 3rd person	82	85	100
▨ 1st person	18	15	0

▨ 1st person ■ 3rd person

Figure 3. 1st vs. 3rd person

Conclusions and suggestions for further research

One of the first rules all interpreters are taught is to always interpret all utterances in the first person and not preface them with the equivalent of "he said/she said…" However, in my years of professional experience I have found this rule extremely hard to put into practice. Firstly, this is because most of the time, the clients address each other in third person. Second, because it is unnatural for most people to speak directly to a person who they know cannot understand them, especially when they know the interpreter does understand them. Third, it is not always completely apparent from whom the utterance has originated. In Figure 3, it is interesting to note that there is little difference between three-way telephone interpreting and speakerphone interpreting. Around 85% of the clients insisted on using third person reference even when I insisted on using the first person. However, this became 100% in the case of telephone passing.

Perhaps the most striking result of this research is that, in spite of all these different scenarios that the telephone interpreter faces, none of them were unique to this form of interpreting. Even in the case of telephone passing, in my work experience as an on site interpreter, I often had doctors and nurses send me into rooms alone with lists of questions. So what is it then that makes telephone interpreting so particularly difficult? I believe that two main areas need to be investigated.

Though certain configurations are not unique to telephone interpreting, perhaps they are statistically more prevalent. In this case, studies should be done to determine if, for example, there is a correlation between lack of visual input and the frequency of omissions and nonrenditions and if this difference effects the efficacy and accuracy of interpreting in public service settings.

Though there are indeed obvious differences between telephone and face-to-face interpreting, some of the implications of these differences are not all that obvious. My suspicion is that the interpreter troubles stemming from overextending access to the interpreter are unfamiliar to most clients. In other words, by making themselves available to a larger and larger public, interpreters are stretching their capacities to the limit.

This shared frame of reference became apparent to me after my work in rather small neighbourhood health clinics, with a small medical staff, and only dealing a small section of the patient population (i.e. monolingual Spanish-speaking patients who lived in the neighbourhood). My second interpreting position was in a large metropolitan hospital complex that served a large area of central Texas and included many types of services that I had not dealt with before (oncology, trauma, cardiology, pastoral care, etc.). However the largest jump has been from those two rather intimate work settings to interpreting over the telephone. I have had to deal with completely unknown professionals in fields in which I had no previous interpreting experience (banking, hotel reservations, etc.). Furthermore, I was dealing with dialects of Spanish that I found rather difficult to comprehend such as Puerto Rican, Cuban, Dominican, etc. (99% of my previous experience had been with Mexican Spanish). Even more troublesome, given that we do not share the same geographic location, I found it difficult to understand the C2's attempts to pronounce place names and physicians' names that were not a problem when I worked in a more intimate environment, where I usually could guess what my clients were trying to say.

Future research should study how semantic field effects interpreter accuracy, how the interpreter's physical distance and lack of a shared frame of reference can make interpreting far more difficult. Unlike those investigators who want to see something inherent in telephone communication that renders it linguistically unsuitable for quality interpretation, greater emphasis should be placed on the extra linguistic, situational demands being placed on interpreters who are suddenly being made available to a vast and heterogeneous population of non-English-speaking clients.

With the present advances in technology, telephone interpreting is only going to continue to expand, even into the domain of the courts. For example, in a recent survey of court interpreter program coordinators in 25 States in the U.S. some 89% of them declared that they are already utilizing commercial telephone interpreting services, Duncan (2001). Rather than make unbiased claims about the quality of these services rigorous research needs to be carried out on large corpuses of real data and unbiased comparisons need to be made between these modes of interpreting before any judgement should be rendered about the adequacy of this method of service delivery.

References

Duncan, L. 2001. *Remote Court Interpreting: Development of a Pilot Project in California.* California Administrative Office of the courts. San Francisco, California.

Hopper, R. 1992. *Telephone Conversation.* Indiana University Press

Mintz, D. 1999. "Hold the Phone! Telephone Interpreting Scrutinized." *Proteus* Winter, Vol. VLL, No. 1.

Niska, H. 1998. "What is remote interpreting?" From the workshop "Quality issues in remote interpreting" in Vigo, Galicia, 26 March 1998 (Conference "Anovadores de vos, anosadores de nos", 25–27 March 1998).

Niska, H. 1997. "Testing community interpreters: a theory, a model and a plea for research" (lecture given at the Symposium on Community Interpreting in Bloemfontein, South Africa, 6–7 October, 1997).

Oviatt, Sharon L. & Cohen, Philip R. 1992. "Spoken language in interpreted telephone dialogues", in *Computer Speech and Language* 6, 277–302.

Vidal, M. 1998. "Telephone Interpreting: Technological Advance or Due Process Impediment", in *Proteus* Vol. VLL, No. 3 – summer 1998.

Wadensjö, C. 1998. *Interpreting as Interaction.* London & New York: Longman. Language in Social Life Series.

Wadensjö, C. 1999. "Telephone Interpreting and the Synchronization of Talk in Social Interaction". In *The Translator*, 1999, vol 5: 2, St.Jerome Pub. Manchester, UK, 247–264.

PART III

Interpreters in the community

Studies of macro dynamics

Interpreter-mediated police interviews

Working as a professional team

Isabelle A. Perez and Christine W. L. Wilson
Heriot-Watt University, Edinburgh, Scotland

This study builds on the researchers' experience in delivering regular training since 2000 on "working through interpreters" to Scottish police officers. Whilst most previous research has focused on the interpreter's role, the emerging issues emphasise the role of the police professional working alongside the interpreter. The study explores initial perceptions of potential problems and expectations relating to interpreter-mediated interviews, comparing attitudes preceding and following 'Phase I' training. It then highlights and discusses relevant areas emerging from the initial findings which may inform the development of 'Phase II' training and the revision of police guidelines. Ultimately, it concludes that "working with/through interpreters" training should be integrated into interview skills training as part of the basic training of police officers.

Introduction

In performing their professional function, Scottish police officers are increasingly required to work with or through interpreters (Perez & Wilson 2005). This raises a number of questions regarding the impact of interpreting on the police officer's professional role and, conversely, the impact of the police officer on the professional performance of the interpreter.

Studies relating to interpreting in the legal domain tend to concentrate on work in court rather than with the police (Brennan 1997; Hertog 2001); although the studies by Fowler (2003) and Krouglov (1999) focus on the interpreting activity and the role of the interpreter in police settings in England. The present study explores the role of the police professional working alongside the interpreter.

Working environment of the Scottish police

This study refers specifically to the Scottish police – there is no national police force serving the United Kingdom as a whole.[1] Indeed, even within Scotland there is no 'national' police force, but rather eight independent police forces each headed by a Chief Constable whose duty it is to ensure their police force complies with the instructions of the Lord Advocate (the senior law officer in Scotland).[2]

The current environment in which Scottish police officers' work has been shaped by events in recent history such as cases leading to charges of institutional racism and the associated reports, and the Asylum Dispersal Policy impacting on Glasgow from 1999.[3] In the three years to January 2003, 10 000 people seeking asylum arrived in Glasgow and there are around 8 000 people living in the Glasgow area who arrived as asylum seekers, of 67 different nationalities, speaking over 40 different languages (HMIC 2003: 6.2–6.3).

In parallel, a number of legislative developments have redefined the working environment of the police: for example, the Race Relations (Amendment) Act (2000) has required all police forces to produce a Race Equality Scheme.[4] These legislative developments have driven forward the need to address the problem of "language barriers" and, significantly, they have informed the publication of the *Lord Advocate's Guidelines to Chief Constables on investigating racial crime* which include specific directions regarding the provision of interpreters in police work.[5]

More generally, the work of Scottish police officers is governed by the Scots Law principle of procedural *fairness* both to the accused and to society at large. Moreover, every police officer is *individually* and *personally* responsible for ensuring that the evidence gathered (e.g. in interviews) is *admissible as evidence*

---

1.   The Scottish Office Information Directorate (July 1995).

2.   The legislative system in Scotland differs from that in the rest of the United Kingdom and Scottish police powers and duties are defined in the *Police (Scotland) Act 1967* (as subsequently amended). See www.scotland.gov.uk/library/documents/police.htm

3.   Murder of Stephen Lawrence (1993). *The Stephen Lawrence Inquiry – An Action Plan for Scotland* (2001) www.scotland.gov.uk/library2/doc01/sli-03.htm; Murder of Surjit Singh Chhokar (1998). Report by Dr Raj Jandoo (2001); HMIC Thematic Inspection on Race Relations *Without Prejudice?* Led by Mr William Taylor, HM Chief Inspector of Constabulary (Report launched 2001) www.scotland.gov.uk/hmic

4.   Disability Discrimination Act (1995); The Human Rights Act (1998); The Immigration and Asylum Act (1999); Race Relations (Amendment) Act (2000).

5.   The *Lord Advocate's Guidelines to Chief Constables* (2002) include "Assessment of language needs and cultural sensitivities" www.crownoffice.gov.uk/publications/newpublics.htm

in court; failure could lead to a case being thrown out of court and dismissed. Consequently, police officers are instructed to note everything said and done *verbatim*. Police officers are also trained in specific interview skills and must follow strict procedures: for example, cautions and certain frozen forms of words must be administered as part of the legal process and the person being interviewed *must understand* these words.[6] At present, the view is that cautions etc. can only be administered to non-English speakers if an interpreter is *physically present* (thus excluding telephone interpreting).

Finally, in Scotland, a person may only be detained under caution for questioning for a *maximum of six hours* before being charged. It is important to note that this six-hour period commences the moment a person is detained (e.g. put into the police car) and not from the time the actual interview begins. Therefore, if an interpreter is required and it takes four hours for the interpreter to arrive, only two hours remain to question the person detained before s/he must be charged or released.

Scottish police and interpreting

The researchers contacted the eight Scottish police forces to clarify policy (spring 2004).

Only four of the eight Scottish police forces have "current" translation/interpreting policy documents or guidelines in place: three other forces are in the process of drawing up or reviewing documentation and the fourth offers a minimum of information posted on a wall. Two of the existing sets of documentation focus primarily on logistical matters (locating and booking interpreters etc.), whereas the other two sets are very comprehensive – one gives fairly in-depth guidance regarding linguistic matters.

Secondly, all eight forces prefer "face-to-face" interpreting (having an interpreter physically present during interviews), but all regularly use telephone interpreting services.

The final point relates to the training of police officers to work with or through interpreters. The researchers consider that the issue of training is potentially fundamental to the professionalisation of interpreting in settings involving police officers. On the one hand, because no matter how well-trained and competent an interpreter may be, if a police officer does not "allow" him/her to "do his/her job", the interpreter's performance will not be satisfactory. On the other hand, a police officer trained to work with interpreters may be able to ensure that interpreting is

---

6. Strathclyde Police Force Training (1996).

conducted more professionally, even when it is necessary to work with linguists with no interpreter training.

Training of police officers

Unfortunately, there is *no training* in working through interpreters offered to new recruits as part of their basic training by any Scottish police force. At best, new recruits will be told that they need to book an interpreter in particular circumstances: knowledge regarding interpreting tends to be acquired "on the job" from supervising officers who may themselves be ill-informed.

Occasionally there are informal and reciprocal arrangements between certain interpreting-service providers and local police stations.

The majority of training offered to Scottish police officers in working with or through interpreters has been provided by the researchers (Phase I training). Since 2000, Isabelle Perez and Christine Wilson have been training police officers of all ranks from across Strathclyde Police. Strathclyde Police is the largest police force in Scotland: with 7 517 officers it employs almost half the total number (15 713) of police in Scotland (Scottish Executive, June 2004). The researchers have trained approximately 500 officers.

Since 2001, the researchers have also provided training at national level at the Scottish Police College: training officers from all eight Scottish police forces as part of their training to become interview skills trainers.[7] The researchers have trained approximately 270 officers.

Phase I training

The Phase I training sessions provided by the researchers aim mainly to raise awareness regarding interpreting and to provide basic level guidance on how best to work with and through interpreters.

---

7.   Central Scotland Police; Dumfries & Galloway Constabulary; Fife Constabulary; Grampian Police; Lothian & Borders Police; Northern Constabulary; Tayside Police; Strathclyde Police www.scottish.police.uk

Background to research study

Sample

Responses were collected from 252 police officers over the course of 20 training sessions. Of this total, 145 had no previous experience of working with an interpreter, whilst 107 had some previous experience, albeit limited and in many cases with untrained interpreters.

Methodology

Immediately prior to Phase I training, all police officers were asked to indicate what *they perceive to be the main source of difficulty when working through an interpreter*, or if they had previous experience, what *they had found to be the main source(s) of difficulty when working through an interpreter*. The question was fairly open and respondents could offer more than one answer, but they had to respond quickly and spontaneously at the opening of their training session. The data collected is analysed under Data Analysis (Part 1) below.

Following Phase I training, trainees were invited to comment by questionnaire. On the basis of fairly open questions, 20 respondents provided feedback on the usefulness/relevance of Phase I training, its subsequent impact on their professional practice when working through an interpreter, and the content of any Phase II training programme.

In parallel, trained professional public service interpreters (working between English and another spoken language or British Sign Language (BSL)) were also invited to return views by questionnaire on the main difficulties encountered in interpreter-mediated police interviews and any measures which might help counter these. Their responses help set the comments returned by police officers in context (Part 2 of the Data Analysis).

Data analysis

Part 1

There are seven main areas of concern for police officers with (PWs) or without (PW/Os) prior experience of working through an interpreter, as outlined in Table 1.1 as a percentage of the total number of respondents in each category.

Table 1.1. Police responses: Areas of concern

Total responses	PW/Os 145	PWs 107
Logistics	26%	27%
Accuracy	29%	31%
Trust	16%	14%
Conversation Flow	30%	19%
Interpreter's Knowledge / Police Procedures	14%	8%
Interpreter's Skills & Role	17%	22%
Police Officer's Role	9%	7%

Logistics

The issue of logistics is perceived to be a major problem by 26% of PW/Os, both in terms of *availability* – explicit repeated concerns are expressed regarding "locating an interpreter" and "locating a suitable interpreter" – and *time* "to locate a (suitable) interpreter" but also and repeatedly "for the interpreter to arrive (at the police station)". The latter must be considered in the context of the Scottish six-hour detention rule and, therefore, it receives particular emphasis in the responses provided by 27% of PWs.

This group also describes *ad hoc* solutions resorted to in real situations (e.g. "could not get one through Strathclyde Police so turned to Immigration Office in Glasgow", "could not get one to Aberdeenshire in time, so used a Police Constable with language skills"), as well as the problems which may arise at different stages in the judicial process (e.g. the "problem when case reached court because 2 interpreters required: 1 for the prosecution and 1 for the defence", "problem trying to coordinate suspect interview with lawyer, interpreter, police, suspect because of availability").

Accuracy

A primary area of concern for PWs (31%) and PW/Os (29%) is related to the accuracy, faithfulness and/or completeness of the interpreted version and its associated impact on the success of the interview. PW/Os make multiple uses of the terms "accurate" and "accuracy" and, in a significant number of cases, there is explicit concern regarding "(police officers') questions being put across "accurately" and, in fewer cases, to "accurate replies being conveyed back". The focus appears to be on the potential loss of information and/or misinterpretation and the negative consequences this would have for police officers. Respondents often and explicitly make a correlation between a perceived lack of accuracy and possible problems of understanding (presumably on the interpreter's part).

Accuracy also features repeatedly in PWs' comments, with particular emphasis on whether the interpretation accurately conveys the police officer's original questions. This group makes numerous references to "*not knowing* (whether you are getting an accurate interpretation)", in other words they clearly and explicitly regret what they perceive to be lack/loss of control on the part of the police officer, which was only hinted at by PW/Os.

Trust

Concerns regarding accuracy are closely linked to "trust" mentioned by 16% of PW/Os, either with no other qualifier or with explicit reference made to the interpreter: "trusting that the interpreter has interpreted what is being said correctly". So reliance on interpreters – and therefore presumably the perceived surrender of control – is perceived as problematic even by those with no prior experience of situations involving interpreting.

Similar concerns were voiced by 14% of PWs, but, more inclusively, they raise the issue of "trust between parties". A number of comments focus on the importance of rapport building "between the police officer and interpreter" or "between the other parties".

Conversation flow

Focusing on the interpreting process, 30% of PW/Os anticipate difficulties relating to "conversation flow". Comments fall into two equally significant categories: those who regret the *loss/interruption of the flow* of the interview/questioning (i.e. that there has to be an interpreter at all) and those who raise the issue of *pace* which is vital in these settings (typically, "the speed at which conversation can take place").

However, PW/Os' concerns may be partly inspired by fear of the unknown, as the proportion of PWs with similar concerns is significantly lower (19%). Some PWs qualify their answers by stating that interruption of the flow of the interview "is not the fault of the interpreter", although several of them also make specific references to the impact on interviewing techniques – "it is difficult to challenge replies" or "allows the suspect time to gauge reply".

Interpreter's knowledge of police procedures

In view of the emphasis often given to interpreters' knowledge of police or legal procedures, it is perhaps surprising that this is not given priority as a perceived (14% of PW/Os) or observed (8% of PWs) concern. Nonetheless, references to both "terminology" and "procedure'" are usually introduced negatively as "lack of (interpreter) understanding" or "lack of knowledge".

Interpreter's skills and role

In contrast, the interpreter's knowledge is questioned by 17% of PW/Os and 22% of PWs, both in terms of their skills and understanding of their role. Frequent reference is made to instances where the interpreter's skills may or do fail to satisfy the demands of police work: ranging from the ability to deal with slang and local accents to acting impartially and demonstrating cultural competence.

PW/Os' remarks are expressed in fairly general terms (e.g. "interpreter's opinions and prejudices", "bias", "cultural pressure and collusion") whereas PWs report on a wide range of role deviations ("asides with interviewee", "interpreter becoming too involved", "advising complainer", "behaving like lawyer", "making up own mind that suspect was guilty"), as well as numerous cases of what is generally termed "lack of cultural knowledge".

Role of police officer

Significantly, fewer police officers mention their own role as a subject of concern, nevertheless 9% of PW/Os and 7% of PWs comment respectively on the perceived need to identify the correct language and ask simple/short/jargon-free questions, and on the observed need for adjustments to their input in terms of speed, slang or jargon.

Only PWs raise the issue of the "necessary (interpreter's) briefing" and, in referring to problems of communication management ("police officer addressing interpreter", "suspect addressing interpreter not police officer"), hint at the desirability of training for police officers, further supported by comments such as "my lack of knowledge..." and "I video-ed the exchange so that others could benefit".

Successful outcome

Explicit positive comments are returned by 13% of PWs on the basis of previous successful problem-free experiences. However, they warn that success depends on three rules: that the interpreter is pre-briefed, that "I should speak slower and without slang" and that the interpreter is available.

Comments

Finally, comments from both groups of respondents refer to the necessity of thorough planning or preparation for interpreter-mediated police interviews, and to a range of wider policy issues such as: the subsequent use of police interview material in court settings or concern regarding the proper handling of interpreting issues by other professionals (upstream from the police) within court settings, as well as the need for a regularly updated, national list of registered interpreters.

Part 2

The profile of police respondents involved in the study following Phase 1 training is outlined in Table 2.1. Most respondents are detective sergeants/inspectors working in the Criminal Investigation Department (CID). Most are also interview advisors who contribute to the training of officers in interviewing at local level.

Although 9 respondents claim to have received training as part of basic police training, it has been impossible to trace this to any formal training initiative. Based on other information regarding the content of basic training for new recruits, it is assumed "basic training" refers to minimal input regarding the circumstances when an interpreter must be booked and information on the basic logistics of booking an interpreter.

Results based on the questionnaires returned are summarised in Tables 2.2 to 2.5.

Table 2.1. Profile of police respondents

Total: 20 respondents		
Rank	Detective Inspector	4
	Detective Sergeant	14
	Inspector	1
	Sergeant	1
Area	Criminal Investigation Department (CID)	14
	Major Crime	2
	Drugs/surveillance	1
	ACPOS* secretariat	1
	Professional standards	1
Training	Basic training	9
	Phase I training	20
Experience	PWs	14
	PW/Os	6
	Telephone interpreting	5

* Association of Chief Police Officers in Scotland

Table 2.2. Particularly useful / relevant insights from Phase I training

Total: 20 respondents	
Understanding of interpreter's role and interpreting process	14
Importance of pre-briefing	6
Interpreter's perspective/difficulties	5
Communication management: directly addressing interviewee	3
Understanding of best practice	3
Confidence booster	3
Need to prepare/plan	2
Police and non-English speakers' perspective	2
Understanding specific cultural requirements	1
Need for qualified interpreter	1

Table 2.3. Resulting modifications to professional practice

Total: 20 respondents	
Knowledge transfer	5
Change style/format of interview	5
Better planning, involving interpreter	4
Briefing/debriefing of interpreter	4
None mentioned	4
Suggestion to tape-record interview	1

Table 2.4. Unanswered questions for future training

Total: 20 respondents	
None mentioned	17
More practice, less theory	1
Obtaining feedback from interpreter	1
More on ethical issues ("discretion")	1

In considering what was most beneficial or relevant in Phase I training, 14 respondents found the insight it gave them into the interpreter's skills, the interpreter's role and "how it all works" (i.e. the interpreting process) particularly valuable. Consequently, 3 respondents claimed the training had given them confidence to cope in interpreter-mediated situations as they realised interpreting need not prevent them conducting an interview successfully with accurate transfer of in-

Table 2.5. Other comments

Total: 20 respondents	
None mentioned	10
Valued input for both police and interviewees	3
Need to tape-record interpreted interviews?	2
Refresher/follow-up would be useful	1
Dialogue with interpreter essential	1
Status of interpreter's notes	1
Remaining concerns (various)	3

formation. However, the responses demonstrate an awareness that the interpreted-exchange should be managed in a particular way and that the police officer shares the responsibility: for example, by addressing the interviewee directly (3 mentions). There is also recognition of the need to pre-brief the interpreter (6) and to carefully plan the interview (2). Respondents also acknowledge the difficulties faced by other participants, primarily the interpreter (5), but also the non English-speaking interviewee.

Actual or potential changes to professional practice following Phase I training include better planning, including allowing more time for preparation, and involving the interpreter in this process (4 mentions) both to brief the interpreter and to obtain suggestions or feedback from him/her (4).

Five respondents mentioned making changes to the format of the interview: improving the "layout" (in order to facilitate a 3-way exchange rather than two 2-way exchanges), adjusting questions so that they are precise and unambiguous and speaking directly to the interviewee.

Phase I training has had a major impact on knowledge transfer (5) as trainees use input and documentation from Phase 1 Training to brief interviewing officers within their police force. In one case, a local *forum* was set up involving interpreters, senior interviewing officers, interview advisors and detective sergeants "where best practice could be confirmed".

Police officers were unable to identify any significant unanswered questions although they requested more "hands on" training. Mention was made of more discussion of ethical dilemmas with particular reference to "discretion" i.e. when an interpreter may elect not to accept an interpreting assignment or feel unable to continue interpreting for a range of reasons (e.g. skills related, conflict of interest, otherwise unsuitable, etc.). One response, demonstrating willingness to teamwork, requests training in handling feedback from interpreters during interview and in de-briefing.

Other comments return explicit positive feedback regarding Phase I training and indicate the desirability of further training. The issue of dialogue with the interpreter before, during and following interview is raised again, so Phase II training should look at this in more detail. Questions relating to the status of interpreter's notes (to assist interpreting, but not as an exhibit) and the recording of interpreted interviews (only suspect interviews are systematically recorded), as well as concerns relating to logistics, and trusting and vetting the interpreter may also inform Phase II training.

Interpreters' feedback

Only 7 questionnaires were returned by interpreters, but the respondents all have experience of working in police settings and represent both English/BSL and English/other spoken language interpreters.

The interpreters were asked about the main difficulties/problems they had encountered when working as an interpreter in police situations and were invited to suggest any measures to counter or solve these difficulties/problems.

Although few in number, there was strong consensus amongst the questionnaires returned, so the responses are likely to be indicative of the main trends. The main problems and potential solutions indicated by the interpreters are listed below.

Problems
– Police have inadequate knowledge of how to work with interpreters
– Police do not understand the (interpreting) process and what is involved
– Police (and/or interviewee) put the interpreter in an advocate's role
– Lack of briefing/preparation, often due to short notice for assignments
– Nature of police questioning is fixed and does not allow for cultural disparity
– Adverse working conditions for interpreters

Solutions
– Training for police officers on how to work with interpreters, including recommendations for in-depth analysis of the process through role-plays etc.
– Training for interpreters, including specialised post-qualification training for police and court assignments
– Better dialogue between police and interpreter at all stages
– Development of a clearer professional role for interpreters
– Police to pay interpreters to be on standby

Phase II training

The question is, now that a degree of mutual understanding has been attained, how Phase II training can build on this.

The consensus is that everyone needs more training:

- trained, experienced *interpreters* want police officers to have more training,
- *police officers* want the training of interpreters to be more extensive.

It is unrealistic to expect all interpreters to be trained in interview skills to the level required of police officers. However, if police officers understand the interpreting process, they may *adjust their strategy to accommodate interpreting* and *brief the interpreter appropriately*. Potentially, a police officer may even make decisions to resolve a dilemma regarding interpreting which that police officer would feel able to defend in court.

The P.R.I.C.E. Model

The **PRICE Guide to Interpreting** is proposed by the researchers as a model for professionalising the integration of interpreting into police settings and activities. The mnemonic PRICE describes a structured approach to interviewing in which Scottish police officers are trained (Force Training & Recruitment Centre 2003). It represents:

- Planning and preparation
- Rapport building
- Information gathering
- Clarifying, confirming and closing
- Evaluating

Phase II training will involve the "mapping" of interpreting onto these existing guidelines to ensure that interpreters and interpreting are integrated into the interview process and that police officers, and interpreters, are aware of how the two activities (police interviewing and interpreting) dovetail with each other.

A few examples follow to illustrate the potential of the PRICE model as a basis for the development of an integrated strategy incorporated into initial interview skills training for all police officers.

Planning and preparation

It is worth noting that PRICE warns that time must be given to planning and preparation or some interviews will be doomed to failure – even when interpreting is not involved.

PRICE advises that thorough preparation will avoid the possibility of the second officer inadvertently interrupting or breaking a *planned silence* between questions. Interpreters need to know that some silences are deliberately planned (e.g. to consider how they place interventions).

Rapport

"Social rewarding" is discussed as part of rapport building between interviewer and interviewee. How this functions through an interpreter needs to be considered.

Information gathering

Police officers use a range of skilled questioning techniques to gather information. Their training instructs that when using "free recall" they must not interrupt for any reason. Therefore, how to incorporate interpreter interventions needs to be explored.

Police officers must avoid leading question or prompting the witness so interpreters must avoid introducing any such into their translated version, whilst police officers need to be aware of the difficulties for interpreters working in certain languages.

Clarifying, confirming and closing

Police officers ask probing questions and revisit a topic (e.g. to check whether responses are consistent) so interpreters must avoid "editing" because they feel a point has already been addressed.

Evaluation

Evaluation includes the police officer's self-evaluation and should, therefore, include evaluation of his/her performance in an interpreter-mediated situation.

Conclusion

PRICE indicates that the end product of an interview should be a partnership between the police officer and the interviewee. Therefore, in an interpreter-mediated interview, the police officer and the interpreter must form an *interviewing/interpreting team* in partnership with the interviewee.

Professionalisation of interpreting in police work

The professionalisation of interpreting is not solely a question of training more professional interpreters to work competently in police settings, it is also about training police officers to be able to work "professionally" through and with interpreters (i.e. in a way which allows them to apply, perhaps adapt, their professional skills and training). Fundamentally, it is about enabling police officers and interpreters to work as a professional team, in complementary partnership, so that working through an interpreter has the minimum disruptive or negative impact on the interview thereby ensuring fairness to both the accused and to society at large.

References

Brennan, M. & Brown, R. 1997. *Equality before the Law: Deaf people's access to justice.* Durham: Deaf Studies Research Unit.

Fowler, Y. 2003. "Taking an Interpreted Witness Statement at the Police Station: What did the Witness Actually Say?" In *The Crtical Link 3: Interpreters in the Community*, L. Brunette, G. Bastin, I. Hemlin, & H. Clarke (eds), 195–209. Amsterdam and Philadelphia: John Benjamins.

Her Majesty's Inspectorate of Constabulary for Scotland. 2000. *Without Prejudice? – a thematic inspection of police race relations in Scotland.* Edinburgh: Scottish Executive.

Hertog, E. (ed). 2001. *Aequitas: Access to Justice across language and Culture in the EU.* Antwerpen: Lessius Hogeschool.

HMIC. 2003. *Pride and Prejudice: A Review of police Race Relations in Scotland.* Edinburgh: Scottish Executive.

Jandoo, R., Dr. October 2001. *Report of the Inquiry into the liaison arrangements between the police, the Procurator Fiscal Service and the Crown Office and the family of the deceased Surjit Singh Chhokar in connection with the murder of Surjit Singh Chhokar and the related prosecutions.* Vol. 1. Edinburgh: Scottish Parliament.

Krouglov, A. 1999. "Police Interpreting: Politeness and Sociocultural Context." *The Translator* 5 (2): 285–302.

Perez, I. A. & Wilson, C. W. L. 2005. *Translating, Interpreting and Communication Support: a review of provision in public services in Scotland.* Edinburgh: Scottish Executive.

Scottish Executive. 2004. *Police powers and functions.* www.scotland.gov.uk/library4/JD/JD-BSU/00017377.aspx Edinburgh: Scottish Executive.

Stephen Lawrence Inquiry Steering Group. February 2001. *The Stephen Lawrence Inquiry – An Action Plan for Scotland.* Edinburgh: Scottish Executive.

Strathclyde Police Force Training. 1996. *Training for the Future.* Glasgow: Strathclyde Police.

Force Training & Recruitment Centre. February 2003. *Investigative Interview Course Booklet.* Glasgow: Strathclyde Police.

The Scottish Office Information Directorate. July 1995. *Factsheet 23: The Police in Scotland.* Edinburgh: The Scottish Office.

Community interpreting in Poland

Małgorzata Tryuk
University of Warsaw, Poland

The article aims at identifying the problems connected with community interpreting in Poland on the eve of Poland's accession to the European Union. It presents the results of an investigation carried out in a sample group of different types of community interpreters in Poland and discusses a questionnaire conducted among sworn translators rendering this kind of service. The questionnaire dealt mainly with such parameters as job satisfaction, job preparation, education and self-education, norms in community interpreting (faithfulness, comprehensibility, dialogue coordination), the role of an interpreter and ethics of community interpreting. The article ends with proposals for community-oriented education of interpreters and the perspectives for the emergence and professionalization of this kind of interpreting in Poland.

Introduction

When Poland is compared with other countries, in which community interpreting is a full-fledged variety of interpreting, one notices the lack of interest in this kind of activity on the part of Polish state administration and professional groups making, elsewhere, extensive use of the services provided by community interpreters (court, police, health service, immigration offices and customs, as described at earlier Critical Link conferences by, Dubslaff & Martinsen 2003; Angelelli 2003; Bot 2003 and many others). Professional groups of translators and interpreters themselves do not show a significant involvement in this area (except those based in courts). At the same time, the increase of Poland's contacts with other countries, the opening of the frontiers and a growing wave of immigrants and refugees are paralleled by a growing need for community interpreting that is overlooked by the administration. Another Polish peculiarity is the lack of community-oriented training of interpreters and the lack of generally accepted and recognized qualitative standards of community interpreting. Neither the norms provided by the professional organizations nor the existing code of sworn translators fully satisfy the needs of the translators and the market.

In spite of the fact that extensive research in the area of community interpreting has been conducted worldwide for many decades now (see e.g. Roberts 1997; Niska 2002; Zimann 1994), there has not been any systematic observation or analysis of either the market of community interpreting (i.e. the settings in which an interpreter is a participant) or the attitudes and perceptions of interpreters across settings – crucial in understanding the interpreters' perceptions of their own roles, their beliefs, and their behaviour in practice. Another unexplored area is the way in which the interpreters' roles and work is perceived by the recipients of their activity (e.g. judges, policemen, prosecutors or doctors) (cf. Pöchhacker 2000).

Pilot study

At the end of 2002 and at the beginning of 2003, I conducted an anonymous pilot questionnaire among interpreters affiliated with professional organizations endorsing community interpreting (Tryuk 2004). The questionnaire consisted of several multiple choice and open-ended questions. The multiple choice questions covered four sets of following issues:

1. the characteristics of the settings in which the interpreters work and the mode of their interpreting,
2. job satisfaction and job preparation,
3. the applied norms,
4. the applied ethics.

The open-ended questions called for specifying the languages the interpreters used and referred to some specific issues connected with their performances (i.e. the best or the worst interpreting-related experience). The questions also dealt with possible solutions of problems involved in training and in defining norms or ethics of community interpreting. As they triggered many comments, I decided to carry out a separate analysis of these qualitative data.

Analysis and additional data

Out of 300 copies of the questionnaire, distributed through the Internet, by post as well at conferences or other professional and personal meetings, 95 were filled in and returned. I also conducted 5 taped 1-hour long interviews with sworn translators specializing in interpreting in specific settings (police and court, legal, medical and at asylum hearings). The respondents represented professionals from all over Poland, working with the following languages: Arab, Belorussian, Bosnian, Croatian, Czech, Dutch, English, French, Hebrew, German, Italian, Lithuanian, Polish – as a foreign language, Russian, Serbian, Slovak, Spanish, Turkish and Ukrainian.

In the first set of questions the respondents indicated that community interpreting in Poland takes place in the following institutions and settings: courts (59 cases), police stations (49), hospitals (13), border guard offices (9), refugee centres (5), sessions of psychotherapy (2) and other (59) – a category including notaries and lawyers' offices (12), churches of different denominations (11), municipal and *voivodship* (regional) offices (9), registries (6), custom-houses (3), public prosecutor's offices (2), banks (1) and one emergency ward.

The answers referring to situations in which either consecutive or simultaneous interpreting (e.g. at press conferences, training courses or at scientific conferences) was required were not included in the current research. None of the respondents mentioned over-the-telephone interpreting.

In the set of questions on job satisfaction, a considerable number of answers were positive evaluations (75). Only 10 respondents were unsatisfied. 70 people considered themselves well-prepared for their jobs; 25 thought they were not. As was evident from other answers given in this group of questions, the latter claimed the following factors responsible for this situation:

1. the interpreters think they do not have an adequate knowledge of the terminology in the specific discipline;
2. they signal lack of knowledge of interpreting theory and in the majority of cases would be willing to undertake specialist studies in this area, especially some kind of training in interpreting;
3. they do not have access to all the documents essential for making the interpreting much easier.

These answers are evidence of the widespread 'terminological bias' among the respondents, i.e. they view translation and interpreting as basically concerned with the knowledge of specialist lexicon which, in turn, should guarantee satisfying the requirement of faithfulness in interpreting.

Another group of respondents pointed to the significance of professional knowledge (in law, medicine, etc.) and the accessibility of documents (in, for example, court trials) which are quite important for making the interpreting reliable.

In the comments accompanying the answers the respondents add that they would be eager to avail themselves of courses in a particular area of interest (e.g. law, medicine, psychology), in specific terminology, in the theory of translation and interpreting, as well as training in the administration and offices in the countries in which a particular foreign language is spoken.

There is also a group of answers which seem to contradict the widely recognized rule of non-involvement of an interpreter. The respondents signal the need to meet the person for whom they are interpreting in advance, to meet the 'main characters of the show', and they even add that it would be desirable to talk to parties involved. In their opinion, it would help them acquaint themselves with the subject matter of the particular cases, thus making the 'live' interpreting much easier. Some admit to discussing, usually with one party involved, the matter in question. This direct contact is for the respondents quite helpful in interpreting and most of them reject the hypothesis that it could at the same time inadvertently influence and bias their views on the standpoints presented by all parties.

Some respondents expect active co-operation on the part of their clients, e.g. they would welcome recommendations as to the literature worth consulting in order to better understand the particular issue and to be better prepared for the job. In the answers on job satisfaction I also found definitions of the perfect or ideal interpreter – the way s/he is perceived in Poland. One respondent writes:

(1)   I am very pleased with my job of an interpreter. My employers often thank me and praise me, but I think that the best evidence of a job well done is a situation when the interpreter 'is forgotten', because this means that the interpreter has been invisible, which is the evidence of a well completed task.

In the comments to the open-ended questions in this set, some express lack of confidence in their competence, of both linguistic and translational nature, and voice frustration stemming from their clients underestimating their skills. These opinions reflect the following two standpoints:

1.   most interpreters are not very self-confident – they do not trust their knowledge and their skills, they doubt their own professionalism because they are not lawyers or medical doctors and they are not sufficiently acquainted with the terminology in the field; these respondents say they translate literally, which, in their opinion, is the only safe method of dealing with the situation and they also try to be as invisible as possible for the clients, since the ideal interpreter is the 'transparent' one;

2.   few interpreters are fully aware of their competences; they are the true professionals and they are the ones who know how to interpret and they cannot be easily and readily replaced.

In the view of the respondents, job satisfaction is also closely related to the whole atmosphere, the quality of interpersonal contacts, the intellectual rapport and the level of cultivation of the participants of the encounter. The respondents provide an example of court-police context, in which neither the pay nor the attitude of the court and police officers motivate to improve one's work.

There is also a group of interpreters, who, in any circumstances, would act as 'good Samaritans' and attempt to form good relations with one of the parties, though not necessarily with the wronged one or the party in need of help. Regrettably, there are also cases when an interpreter assumes the role of the representative of the justice system, the police, or the public prosecutor office. Occasionally, an interpreter would leave his/her role and remain available outside of the interpreting assignment – to offer additional information, call a taxi, etc. Finally, there is also a group of 'interpreters-as-observers' who treat their job as an opportunity to observe and learn about human behaviour in extreme situations.

The next set of questions concerned norms in interpreting. There were three answers proposed in the questionnaire:

1. faithful equivalence of messages in the source and the target languages – 60 positive answers;
2. comprehensibility of the message – 79 positive answers;
3. ensuring communication between the parties of the encounter, co-ordination of the verbal exchange (Wadensjö 1998) – 65 positive answers.

So, the conclusion drawn from the above is that the comprehensibility of the message and ensuring the communication between the parties is more important that the faithfulness of the message. Other norms enumerated by the interpreters were: loyalty to both parties, transparency, impartiality, levelling the differences between the parties, mediation, explanation of the cultural differences and adequacy. Such adequacy, in the opinion of the respondents, guarantees communication between the participants and does not force the interpreter to assume the role of the co-ordinator in the conversation. Some of the interpreters consulted consider all the three mentioned parameters – faithfulness, comprehensibility and co-ordination – equally important in the process of interpreting. Others emphasize the significance of either faithfulness or comprehensibility. The answers, however, indicate that the notion of faithfulness in interpreting is susceptible to different interpretations and the following comments lend evidence to it:

(2)   Definitely, faithfulness is the most important, because this is our task; comprehensibility of the message comes secondary, because if anything is not clear for the client, then the explanation is instantly offered to him in the process of interpreting.

or:

(3)   Faithfulness of the message is when the other party demands to translate literally.

Strict observance of the faithfulness principle may, in the respondents' opinion, lead to incomprehensibility, but then as one respondent admits:

(4)   If some faulty wording occurs in the source language, I don't try to force the improved version.

As a rule, however, interpreters try to faithfully render the content of the utterances, but they signal that making cultural and systematic adjustments cannot be avoided. In some situations, e.g. in negotiations, the comprehensibility is deemed by some respondents more important than faithfulness, even an absolute priority. Comprehensibility may be achieved by means of additional explanation, but this seems to be exceeding the role of the interpreter, as one person states:

(5)   In the notary office, I occasionally explain, in consultation with the attorney or a notary, the legal intricacies.

For most respondents, comprehensibility occurs when the participants in the verbal exchange understand each other well; the respondents thus conclude that the interpreter should not interpret literally but according to the rule 'what the client meant'.

The answers about the final parameter enquired here allowed me to distinguish two tendencies:

1.   it is not the role of the interpreter to act as a dialogue co-ordinator, it does not belong to the interpreter's scope of duties; in some situations the interpreter is like a pane of glass and acts as if s/he were not there, in others the interpreter is merely not a fully active participant; according to some enquired interpreters, the attempts to co-ordinate conversation usually have 'pathetic' outcomes, and these are the respondents who think that the interpreter should be transparent so that the dialogue participants are not aware of the interpreter's presence;
2.   it is the task of an interpreter to integrate the three norms, ideally in such a way that s/he stays in the background, remaining invisible.

The set of questions on the ethics of interpreting was aimed at defining the ethical rules and limits that any interpreter should observe, in other words what the interpreter can and cannot do while performing his/her professional duties.

As a rule, the interpreters respondents admit that one is not allowed to add or omit information, make comments or suggestions directed at any party as it would worsen the quality of interpreting understood in the terms of faithfulness and/or comprehensibility. One is not allowed to show one's emotions or opinions. One is not allowed to misinterpret the message for the sake of better stylistic effect. One is not allowed to actively participate in communication. Interpreters should not translate vulgarisms or swear words. Their main task is to stay impartial, and so they should not act against anybody's interests, they should not prompt any party what to do or how to act in order to gain advantage. The interpreters are at the same time aware they may offer additional comments, making clear, however, that they are the authors of those additions. One of the instances when such additions are necessary is when the nuances of the Polish law are referred to. Loyalty towards the wronged party or the disadvantaged party is also understood as an expression of ethics in interpreting. The respondents state that the interest of one party should not influence their work, as in:

(6)   I may prevent the private interest of the state officials from prevailing over the binding rules and regulations.

(7)   I can't fulfil the wishes aimed at undermining the faithfulness of interpreting.

The interpreter may modify the original text by reasonably simplifying the speakers' productions (e.g. in case of complicated syntax or sophisticated terminology); s/he may also express the idea more clearly, without changing the general sense. Some respondents justify the interpreter's interference in the dialogue, even assuming the role of the main character in the exchange; one of them states:

(8)   In a divorce case, I let myself comment if there is a chance of reconciliation.

Interestingly, this very person adds:

(9)   I can't and won't help the delinquent. I am a court employee. I am not concerned with the opinions of the other party.

The question about who decides about the method of translation (the interpreter or the employing party), most frequently elicited the answer: the interpreter. S/he is the one who takes decisions about his/her action, i.e. what s/he can and cannot do (33 answers). The next largest group wrote that how the interpreter translates is decided by one of the parties involved in the encounter (10 answers), and only 8 persons stated the interpreter and the party employing their services decide about it together. It appears that here the interpreters perceive themselves as professionals, fully responsible for their decisions while interpreting, which in a way contradicts the comments offered in the part of the questionnaire on job satisfaction.

It is evident from some answers that for a group of interpreters the most important thing is to stay in the background and observe the rule of impartiality. The primary goal is the clients' satisfaction and the interpreter is merely an instrument and is required to adjust to the client's expectations. Judging from these answers, and from my general experience of talking with colleague interpreters, this approach, in which an interpreter plays an ancillary role, is by no means uncommon.

There was also a point in the questionnaire when I asked whether the interpreter comes to an agreement with the party s/he works for as to what would be expected from him/her, and unexpectedly 78 people provided positive answers.

Another important issue for the interpreter's ethics is the knowledge of the deontological code. Here, although 61 respondents answered that they knew such codes exist and are binding, only 13 of them admitted being familiar with and referring to the Polish code for court translators (Kierzkowska 1991). I also posed a question about what other codes the interpreters refer to, or are familiar with and the answers included: one's own code of conduct, the moral code or the code of ethics, and finally, the Decalogue.

The questionnaire was supplemented by a series of interviews, from which there emerges a more complex picture of an interpreter and his/her role. One interpreter for example, defined his role in the communicative event in the following way:

(10)   My personality shows. I partly organize this meeting, I smile at the policeman (but not at the other party). I do not remain in the background, I am creative and mediate in the area of formalities (e.g. *Some tea?*). […] I am perceived by the parties as co-operating with each of them.

The above statement indicates how far this interpreter is from non-involvement, impartiality and neutrality, and the rules he is obliged to observe. The same interpreter admits that one is not allowed to develop a liking for, or any other feeling for the delinquent, although these feelings may be hard to resist, e.g.:

(11)   There might be the urge to punch someone's head.

Another interpreter, a frequent participant in negotiations and refugee hearings, admits playing a special role in encounters, e.g. he takes turns as if he were a full-member of the negotiating party. He even demands:

(12)   More of an interpreter in interpreting – he is physically present (not transparent), this is someone who has a role to fulfil, and what the role is – depends
on the situations.

Conclusions

The results of the questionnaire allow me to draw several conclusions about the
situation of community interpreters in Poland. The behaviour and role of an interpreter are modelled after those developed for conference interpreting, according to which an ideal interpreter is impartial and emotionally detached, whose
sole aim is faithful rendering of the message in the target language. This 'ideal
interpreter' is virtually invisible. This invisibility has been somehow sanctioned
by placing conference interpreters in booths or by removing them to behind the
scenes. This is not the case for interpreters working in courts, at police stations,
or accompanying patients at medical examinations. The ideal of an invisible and
impartial interpreter is exceptionally difficult to achieve in the settings in which
community interpreters act. Firstly, the physical presence of an interpreter cannot
be disregarded or ignored, even in such intimate contexts as medical examination,
since s/he participates in the dialogues. Secondly, it results from the practice of
community interpreting that impartial and faithful translation is not sufficient in
achieving the desired effect. When there is some conflict of interest or the lack of
trust, the interpreter, provided s/he does not want the interaction to end in failure,
undertakes the effort of mediating, presenting the rationale and motives of both
sides, encouraging mutual understanding, both linguistic and cultural. He acts,
then, as a mediator. Occasionally, a community interpreter, a link between 'the
weaker' and 'the stronger' party, may feel the obligation to assist the weaker one
and act as his/her advocate.

The answers provided by the respondents are also evidence that there is a
generally recognized need to determine the status of a community interpreter,
even if this label is not used by them. They also postulate to 'professionalize' this
kind of activity, which is connected with specifying clear standards and norms of
what is and what is not the interpreter's duty, and defining what constitutes evident abuse of an interpreter's power. Defining the role of a community interpreter
and establishing the norms is clearly not an easy task due to, among other factors,
varied settings in which community interpreting take place – behaviour in each
of the settings originates from a different tradition and is governed by a different
set of rules. The needs of people assisted by interpreters also vary (i.e. the require-

ments of professionals of Medicine and Law on the one hand, and the wants of lay people seeking medical and legal help on the other).

It is difficult to predict what future course of development community interpreting will assume in Poland in the months and years to come: whether it will become a professional activity fully corresponding, in terms of its significance and recognition, to that of a conference interpreter, or, just the opposite, it will be approached as a kind of work performed by more or less linguistically skilled volunteers applying an arbitrary range of norms and standards.

It is equally difficult to specify what further professionalization of this kind of activity means. The need for community interpreting will probably be directly proportional to the scale of migration and the officially adopted attitude of the authorities to this process. It is, of course, common knowledge that migration in Poland is on the rise.

There is no single and indisputable answer to the problems posed above. One thing, however, remains obvious: there should be some norms elaborated, norms, which are general enough to embrace all the diverse situations and places in which a community interpreter is needed. These norms should not merely mirror the set of norms and standards adopted for conference interpreting.

It seems that the best and most justified solution would be to initiate training for community interpreters in institutions training translators and interpreters, by analogy to courses provided for court and legal translators/interpreters within the programme of postgraduate training in translation/interpreting offered by the University of Warsaw. The next step would be to make the public administration, institutions, and organizations formed to serve and service the migrating populations aware of the problems inherent in this type of interpreting. This kind of approach is a prerequisite of properly defining the needs, expectations and modes of co-operation between public administration officials, immigrant foreigners and the interpreters.

References

Angelelli, C. 2003. "The Interpersonal Role of the Interpreter in Cross-Cultural Communication: A Survey of Conference, Court and Medical Interpreters in the US, Canada and Mexico." In *The Critical Link 3: Interpreters in the Community*, L. Brunette, G. Bastin, I. Hemlin., H. Clarke (eds), 15–26. Amsterdam/Philadelphia: John Benjamins.

Bot, H. 2003. "The Myth of Uninvolved Interpreter Interpreting in Mental Health and the Development of a Three-Person Psychology.", In *The Critical Link 3: Interpreters in the Community*, L. Brunette, G. Bastin, I. Hemlin, H. Clarke (eds), 27–35. Amsterdam/Philadelphia: John Benjamins.

Dubslaff, F. & Martinsen, B. 2003. "Community Interpreting in Denmark.", In *The Critical Link 3:Interpreters in the Community*, L. Brunette, G. Bastin, I. Hemlin, H. Clarke (eds), 113–125. Amsterdam/Philadelphia: John Benjamins.

Kierzkowska, D. 1991. *Kodeks tłumacza sądowego*, Warszawa: Wyd. TEPIS.

Niska., H. 2002. "Community Interpreter Training: Past, Present, Future." In G. Garzone & M. Viezzi (eds), *Interpreting in the 21st Century*, 135–146. Amsterdam/Philadelphia: John Benjamins.

Pöchhacker, F. 2000. "The Community Interpreter's Task: Self-Perception and Provider Views." In *The Critical Link 2: Interpreters in the Community*, R. Roberts, S. Carr, D. Abraham, A. Dufour (eds.), 49–65. Amsterdam/Philadelphia: John Benjamins.

Roberts, R. 1997. "Community Interpreting Tomorrow and Today." In *The Critical Link: Interpreters in the Community*, S. Carr, R. Roberts, A. Dufour, D. Steyn (eds), 7–26. Amsterdam/Philadelphia: John Benjamins.

Tryuk, M. 2004. *L'interprétation communautaire. Des normes et des roles dans l'interprétation.* Warszawa: Wyd.TEPIS.

Wadensjö, C. 1998, *Interpeting as Interaction*, London and New York, Longman.

Zimann, L. 1994. "Intervention as a Pedagogical Problem in Community Interpreting." In *Teaching Translation and Interpreting 2: Insights, Aims and Visions,* C. Dollerup & A. Lindegaard (eds), 217–224. Amsterdam/Philadelphia: John Benjamins.

Alternative futures for a National Institute of Translation

A case study from Malaysia

Roger T. Bell
University of Westminster, London, United Kingdom

Governments, worldwide, face a paradoxical situation. National development depends on reliable information (often only initially available in a foreign language) but there are, normally, no mechanisms in place for assessing the quality of translated and interpreted information.

The response has frequently been to attempt to control the typically chaotic market through a state-appointed regulator with power to accredit training programmes and monitor both the suitability of the product and the behaviour of the service providers. Malaysia has had such a *de jure* regulator – the Malaysia National Institute of Translation – since 1993 but progress towards *de facto* regulation and control has been slow.

In this paper use is made of "systems thinking" to describe the Institute as a problematic "human activity system" moving uncertainly towards a number of as yet ill-defined alternative futures which are evaluated and used as a source of suggestions for improving the present problem situation.

Introduction

The professionalisation of interpreting in the community may be seen as a special case of the process of professionalisation in general and of language services in particular. Equally, since the social contexts in which this takes place are necessarily heterogeneous, a range of responses can be anticipated, institution- or profession-driven, and extending in terms of the provision of language services from none, through the *ad hoc* to the generic (Ozolins 1999).

The focus of this paper is a situation in which, underpinned by rights in the constitution, a state has created a government-owned company to take control of the translation "industry" and to provide translation and interpreting services but, it will be argued, in spite of its powerful *de jure* status, the institution has so far failed to attain the goals set out in the original remit.

The study forms part of a series of activities which should be regarded as "work in progress" rather than a completed project. It is both a follow-up of earlier work on the design of an accreditation system (Bell 1998) and a description of the institution involved (Bell 1999). It is also a response to a methodological suggestion made at The Critical Link 3 (Ibrahim & Bell 2003: 220) and an input to research on the issue of who is to regulate (an institution or the profession) and how they are to go about it (questions of accountability, transparency and equity: Bell 2007 forthcoming), which will only be raised here in the context of the evaluation of alternative futures for the organisation.

Although the case study is set in a single institution within the unique cultural, linguistic, political and economic context of a specific state (Malaysia), and at a particular time in its development (approaching the 50th anniversary of Independence in 2007), it is hoped that its value will lie less in the "facts" it reports than in the methodology used in the investigation which may be of wider applicability and provide suggestions for similar problem-solving studies elsewhere.[1]

Background to the case study

In Malaysia, with the exception of court interpreting, there is no organised public service interpreting (see Ibrahim & Bell 2003 and Ibrahim in this volume) and any move towards accreditation, monitoring and quality assurance for translation and interpreting has, so far, been essentially institution- rather than profession-driven. Exceptionally, however, one professional association – The Malaysian Translators' Association (PPM) – does provide training programmes for members but these are, as yet, not accredited or recognised by employers or educational institutions.

Overall, the situation remains essentially static with a chaotic, unregulated market in which clients continue to assume that mere assertion of "bilingualism" is sufficient qualification and, as a result, engage untrained volunteers or freelancers who can offer no assurance of the quality or appropriateness of the service they provide.

An official regulator does exist, in principle, at least. The Malaysia National Institute of Translation (the *Institut Terjemahan Negara Malaysia Berhad*: IT-

---

1.   It should be made clear that the study, though supported by ITNMB, makes no claim to officially represent the views of the organisation. It is, by definition, the product of the individual perceptions of the researcher and a record of the activities in which he engaged on behalf of the organisation.

NMB) was set up jointly by the Ministries of Finance and Education in 1993 as the sole official translation agency in the country, and charged (under the terms of the original Corporate Statement) with the dual responsibilities of 1) "creating a translation industry within 5 years" (i.e. by 1998) and 2) "providing translation, interpreting and information exchange services at national and international levels". The corporate philosophy is plainly stated in its Mission Statement:

> Towards the removal of language barriers through excellence in translation and interpreting services for national development

In practice, and in sharp contrast with the equivalent regulator for private tertiary level education (including languages) – the National Accreditation Board (the *Lembaga Akreditasi Negara*: LAN) – which was created by the Ministry of Education in 1997, there has been little advance during the last twelve years towards the creation and implementation of the regulatory process.

It is not, however, the purpose of this paper to describe these last twelve years in detail and certainly not to attempt to assign blame for the present situation but to provide a clear description of the system (based on an on-going investigation begun by the writer in 2003) and to look forward to the next ten years.[2]

Underlying this study is a two-part question, to which it provides a partial and provisional answer: "What is ITNMB and what does it want to be?" Given an answer to the first part of the question, the second part can be addressed by proposing a range of alternative futures for the Institute which can begin the move from the *de jure* to the *de facto* by devising and implementing policies which satisfy the terms under which the Institute was initially created.

That such a question still needs to be asked is an indication of the problematic situation in which the Institute finds itself and so the orientation of the paper is not merely towards description but, and more significantly, towards problem-solving and the presentation of a generalisable methodology for approaching situations of this kind.

Methodology: Description and problem resolution

Current thinking on organisations (particularly in "systems thinking" and the associated soft systems methodology (SSM) which forms the basis of this study[3]) recognises:

---

2. A description of the structure and functions of ITNMB follows on pages 111–113.

3. Checkland (1999) provides a comprehensive introduction.

1. that organisations are not fundamentally *structure* but *system*: "an entity that maintains its existence and functions as a whole through the interaction of its parts" (O'Connor & McDermott 1997);
2. that such systems are *purposeful*: they consist of processes which transform input into output;
3. that these processes are a function of the *relationships* and *interactions* between individual role-players;
4. that these relationships and interactions are, necessarily, *functional* rather than *formal*: the result of individual beliefs, attitudes and values and of the *world-view* and "culture" of the organisation itself;
5. that this complexity makes such a *human activity system* (HAS) difficult to define and describe, since the number and nature of the component parts and their relationships are in constant flux, making it inherently *problematic* and *fuzzy* and its operation only probabilistically predictable;
6. that research into systems of this kind will be essentially *qualitative* rather than *quantitative* with "results" that are indicative of *trends* which are not amenable to statistical demonstrations of significance since they are no more than "provisional truths" about the nature of the system (Stansfield 1997);
7. that the description and explanation of "problems" in such a system is made virtually impossible by the complexity of the system itself and that, therefore, any "solution" can constitute no more than a range of alternative futures for the system rather than a final, 100% effective "miracle cure".

The modelling and problem-solving process constitutes an attempt to "make sense" of the system by reaching a deeper understanding of its nature and that of its malfunctions which, in itself, will suggest ways of improving the problem situation.

Since multiple inputs are essential to the creation of such insights, the methodology is both *bottom-up* and *top-down* (the perceptions of all involved are valued equally) and involves three stages subdivided into seven steps, which are *interactive* (information is constantly exchanged between all involved, groups and individuals), *cascaded* (stages in the process are arranged in a non-linear manner which permits them to be activated in parallel rather than in series), *iterative* (states are returned to and reactivated as information from other parts of the process become available, resulting in constant revision).[4]

---

4.   See Bell (1991:44) on modelling the translation process.

Table 1. The modelling process

Stage		Step	
1	Description	1	problem recognition
		2	description
		3	root definition
		4	conceptual modelling
2	Contextualisation	5	comparison of models with reality
3	Planning and action	6	identification of and evaluation of feasible and desirable changes
		7	action to improve the problem situation.

Problem recognition

Problem solving cannot start until a sense of unease about the *status quo* emerges (Checkland & Scholes 1990): "a mismatch between 'what is' and what might or could or should be" (Checkland 1999: 155) but without a clear definition of what the problem is, only the realisation that there is a problem which requires attention: the present state of the system is in some way unsatisfactory and, if left alone, will evolve into even less satisfactory future states.[5]

Description

The description of a HAS depends on the specification of six key variables: transformations, customers, actors, world-view, owners and environment:[6]

1) ITNMB is a government-owned company engaged in an input-output process (a series of *transformations*) consisting of the provision of languages services – translation (and publication), interpreting, and language, translator and interpreter training – which are carried out for and by a range of individuals (some of whom play multiple roles):
2) the *customers* (individuals and organisations, public and private, who are the beneficiaries of the process) and *actors* (who run the process): some three dozen full-time employees; in-house translators, editors, management, administrative and support staff supplemented, as required, by a substantial number of freelance trainers, translators and interpreters.

---

5. A General Systems Theory orientation (see von Bertalanffy 1968).

6. These are conventionally labelled by the acronym CATWOE, with *Weltanschauung* for "world-view".

3) the organisation operates under several constraints, internal and external:

a) its own *world-view*: "a statement of belief about what the business is, should be or should provide";[7] its vision and mission,

b) the *owners* (or *stakeholders*) who have the power of veto over the organisation's activities and therefore may also be *decision takers* "who can alter its content (its activities) and their arrangements within the system ... and decide re-source allocation within the system" (Checkland 1999: 294): here the major stake-holders are (on behalf of the people of the country) the two ministries, Education and Finance,

c) the *environment*: the social, economic and political context in which the or-ganisation operates (the expectations of the clients, the ruling elite and the public at large).

In addition, the recognition of the existence of problems and the desire to do something about them calls for two further roles:

a) *problem solver*: "a person or persons anxious to bring about improvement in the problem situation" (Checkland 1999: 316); here the Chairman of the Board of Directors, the Executive Director, and the researcher

b) *client*: "who wants to know or do something and *commissions* the study ... [implying] that he can cause something to happen as a result of the study" (Checkland 1999: 294); here the Chairman, who is also a decision taker and a potential problem solver.

Root definition

Bringing these variables together leads to a "rich picture" of the situation, which is reduced to its "essence": the root definition.

> ITNMB is a government-owned company which converts texts – spoken and written – in one language into equivalent texts in another and provides training in languages, translating, and interpreting by means of the actions of skilled and experienced individuals (translators, interpreters and trainers) for public and private clients in order to further national development through the reduction of communication barriers caused by language.

---

7. Source: http://project.fast.de/ADDE/Guidance/Concepts/Catalog.htm

Conceptual modelling

The crucial next stage is identifying and presenting the conceptual models (frame-works/mind sets) of those involved, since these both define the system and explain the degree to which it is malfunctioning.

The models outlined here derive from discussions with role players starting in 1999, initially in the context of devising an accreditation scheme for transla-tors and interpreters and, in early 2003, a traditional SWOT analysis – **S**trengths, **W**eaknesses, **O**pportunities, **T**hreats – conducted by means of an informal, confi-dential, one-to-one guided conversation[8] with each member of staff.

Although it is unusual to find a consensus on either the perception of the nature of the "problem" or its "solution" – both are functions of individual and group attitudes, assumptions and expectations[9] – staff, stakeholders and clients alike believe that the system has become severely dysfunctional and that urgent action needs to be taken if the Institute is to satisfy the terms under which it was established 12 years ago.

Both the ministries and ITNMB itself, concur on the prioritising of transla-tion services and training, differing only on implementation but this is the root of the dysfunction: the competing world-views of the Owners and their resultant models (i.e. alternative answers to the question "what is ITNMB?").[10]

From its inception in 1993, the organisation has been bedevilled by the re-quirement to play two mutually incompatible roles: profit-making commercial enterprise and non-profit-making communication hub.

The Ministry of Finance, which provided substantial start-up funding, ex-pects ITNMB to perform as a successful business: a limited company[11] supplying translation and training services.

The Ministry of Education, in contrast, expects ITNMB to act more like a Statutory Board or Body whose major role is to make a significant contribution to education and national development but (like the British "Charity") is under no obligation to make a profit.

ITNMB's own conceptual model of the world and its place in it, is clearly stated in its website. The current version (June 2005) emphasises translation, in-

---

8. See Bohm (1987) and Stanfield (1997) for an outline of the methodology.

9. *Quot homines, tot sententiae*: "many men, many minds/thoughts/questions", as Terence put it more than two millennia ago.

10. A fact which was remarked upon by almost all those interviewed during a preliminary investigation of staff perceptions and attitudes (Bell 2003).

11. Hence the "Berhad" (company) in the name.

terpreting and information transfer, and translator training: essentially the activities expressed in the root definition and those stressed by the Owners.

Comparison of models with reality

The tension between the three models has led to less than satisfactory performance in either role. Simply put, ITNMB has never been commercially successful and, although it breaks even on a month-by-month basis, neither translation, nor interpreting, nor training has ever run at a profit and has certainly not fulfilled the hopes of those who expected ITNMB to be quoted on the Kuala Lumpur Stock Exchange within five years of its creation.

The demand is undeniable, but ITNMB has never conducted a market survey to quantify its size or characteristics and can provide no more than ad hoc quality assurance mechanisms to ensure "excellence in translation and interpreting services" (Mission Statement).[12]

Identification and evaluation of feasible and desirable changes

If the situation is to be changed for the better, plans need to be made and implemented through the "3 I" process: *identification, implementation* and *iteration.*

1) feasible and desirable changes (alternative futures) have to be identified and evaluated and 2) action needs to be taken to improve the problem situation which, itself, is subject to 3) evaluation:[13] *monitoring* of the process (to provide feedback and permit systemic adaptation) and summative assessment of the results: *retrospective validation* and *evaluation,* to provide feedback to ensure the continuity of the dynamic process i.e. the identification of new alternative futures.

ITNMB was originally charged with:

1. Creating a translation "industry" (the initial deadline of 1998 is long past) and
2. Providing translation, interpreting and information exchange services

In the absence of evidence to the contrary, it must be assumed that the terms of the original remit still stand and the answer to the second half of the question ("what does ITNMB want to be?") must contain a specification of alternative

---

12. Little use is made of CAT to increase productivity and reliability, which is left to the in-house editors.

13. The "3 E's" of classic SSM (Checkland 1999. A25): *efficacy, efficiency* and *effectiveness.*

goals at which the system must aim in order to satisfy or move towards satisfying these requirements.

Alternative futures

Keeping to the order of the original remit, ITNMB can structure itself as any one or a combination of any of the following:

1. An *accreditation agency* certifying translator and interpreter competence and, thereby, providing quality assurance for language services.
2. A *professional association* for translators and interpreters providing a point of reference for service providers.
3. A commercial *translation house* providing translation and interpreting services and, jointly with other publishers, producing books and other materials for sale to the public.
4. An *academic institution* providing, in co-operation with local universities, training for translators, interpreters and other language service providers.
5. An *information hub* providing a mechanism for bringing language service providers and potential clients together.

Evaluation of the alternatives

The next step is, ideally, to subject each of these alternative roles – some of which ITNMB already plays, if only in part – to comparative evaluation against the criteria of *desirability, feasibility* and *acceptability*: to what extent is each 1) conducive to improvement?; 2) achievable?; 3) culturally appropriate?

The implications of selecting each of the alternative futures are presented informally below:

1. If ITNMB is to "create" the "industry", it must (at least initially) become the regulator but, in spite of discussion over more than seven years, that goal is no closer. Regulation requires both an accreditation process, which is transparent and robust and a register of accredited translators, interpreters, and other language service providers.[14] There is, however, a potential conflict of interest between ITNMB in this role (as a body making an award) and in role 4 (an institution running courses leading to that award (see Bell 2005 on this).

---

14. See Chesters (2003) on this in the UK context.

2. ITNMB keeps a register of available translators and interpreters which it uses to outsource services and this may be seen as the start of the creation of a professional association. The move seems likely to put the Institute into direct conflict with the well-established 1000-member Malaysian Association of Translators (PPM) and, potentially, with the 300-member Union of Court Interpreters (KJM).

3. This is ITNMB's core business[15] but, lacking adequate market intelligence and faced with high overheads (both maintenance and salaries) and no value-added service to offer (such as guaranteed appropriateness or faster delivery), ITNMB is hard pressed to compete with other providers, except where it has a captive clientele (e.g. overseas visitors, students or workers or government departments for which it translates official documents).

4. Providing training programmes which lead to an academic or professional award assumes academic credibility, which requires the validation of the courses by a recognised tertiary institution or professional association, the upgrading of facilities and the hiring of top-class trainers.

5. ITNMB already uses its list of translators and interpreters to outsource services (for example, English-French and Arabic-English conference interpreters for international meetings). To extend this facility would have substantial financial implications, particularly if the Institute hosts a web-based list of providers and clients to which access is free (as CILT does with BLIS).

In short, since the first of these goals has manifestly not been reached and the rest only partially, it is self-evident that improvement can only come about through major change in both planning and implementation but, as Drucker (1973: 128) rather pithily puts it: "the best plan is *only* a plan, that is, good intentions, unless it *degenerates into work*" (original emphasis) and what must come next is action.

Action to improve the problem situation

Once ITNMB has decided on a policy which states the direction it wishes to take, and long terms goals have been set, the next step will be to commit resources – financial and human – to the implementation of the decisions: the means must be provided and agents appointed to carry out the policy.

Whatever decision is reached, a number of actions stand out as urgent, including:

---

15. The website, significantly, glosses the name of the organisation with the phrase "Malaysia's Number 1 Translation Agency".

- Conducting an in-depth study of the issues surrounding regulation and accreditation, including the implications of setting up a rival professional as-
  sociation to PPM.
- Commissioning a professional market survey to discover the nature and extent of the market for language services.
- Upgrading translation hardware and software, particularly the introduction
  of translator memory systems.
- Providing continuing professional development for staff translators.
- Installing a conference interpreter training suite, designed to AIIC specifications.
- Bringing library facilities up to postgraduate level.
- Agreeing course accreditation arrangements with appropriate tertiary institu-
  tions.

A good deal of positive action has already been taken, including:

- Appointment (2004) of a new Chairman of the Board of Directors (replacing
  the *ex officio* Minister of Education) and (2005) of a new Executive Director
  (for the first time since 1995 from outside the ranks of retired Ministry of
  Education Officers[16]) bringing with them substantial commercial and legal
  experience and contacts.
- A series of two-day planning workshops dedicated to working towards a
  5-year plan were held, facilitated by an internationally known consultancy
  group and involving senior management and staff, and – significantly, for the
  first time – the Board of Directors.
- Consultation with relevant organisations in the UK on accreditation and
  membership (Institute of Linguists), information exchange services (CILT),
  and training (University of Westminster).
- The appointment of two English language editors to strengthen the in-house
  translation team (2003).
- Co-operation with MIMOS on the development of a machine translation sys-
  tem.
- Workshop on translator-memory software (DVX).[17]
- Refresher programme for conference interpreters (bidirectionally, English-
  French and English-Arabic) in preparation for the Organisation of Islamic
  Conference (OIC) meeting (2003).
- Modular programme for translator training (2005).

---

16. Retirement age in Malaysia is 55.

17. Atril.

Conclusion

It is surely now accepted that the quality of the provision of translation and interpreting services is too important to the world to remain an amateur occupation and that some degree of regulation is essential.

In Malaysia, it is far from clear whether such a regulator can easily emerge from the existing associations or unions or whether some system outside them, such as ITNMB, would be more appropriate, either acting alone or in concert with them.

Either way, ITNMB has a significant role to play and the developments over the last two years give rise to cautious optimism.

Malaysia could well be on the way to becoming one of the first Third World countries to set up and run a national system for the regulation of the profession and, thereby, gain control of the infrastructure of translation and interpreting services for the people as a whole.

Just how this will be achieved and over what time scale waits to be seen but the first steps have been taken and, as has been demonstrated in other professions, the process of professionalisation, like a heavy fly-wheel, is difficult to start but, once started, virtually unstoppable.

References

Bell, R. T. 1998. *Memorandum from the Minister of Education: Proposal for the establishment of a national accreditation council for translators and interpreters* Cabinet Paper ITNM (limited circulation).

Bell, R. T. 1999. "Regulating translating and interpreting: the Malaysian Experience". In *Proceedings of the Conference on the regulation of the translation and interpreting profession in South Africa* Pretoria: PANSALB 102–105.

Bell, R. T. 2003. *ITNMB Five Year Plan 2003-2008: survey of staff perceptions, attitudes and suggestions* submitted to the Board of Directors April 2003 (internal circulation).

Bell, R. T. 2007. "Providing 'ethical' Service in Translation: who will guard the guardians?" *The 2nd International Conference on Language, Linguistics and the Real World: Language and Linguistics Serving the Community; Practical and Professional Challenges* (in press).

von Bertalanffy, L. 1968. *General Systems Theory* Harmondsworth: Penguin.

Bohm, D. 1987. *Unfolding Meaning: a weekend of dialogue with David Bohm*. New York: Arc.

Checkland, P. 1999. *Systems thinking, Systems Practice*. Chichester: Wiley.

Checkland, P. & Scholes, J. 1999. *Soft systems methodology in action*. Chichester: Wiley.

Chesters, R. 2003. "The Diploma in public service interpreting" *The Critical Link* 1.(1–7).

Drucker, P. 1973. *Management: tasks, responsibilities, practices*. New York: Heinemann.

Ibrahim, Z. & Bell, R. T. 2003. "Court Interpreting: Malaysian Perspectives" 212–222 *The Critical Link 3 interpreters in the Community* Amsterdam: John Benjamins.

Ibrahim, Z. 2006. "The interpreter as advocate – Malaysian court interpreting as a case in point" (this volume).

O'Connor, J. & McDermott, I. 1997. *The art of systems thinking: essential skills for creativity and problem solving*. London: Thorsons/HarperCollins.

Ozolins, U. 1999. "Communication needs and interpreting in multilingual settings: the international spectrum of response". *The Critical Link 2 interpreters in the Community*, 21–33. Amsterdam: John Benjamins.

Stanfield, B. R. ed. 1997. *The Art of Focused Conversation: 100 ways to access group wisdom in the workplace*. Toronto: Canadian Institute of Cultural Affairs.

Websites

AIIC, International Association of Conference interpreters, www.aiic.net
Atril, www.atril.com
BLIS, Business Language Information Services, www.blis.org.uk
CILT, National Centre for Information on Languages, www.cilt.org.uk
IoL, Institute of Linguists, www.iol.org.uk
ITNMB, Institut Terjemahan Negara Malaysia Berhad, www.itnm.com.my
LAN, Lembaga Akreditasi Negara, www.lan.gov.my
MIMOS, The Malaysian Institute of Microelectronic Systems, www.mimos.my
University of Westminster, www.westminster.ac.uk

The interpreter's 'third client'

Interpreters, professionalism
and interpreting agencies

Uldis Ozolins
La Trobe University, Melbourne, Australia

Interpreting agencies are crucial in determining outcomes in community interpreting, but have been little studied. We analyze the role of agencies in the
context of changing employment practices in the field, where more interpreters now work as freelancers. We identify problematic issues for both parties
in agencies' relations with interpreters: agencies vary in their expectations of
interpreters, their own work practices, and engagement in professional issues;
interpreters vary in their own required business practices and professionalism, and the ability to see the agency as their client. Agencies also crucially set
expectations of end-user clients who purchase language services. The growing
prominence of agencies may lead to greater emphasis by public policy bodies in
demanding codes of industry practice and ultimately accrediting agencies.

Introduction

This paper looks at the crucial role played by interpreting agencies in determining
the industrial, ethical and professional environment in which interpreters carry
out their work. While some community interpreters around the world are full-time
employees, and some are voluntary workers, an increasing trend is for interpreters to be free-lancers who work in many different institutions, and largely obtain
work through interpreting agencies. Such situations are clearly predominant now
in some of the countries that have provided the lead in developing interpreting
services (e.g. Australia, Sweden) where former provision by government services
is now increasingly provided by a variety of agencies including private agencies
(Ozolins 1998; Niska 2004). Such arrangements of course reflect longstanding
practice in conference interpreting and in translation – most interpreters and
translators of any kind will get the bulk of their work through such agencies; the

single practitioners who have a direct relation with a client or client institution are in the minority.

Agencies are of many kinds. While the growth of private agencies, as mentioned, is apparent in many countries, other agencies, as we shall see, can be non-profit community based, or government-controlled agencies, or alternatively agencies that cover a specific institutional field. Fortier (1997) and Downing & Roat (2002) for example look at the variety of agencies servicing the health sector in the USA. A further important type of agency is that which provides interpreters for a specific linguistic community (as for example in many countries for sign language interpreting). Referring specifically to the interpreting carried out for immigrants and their contact with host institutions, Sauvêtre (2000) has described the range of services and agencies in Europe, their character determined fundamentally by attitudes to foreign workers and the degree of responsibility taken by the host society to provide language services.

Despite this diversity of origins and jurisdictions, agencies often face a common set of issues in terms of their relation with interpreters, with clients, and with the professional issues that beset the field.

Yet the role of interpreting agencies has received little attention in material on community interpreting, and what literature there is, as cited above, does not focus on actual agency practice, or the link between agency practice and professionalisation. There has been scant examination of how agencies themselves shape expectations of professionalism among end-users, or how they enhance or inhibit professional practice among interpreters. For example, almost no attention has been paid to this link between agencies and professionalism in the four Critical Link conferences since 1995. Other more regular forums such as the American Translators Associations' annual conferences do have a section devoted to 'Agencies, Businesses and Companies', but papers here are almost all didactic in tone, with agency representatives describing how individual practitioners (usually translators) can make themselves more appealing to companies, or addressing business skills. Professional issues as such are rarely encountered, and difficulties with practitioners or clients expressed usually only in anecdotal form. ('40 Ways Project Managers Drive Translators Crazy', ATA 44th conference, 2003, www.ata-net.org/conf2003/abc.htm).

However, crucial aspects of interpreting practice can be influenced by agency action (or inaction), and the practitioner–agency relation deserves closer attention.

The central peculiarity of interpreting agencies in the present state of interpreting is that their service is often misunderstood by their clients (the purchasers of language services), *and* misunderstood by interpreters, *and* not infrequently misunderstood by agency employees themselves.

Crucially, the extremely uneven growth of professionalisation in the community language field means that agencies are not working in a situation where interpreters, clients, policy makers and other relevant parties have common views of their roles and a common understanding of the quality and purpose of interpreting services. Unlike other fields of burgeoning agency work, such as nursing or information technology staffing, interpreting agencies often do not provide a placement of professionals with clear standards and routines of work that are accepted and understood implicitly by purchasers. This issue of standards has been identified as the overwhelming professional issue facing the community interpreting field (Harris 2000).

We deal first with agencies' relations with interpreters; then agencies' relations to purchasers; and finally agencies' crucial role in mediating between both purchasers and interpreters.

Relations with interpreters

The unevenness of professionalism in the interpreting field results from the fact that other professional institutions that could provide predictable standards and professional support for interpreters (e.g. recognised and compulsory training programs, licensing of practitioners, strong interpreter associations) are often absent. The majority of interpreters in community settings may have received *no* training for their work; few systems have strict licensing requirements; and professional associations are often weak and in some cases non-existent.

Thus agencies will typically be confronted with an extreme range of dispositions and behaviour on the part of their contract interpreters; indeed, *from an agency's point of view* the variation of quality, professionalism and business skills among interpreters makes it often difficult to have a professional relationship with practitioners. Difficult interpreter behavior may include a random approach to punctuality (from tardiness in arrival to hastiness in leaving), a 'yes boss' attitude to agency management, failure to communicate on important matters, or pursuing a completely idiosyncratic personal code of ethics and practice. Such practices also challenge the agency's relations with its institutional clients who form negative dispositions to language services overall from this behavior.

Such behaviour, from even a few interpreters, also challenges the agency in that it well knows that such behaviour may be only the tip of the iceberg; as an agency typically does *not* see its interpreters in action in many situations, the extent of unprofessional practice is difficult to determine. While some interpreting practice is public (e.g. courts) and some can be technically monitored (e.g.

telephone interpreting), most practice is never seen by the agency; most agencies must take the interpreter's professionalism on trust.

It is a fundamental dilemma for an agency whether to set about intervening in such situations when it becomes aware of them, or to simply accept that a proportion of its contractors will be unreliable/unprofessional, because bringing about change to such behaviour may call for significant resources and may in fact achieve very little as the gap in understanding of desirable practice on the part of some interpreters and the agency may be unbridgeable.

Curiously, *from the interpreter's point of view*, there seem to be few guidelines by which to understand what their relationship with an agency should be. For example, there is typically *no* mention of agencies in interpreters' codes of ethics. Having been debated, fought over, adopted and refined over past decades, almost all codes of ethics still describe an almost Platonic ideal environment where an interpreter has a direct relationship with the two clients for whom they are interpreting. Typically, one of these clients may be a representative of a powerful institution (Police, health, social security etc.) that has purchased the service, and the other client is often a much less powerful immigrant or Deaf person coming to the institution because of a problem (Garber 2000). Yet all codes of ethics explicitly ignore this power differential through reference to impartiality – an interpreter is there to convey exactly what both parties say. While such an emphasis in a code of ethics may be understandable to achieve a statement of ideal standards, the absence in these codes of any reference to agencies leaves a dangerous 'black hole': all interpreters have (at least) two clients – the two parties they are interpreting for, but not all interpreters understand they also often have a third client – the agency through which they obtain work.

One of the marks of lack of professionalisation among some interpreters is precisely this inability to experience the agency as a client of the interpreter: the agency is the interpreter's client for whom the interpreter performs a service, to interpret for other clients the agency has identified. Thus the prime relationship the interpreter has is with the interpreting agency: this will be their source of income, and this will also be the important relationship if things go wrong or are unclear. The actual institutions where the interpreter interpreted will typically not have direct contact with the interpreter after the event, only with the agency that booked their service.

The rapidity with which discussion at any interpreters' professional association or on-line discussions moves from high points of principle contained in codes of ethics to specific and often endless complaints about the operations of agencies attests to the centrality of agencies in interpreters' experience. Yet it is the aspect of interpreter work least covered in available literature and professional guidance material.

From interpreters' point of view as well, a compounding issue is the disparity among agencies in work practices and standards, leading to differences in expectations and procedures.

A number of such issues in which there is a diversity of approaches by agencies can be quickly assembled:

– Punctuality is a universal requirement for all agencies for their contract interpreters, and punctuality remains the most obvious (and in many cases the only) criterion by which a purchaser of interpreting services can assess an interpreter. Yet agencies will often vary in their advice to interpreters about what to do in cases of not being punctual, and will also vary in what expectations they have of such related issue as length of time to wait, protocols for leaving an assignment, or reporting back mechanisms.

– Agencies may also respond differently – and even individual workers within agencies respond differently – to a host of professionally-related expectations such as when and whether sight translation is appropriate, how to handle oneself if the nature of an assignment is changed without notice, how to ensure breaks in interpreting in long sessions, how to handle cases of personnel not knowing how to work with interpreters, or how to handle clear cases of misunderstanding, or a myriad of other questions

– At an operational level, there can be quite often a chasm of understanding between the managers of an agency (who in many cases do have an in-depth understanding of professional issues) and the telephone operators/booking officers at the agency who often lack any such understanding, and may not have either insight or training to refer matters to managers. Again, agencies may differ markedly on this score.

These differences may be compounded by more internal differences between agencies such as in rates of remuneration, or communicability and approachability of agency staff, all of which calibrate an interpreter's response to that agency.

We see here a fundamental need to supplement existing codes of ethics with *Codes of industry practice*; indeed, if there is a trend to greater reliance on agencies for supply of interpreting services, we will see an increasing need for agencies to attempt to make explicit the practices that are expected not only in their own internal administrative terms, but also taking on a number of the practice issues outlined above and defining standard practice in the industry. Seeing the field as a united industry is not a perspective common to many agencies, as in most countries agencies do not form a recognisable industry body typical of other industries.

At a deeper professional level yet, even in cases where accreditation or some training may be available, there will simply be no other port of call for many practitioners to address professional issues than through an agency. Issues as professionally fundamental as debriefing or supervision (absolutely essential in many other human-related professions) will often not be addressed at all: will an agency see it as its role to debrief or to find debriefing when necessary for an interpreter? Can a practice of supervision exist alongside a view of interpreters as contractors rather than employees? These activities are not part of the role that interpreting agencies have traditionally seen for themselves.

Winnie Heh from Language Line Services in the USA, the world's largest telephone interpreting service, in her contribution to the panel on agencies at Critical Link 4 described how Language Line saw itself as increasingly taking on some roles that might otherwise be performed by professional associations in such matters as debriefing, providing discussion leaders for professional and practice issues faced by their contractors, providing in-service sessions, and developing training and certification programs.

Such significant instances are still rare, and while an agency as prominent in the field as Language Line Services may take such initiatives, for most smaller agencies addressing such concerns quickly raises issues of resources and reach. Linda Okahara, from the non-profit community based Asian Health Services agency in California at the same Critical Link 4 panel on agencies, points out that they 'provide a service which emphasizes training and testing and development of standards. Though it is a challenge given that most of our "competitors" are not necessarily interested' (Okahara 2004). Many smaller agencies are not-for-profit or undercapitalized and work on extremely low margins, with little capacity for any function beyond simply booking and service delivery – in particular, the capacity to address professional issues. We return to this issue below.

Finally here, if the forecast of greater agency involvement in interpreting in the future is correct, then we will encounter situations where interpreters may face significant industrial issues, particularly where interpreters are used to specific work practices of the past. Typically such changes have been from interpreters being directly employed by an institution, such as a hospital, immigration or social security system, to becoming contractors for a private agency; or moving from a charity or community-controlled agency to a corporate business agency.

Such moves have been described in the Australian context. At Critical Link 4, Senada Softic of VITS LanguageLink – a previous government interpreting service now operating as a corporatised agency – outlined the difficult issues of dislocation and trust raised on such occasions, but pointing out that it is possible to secure satisfactory industrial relations outcomes through 'the professionalism on both sides and the partnership that has grown out of it' (Softic 2004).

Agencies and their market

While relations between interpreting agencies and interpreters highlight numerous professional issues that deserve better recognition, equally important in understanding the operations of agencies is their relation with their market – the purchasers of interpreting services.

Heh points out that 'in some cases, the market had/has no expectations or false expectations that we as an agency have to address' (Heh 2004). In many cases these false expectations may mirror those of interpreters already outlined, including on occasions fundamental miscomprehension of interpreters' role, not knowing how to work with interpreters, and having confusing or contradictory administrative demands.

Other expectations may relate more to aspects of agencies *qua* agencies: price; length of notice but also very often an approach of needing to use language services (often reluctantly) but not being interested in agency explanations of what can or cannot be delivered, a sure clue to a purchaser seeing interpreting as an odious necessity and relating to the agency on that basis.

However, structural factors also condition how an agency relates to its market, in particular its relation to *other* agencies. As Okahara indicated above, competition becomes problematic if competition will significantly be decided on issues of price, but agencies have different views of what is their relation to professional issues such as feedback, training and ensuring standards, and have widely differing enthusiasm for such roles.

For some agencies, however, there is an attempt to educate the market, by advocating the importance of language services, and take advantage of or even professionally contribute to formulating policy mechanisms to mandate access to such services. Importantly, this is not advocacy on the part of an interpreter during their interpreting work (an old chestnut in debates on community interpreting) but having the agency act as an advocate for the field. Okahara gives such an example of her own agency

> that became involved with the issue of health care interpreting as part of our advocacy efforts on behalf of limited English speakers. Ultimately, our vision is of health care organizations to have the in-house capacity and either provide services directly in language through bilingual staff or at least have in-house interpreter capacity for major languages (Okahara 2004).

It is an open question, and one worthy of further research, to what extent market leaders are indeed agencies that explicitly have developed their prominence because they have taken on professional issues and enabled their purchasers to see the benefits of this; or whether in fact such professional initiatives occur only after market leadership has been gained through more operational cost and accessibility criteria.

Mediating the relationship: Agencies, interpreters and purchasers

The third way in which agencies are central to issues of professionalisation is that they are in a crucial position of mediating between purchasers and interpreters. At the most general level, as already noted, there is often extreme variation among agencies in their degree of interest in professional issues. Will agencies do any more than simply expect the interpreter to turn up on time at and not be the object of complaints? Yet when the relation between an interpreter and a purchaser is for any reason perceived by either of them as being less than adequate, the agency is critical in how it can resolve this issue: a number of the issues examined earlier in the relations between interpreters and agencies have further ramifications in agencies' relations with their purchasers as well.

While formal complaints about interpreters from purchasers are generally rare, interpreters are particularly sensitive to the way a complaint or comment against them by a purchaser is handled by the agency: does the agency inform the interpreter? (And not all agencies do on all occasions). Does the agency simply convey the comment and leave it at that? Or does it have a method of discussion and getting to the bottom of it?

At an even sharper end, interpreters may themselves have complaints or unease over their treatment or over practices they observed where they were interpreting: is the agency open to such feedback, and where interpreters feel that an issue needs to be taken up with a purchaser, will the agency do so? Or be too fearful of potentially losing a client?

And even with such issues as debriefing or supervision identified earlier, satisfactory resolutions may come about only through an effective working between agency, interpreter and purchaser, with the agency clearly an active party.

Industrial relations issues, briefly mentioned earlier, also impinge on this 3 way relationship between agencies, interpreters and purchasers. Crucially, contracts or service agreements between agencies and purchasers, where they exist, are in most cases negotiated and finalised without reference to the people who will be carrying them out – the contract interpreters. This leaves the interpreters in the position of being very much price takers, and in only rare instances can they be price makers – a situation particularly compounded by the historical low remu-neration in the community interpreting field, and compounded even more by the overriding reason for contracting out and privatisation of language services: to cut costs, in an ever more prevalent mode of public administration. Agencies and interpreters may be seen as professional partners but the main contractual focus of the agency is with their purchasers, leading to potentially uneasy relations.

Finally here, and in some contrast to the previous point, how agencies re-spond to professional issues becomes a critical issue when attempts are made to introduce regulation or accreditation for agencies rather than just for individual interpreters. A slowly increasing number of countries have, over time, developed accreditation or certification and training, and some have started at a policy level to set standards for individual interpreters (Ozolins 1998). But one move that may be more prominent in the future, partly as a result of greater privatization and dependence on agencies, is the move to *accredit agencies* rather than only individual interpreters. The rationale for this is clear: if agencies, many of which may be private businesses, supply an increasing part of interpreting services, then public policy objectives (ensuring a desirable standard of language services) may mandate that agencies meet certain criteria e.g. preferring to use accredited or trained practitioners, explicitly addressing issues of standards, having complaint and feedback mechanisms, and reporting requirements including reporting on professional issue faced by interpreters in their practice.

The sign language (SL) interpreting field, as with so many other issues, may be further down the road on this than spoken language interpreting. Kyra Pollitt at Critical Link 4 described the beginnings of a voluntary scheme in the United Kingdom to accredit agencies, setting standards that agencies providing SL in-terpreters are encouraged to adhere to. Pollitt first describes the range of differ-ent kinds of SL interpreting agencies, a range mirrored often in spoken language interpreting:

> The situation is complicated by the nature of the agencies involved; some are attached to training organisations, some to major employers in the field, others are run by interpreting colleagues, some by administrators with no insight into interpreting, others by consumer organisations (Pollitt 2004).

While the UK steps so far have been only to have a non-binding, voluntary sys-tem, Politt recounts how even this mild step has resulted in a significant differ-entiation among agencies, and particularly enhanced the power of some of the better interpreters who have had considerable impact on agencies to take their brief on professional issues seriously:

Examples have emerged of the most professional and ethical interpreters using their good practice to change agency practices, and educate agency staff. Whilst, simultaneously, the less educated and less ethical practitioner may find work in abundance from the least scrupulous agencies (Ibid.).

It is likely that concerns for accrediting agencies will increasingly be raised, not for SL interpreting alone.

Conclusion: Researching agencies

Interpreting agencies can play a crucial role in professionalisation or retarding of professionalisation of the field. Yet research in this area presents considerable problems: accounts of agency practices are not common, and there is a danger that agencies, whatever their status, may hide behind considerations of commercial-in confidence out of concern of giving away secrets or revealing anything less than perfect practice on the part of themselves and their contract interpreters.

However, to the extent that much of this area of interpreting is done for the public sector and for public money, requirements of transparency and accountability cannot be denied. Already a small number of agencies do participate vigorously in public and policy debate, and any moves to accredit agencies will lead to a greater prevalence of agencies forming industry bodies and participating even more in public discourse on interpreting.

References

Downing, B. & Roat, C. E. 2002. *Models for the Provision of Language access in Health Care Settings*. The National Council on Interpreting in Health Care. Available at www.ncihc.org

Fortier, J. 1997. "Interpreting for health in the United States.: Government partnerships with communities, interpreters and providers." In *The Critical Link*, S. Carr et al. (eds), 165–178. Amsterdam/Philadelphia: John Benjamins.

Garber, N. 2000. "Community Interpretation. A Personal View". In *The Critical Link 2: Interpreters in the Community*, R. P. Roberts et al. (eds), 9–20. Amsterdam/Philadelphia: John Benjamins.

Harris, B. 2000. "Foreword: Community Interpreting – Stage Two". In *The Critical Link 2: Interpreters in the Community*, R. P. Roberts et al. (eds), 1–5. Amsterdam/Philadelphia: John Benjamins.

Heh, W. 2004. Critical Link 4, Abstract, at www.tolk.su.se/CL42004_abstracts.pdf. p.9.

Niska, H. 2004. *Community interpreting in Sweden*. Stockholm University: Institute for Interpretation and Translation Studies.

Okahara, L. 2004. Critical Link 4, Abstract, at www.tolk.su.se/CL42004_abstracts.pdf. p.9.

Ozolins, U. 1998. *Interpreting and Translating in Australia. Current Issues and International Comparisons.* Melbourne: Language Australia.

Pollitt, K. 2004. Critical Link 4, Abstract, at www.tolk.su.se/CL42004_abstracts.pdf. p.10.

Sauvêtre, M. 2000. «De L'interprétariat au dialogue à trois. Pratique européennes de l'interprétariat en milieu social.» In *The Critical Link 2: Interpreters in the Community*, R. P. Roberts et al. (eds), 35–45. Amsterdam/Philadelphia: John Benjamins.

Softic, S. 2004. Critical Link 4, Abstract, at www.tolk.su.se/CL42004_abstracts.pdf. p.10.

PART IV

Developing local standards

The Swedish system of authorizing interpreters

Leena Idh
The Swedish Legal, Financial and Administrative Services Agency

Everyone who lives in Sweden but is unable to speak Swedish is entitled to the help of an interpreter in their contacts with the authorities in Sweden. Good interpretation provides one important safeguard for individual legal rights. For more than thirty years, therefore, the Swedish state has had a well-established system of authorizing interpreters. Sweden's interpreter authorization is unique in the world today.

Authorization is awarded by the Swedish Legal, Financial and Administrative Services Agency to those who pass its test in interpreting. This test consists of two sections:

1. Written test with questions on Swedish society and terminology into and from Swedish.
2. Oral test in the form of a role-play that may involve, for instance, a visit to a physician or lawyer.

Once authorized, interpreters may then take another test for a specialist qualification as a court interpreter and/or health services interpreter.

The "Kammarkollegiet"

The Swedish state system of authorizing interpreters aims to ensure the availability of interpreters with the knowledge and skills they need to be able to interpret for those who need them in their contacts with, for example, health services or the legal system. If interpretation is not effective, there is a risk that these people may be given the wrong treatment or that their legal rights may be jeopardized.

Interpreters seeking authorization have to take a test arranged by the Swedish Legal, Financial and Administrative Services Agency, *Kammarkollegiet*, in Swedish. The Agency has links with a large number of language experts, from universities and colleges for instance, who provide assistance in constructing the tests and evaluating the results. Whether or not the Agency can authorize interpreters in any given language depends to a large extent on whether experts in the language are available.

The aim of the test is to ensure that the interpreters have the knowledge and skills required to provide high quality interpretation.

In addition to passing the test, interpreters also have to be familiar with, and abide by, "good interpreting practice" (Kammarkollegiet 2004). Interpreters must also comply with the ethical rules that otherwise apply to authorized interpreters. This means that they must remain neutral in the contact between their clients and the representatives of the authorities, and alsothat they are aware of and respect the professional confidentiality that applies to their practice.

Before interpreters can be granted authorization, the Swedish Legal, Financial and Administrative Services Agency checks to ensure that they are trustworthy and suitable, or in other words that they have no outstanding taxes or criminal record.

The Swedish Legal, Financial and Administrative Services Agency is the supervisory agency for interpreters with authorization. This means that anyone who is dissatisfied with the work of a certain interpreter can send a complaint to the Agency. The Agency is then entitled to issue a reprimand to this interpreter or, in serious cases, to withdraw authorization.

The authorization test

The interpreting test is a vocational test and is open to all. The Agency requires no formal qualifications of candidate interpreters, nor does it provide any preparatory teaching.

The test is arranged twice each year. On each occasion tests are offered in about ten languages. The different languages are planned according to a staggered timetable. How often a language is offered depends on the demand of interpreters in that specific language. Those who do not pass a test may therefore have to wait for quite some time before another test in the relevant language is offered again.

The test is divided into two sections: written and oral. The written test contains questions on Swedish society and a test of terminology into and from Swedish. To pass the test interpreters must have full command of Swedish and the other language, in other words they have to be familiar with the means of expression, vocabulary and grammar of both languages. They have to pass the written test with a score of 80 per cent in each section before they are allowed to go on to the oral test. In order to pass the test interpreters must have sound knowledge of terminology and of Swedish life and institutions in areas such as health care, social issues, the labour market, social insurance and law. In addition, interpreters must have adequate insight into the way in which Swedish society functions. Less than 50 per cent of those who take the written test do well enough to be allowed to proceed to the oral section.

The oral section consists of a test of interpretation skills. The candidate interprets a role-play, which is performed on the basis of a written text. This role-play is enacted as authentically as possible and may, for instance, involve a (mock) visit to a physician or a lawyer. The test takes place before a panel consisting of the test administrator and language experts. The task of the panel is to decide whether the interpreter has attained the standard required for authorization.

The interpretation has to be as precise and fluent as possible, without loss of information. The interpreter is entitled to interrupt the interpretation to ask questions to a reasonable extent. In addition to the role-play, the test also includes questions on interpreting techniques and ethics.

Interpreters who want to specialize further can acquire specialist qualifications as court interpreters and/or health care interpreters. This requires an additional test, in which considerably more stringent demands apply to knowledge about life and institutions and terminology in the area of specialization and to interpreting skills than in the test for authorization.

Language trends

At the end of 2004, 846 interpreting authorizations were valid. The number of authorized interpreters was somewhat lower, as some individuals are authorized in more than one language. Authorization needs to be renewed every fifth year. In order to receive re-validation, the individual must have been active as an interpreter or in other relevant lines of work. The number of people with a valid authorization has remained more or less constant during the years, although the languages concerned have varied.

In 2005, interpreters can be authorized in 37 different languages. The need is greater but the shortage of suitable language experts restricts the possibility of increasing the number of languages. The quality of the tests and their evaluation is an important consideration for the Swedish Legal, Financial and Administrative Services Agency. Even though there may be a great demand for authorized interpreters in specific languages, tests are not arranged before they can be offered in ways that will enable standards to be upheld.

Nevertheless, the languages offered in the test reflect demand. This in turn depends on the quantities of people moving to Sweden and the countries that they originate from. In recent years authorization tests have been offered for interpreters in Baltic and Slavic languages, such as Latvian, Estonian, Bulgarian and Albanian. The language in which most authorizations have been awarded is Finnish, but the demand has declined considerably as fewer and fewer Finns are moving to Sweden.

Since 2000, Finnish, Sami and Tornedal Finnish (Меднkieli) occupy a distinctive position in Sweden as minority languages. This means that in certain local authorities, those who speak these languages as their first language are entitled to use them in all contacts with the authorities. For this reason, authorization tests have also been arranged in these languages.

In 2004, tests in Swedish sign language were introduced and arranged for the first time. The requirements are the same as for other languages, but the test is somewhat different in construction.

References

Kammarkollegiet (The Swedish Legal, Financial and Administrative Services Agency) 2004. *God tolksed – Vägledning för auktoriserade tolkar* [Good interpreting practice – guidelines for authorised interpreters]. http://www.kammarkollegiet.se/tolktrans/godtolk04.pdf

Establishment, maintenance and development of a national register

Ann Corsellis, Jan Cambridge, Nicky Glegg
and Sarah Robson
The National Register of Public Service Interpreters, London, UK

Once public service interpreters (PSIs) are trained and assessed, they need a practical professional focus. A national register has obvious advantages for setting professional standards, making accredited PSI skills more easily accessible and making available the widest possible range of language combinations countrywide. Traditionally, linguists have not been a regulated profession but a number of countries are in the process of developing this approach, particularly in the public service context. The main requirements and procedures discussed are:

- Selection Criteria – at different levels
- Code of Conduct and Disciplinary Procedures
- Secure access to the register – and by whom
- Financial basis and budgets
- Administration of registration and annual-registration
- Liaison with public services, interpreters and government bodies

Introduction

The UK National Register for Public Service Interpreters was set up in 1994, and later turned into a non-profit making company (NRPSI Ltd) under the auspices of the Institute of Linguists. The Institute of Linguists is the largest UK language professional body (www.iol.org.uk). It comprises over 6,000 members including interpreters, translators, language teachers and those who use their language skills as part of their jobs. All members are required to meet the published criteria for membership, in terms of qualifications and experience, and to observe a Code of conduct. The Institute of Linguists Educational Trust offers nationally recognised language examinations.

In this paper, three members of the NRPSI Board and one of its managers offer their experiences, including their challenges and dilemmas, as a stimulus for discussion of the professional policies and practicalities involved.

Why have a profession of public service interpreters and translators?

A profession arises where trust has to be engendered. When a client is not in a position to judge the quality of an important service at the point of delivery, structures have to be in place to protect the client, the practitioner and the practitioner's colleagues in their own and other disciplines. This is why people like doctors, lawyers and teachers work within regulated professional structures. The same logic applies to language practitioners because, by definition, clients are not able to communicate in both the languages in question. In the public service context in particular, accuracy and reliability of communication are essential.

What is a profession?

A profession is a group of people, sharing a common expertise, who *profess* to a code of values in order to protect its clients, body of knowledge and colleagues in its own and other disciplines and goes beyond the self-interest of its members. In order to meet what is required by its code, professionals establish national, transparent, accountable and consistent systems which includes:

- selection
- training and in-service training
- assessment & qualification
- registration
- good practice
- quality assurance and disciplinary procedures.

This definition is similar to the one set out in the recommendations arising from the international EU Grotius project 98/GR/131, about equivalency of standards in all member states for legal interpreting and translation, which were accepted by the European Commission. These same principles apply, not only in the legal context, but also to any context in the public services, such as medical or social services.

What is a professional register?

It follows that the details of those who have met the criteria set out under the headings above should be made available through a professional register. Such a register is, therefore, not a list or a directory but the public manifestation of a professional structure and of its integrity. The Code, which members of the register have agreed to observe, is supported by Disciplinary Procedures.

It also follows that the other relevant professions such as medicine and law should, where necessary, extend their own professional structures and expertise to encompass their responsibilities for working with linguists and across cultures and to accommodate the linguists' professional code of practice (Corsellis 2000).

What are the benefits of having a professional register?

Over time, the collective experience has increasingly demonstrated the benefits of having a professional register.

a)   For the public services and their clients

Access to the expertise of reliable interpreters is essential where public services and their clients do not fully share a common language. Otherwise, not only may the quality of public service be diminished, there are potential risks arising from miscommunication.

There is therefore a need to have access to interpreters who have had a prior objective assessment of their language and professional skills and who are required to observe a Code of Conduct and Disciplinary Procedures. Equally, given the number of other languages spoken in the UK and elsewhere, public services need access to a national resource that encompasses a wide range of languages and specialisms. The national structure of the register means that, if interpreters in the language combinations required are not available locally, they can be located elsewhere in the country. That facility is also useful in sensitive matters, such as child abuse or domestic violence, where the employment of locally based interpreters may be inappropriate.

The Register provides a focal point for liaison with other public service professions, government and the public. This in its turn promotes nationally consistent approaches.

b)   For the public service interpreters (and translators)

Public service interpreters (PSIs) and, increasingly, translators, benefit from the existence of a national professional register because it gives them access to a wide range of potential employers. The Register, with its levels of membership, provides a professional structure through which linguists can develop their skills and earn professional status and recognition. If registered interpreters wish to do so, they are eligible to apply for membership of the Institute of Linguists, and thereby participate in the wider family of professional linguists and the mutual support that brings.

While a professional register is not a trades union, the formal qualifications required for registration provide the necessary benchmarks against which employers can set fees. Such qualifications, together with membership of the register, are more likely to attract reasonable fees than those paid to interpreters without either. The National Union of Public Service Interpreters (NUPIT) is a subsidiary of a large trade union to which a number of UK PSIs belong.

The Register, acting as a focus for liaison with other bodies, is in a position gradually to raise awareness in government and public services over the need for standards.

What is the structure?

The National Register for Public Service Interpreters (NRPSI Ltd) is a subsidiary non-profit making company, wholly owned by the Institute of Linguists.

The Board of Directors comprises working public service interpreters, linguists and people with a background in the public services. Four of these give their services on a voluntary basis and receive only expenses, while one sits in his capacity as Chief Executive Officer of the Institute of Linguists.

In the UK professional bodies are formally independent of government, while liaising with it and other bodies. There are, therefore, NRPSI Advisory Groups drawn from senior public service practitioners. They give advice but also act in a liaison capacity between their services and the Register. There is an Interpreters Advisory Group, although, it does not sit often and individual interpreters contact the Register on an *ad hoc* basis with concerns and information.

There is an office team of five full-time and two part-time employees. The Register is financed mainly through a combination of fees from interpreters[1] (new application £77.25 for the first language and £25.00 per each additional language, annual registration £70.50 for the first language and £25.00 per each additional language) and subscriptions from the public services (Public Service Standard Licence £1,000.00.) £31.50 per hour is the fee interpreters receive from, for example, the Metropolitan Police Service although others may offer less.

1.　Fees stated are accurate at time of printing.

What are the selection criteria for registration?

The Selection Panel convenes every four weeks to assess applications against the published criteria set out in the appended Table 1.

Levels of Registration allow for an upward progression toward full status within given time scales set out in bold in the table. This system encourages increased standards and discourages those inclined to continue to obtain employment through the register without going to the trouble of improving their skills.

a)   Interim status:

Three years (by obtaining a full Public Service Interpreting qualification, either the Diploma in Public Service Interpreting, the Metropolitan Police Test or an equivalent public service interpreting qualification) if accepted onto the Register by option b (as stated in the included table).

Five years (by obtaining more than 400 hours of public service interpreting experience) if accepted onto the Register by option a (as stated in the table).

b)   LimitedAssessment:

Two years (by obtaining, a full Public Service Interpreting qualification either the Diploma in Public Service Interpreting, the Metropolitan Police Test or equivalent public service interpreting qualification).

c)   Rare Language:

Annual Review (by obtaining a full Public Service Interpreting qualification either the Diploma in Public Service Interpreting, the Metropolitan Police Test or equivalent public service interpreting qualification if available in those languages – hours will be reviewed also).

Qualifications from the UK or abroad

The UK's National Languages Framework includes National Occupational Standards for Interpreters and Translators. At level 6, these standards are equivalent to C1 (effective operational proficiency) of the Common European Framework and the UK level 7 equates to the European C2 (mastery).

The most usual UK qualification is the Institute of Linguists Diploma in Public Service Interpreting (DPSI), calibrated at level 6 of UK national standards. The DPSI is offered in four specialised options: Healthcare, English law, Scottish law and Local Government related services such as housing, education welfare and social services. Relevant qualifications of an equivalent standard are accepted.

Table 1. Explanatory notes on selection criteria

CATEGORY	QUALIFICATION	PLUS PSI HOURS
FULL STATUS (for each language to be registered or upgraded) Qualification and Hours must be supplied	– CCI/DPSI **OR** – Metropolitan Police Test (post 1997) **OR** – Equivalent Level 6/7 National Interpreting Standards	More than 400 hours of proven Public Service Interpreting experience
INTERIM STATUS (for each language to be registered or upgraded) Qualification and Hours must be supplied for Option B	– <u>Option a</u> CCI (forerunner to DPSI*) or Diploma in Public Service Interpreting (DPSI) or Metropolitan Police Test (post 1997) or equivalent Level 6/7 National Interpreting Standards **OR**	No hours required for Option a but when you upgrade to Full status you will need more than 400 hours of proven Public Service Interpreting experience
	– <u>Option b</u> A degree partly studied in English (or whatever is their second language) <u>with an interpreting and translation</u> component	400 hours of proven Public Service Interpreting experience
LIMITED ASSESSMENT Qualification and Hours must be supplied	– <u>Option c</u> IAA** Assessment **OR** – <u>Option d</u> IND*** Assessment **OR** – <u>Option e</u> Metropolitan Police Test (pre-1997) **OR** – <u>Option f</u> DPSI (ORAL ONLY – all oral components must have been passed)	For each of these options c, d, e and f you must provide 400 hours of proven Public Service Interpreting experience
RARE LANGUAGE Hours	Recognition is given to the fact that there are so called 'rare languages' where the chance to establish assessment opportunities is outstripped by demand for the language. In this category interpreters are admitted on the basis of 100 hours of proven Public Service Interpreting experience only and are reviewed annually.	100 hours of proven Public Service Interpreting experience
* DPSI – Diploma in Public Service Interpreting ** IAA – Immigration Appellate Authority *** IND – Immigration & Nationality Directorate		

- Proven professional experience is substantiated by completing log books, also signed by the relevant public service person.
- Registration is required annually to prove that the individual is still professionally active, which indicates the likelihood of their remaining up-to-date.
- Limited assessment and rare language categories deal with the practical realities of situations where a nationally recognised examination in a particular language is not yet available, or such an examination has not yet been taken or where the applicant has passed a test for working in, for example, immigration services. This at least ensures a measure of proven competence, albeit limited, in a transparent way and a willingness to observe the Code of Conduct. This is preferable to public services employing interpreters of completely unknown abilities.

In addition, the following are required:

- References from two people (from different types of organisations) who know the applicant well, attesting to their good character and professional competence.
- Security vetting at various levels. The basic level, as with all those working in the public services with vulnerable people, ensures the absence of any relevant criminal record.
- Agreement to observe the Code of Conduct is signed by each interpreter before registration. They are all given copies of the Disciplinary Procedures.
- Two passport photographs – one is kept on file while the other is used to produce the ID card, which must be carried by each of the registered interpreters.
- Medical Certificate – this may be required for some interpreters.

What is the Code of Conduct and how do Disciplinary Procedures work?

The Code of Conduct follows the normal pattern and, of course, includes confidentiality and impartiality.

Disciplinary and grievance procedures are essential to preserve the quality of professional practice. The Register has clear published procedures to back up the Code. Complaints about individuals providing interpreting services can either be linguistic or non-linguistic. They may arise from a variety of sources including persons directly requiring interpreting assistance or the agency hiring the interpreter. We have a commitment to fair and open investigations, with all parties receiving copies of the complaint. Cases are decided on a balance of probabilities in linguistic matters and advice is sought from sources of linguistic expertise.

Interpreters found to have breached the code can receive a

- **Warning** (for minor indiscretions).
- **Suspension** pending further enquiry.
- **Demotion** – where the circumstances of the breach are serious and proven on a balance of probabilities.
- **Suspension from the NRPSI** for a determined period where there may be acceptable mitigating circumstances that would preclude expulsion from the NRPSI, e.g. first-time major breaches, lack of judgement in isolated incidents or swapping assignments without authorisation.
- **Expulsion from the NRPSI** – for a major breach of the Code, for further serious breaches for which the interpreter has previously been suspended or for repeated less serious infringements of the Code. In addition, automatic expulsion will result where an interpreter has been found to be working as an NRPSI interpreter whilst serving a period of suspension as outlined above.

Re-admission is not considered after major breaches of the Code. These include:

- Unprofessional conduct likely to discredit the NRPSI (including impairment through drugs or alcohol, sexual misconduct, violence, intimidation or abusive behaviour);
- substantiated allegations of incompetence such as major lapses in interpreting accuracy;
- serious negligence causing unacceptable loss/damage/injury.

Cases are heard by a Disciplinary Panel of three or five members drawn from a pool and comprises of a NRPSI Ltd Director plus

- one (or two) practising interpreters from the NRPSI.
- one (or two) representatives of interpreter users.

There is a right to appeal, which depends on material fact/s coming to light after a Disciplinary Panel hearing. Appeals are heard by the Chair of NRPSI Ltd plus one senior officer from an interpreter client agency – plus a NRPSI interpreter.

The Register: Access and format

The Register is available to Public Service Organisations on CD-Rom and in a hard-copy which will soon to be replaced by a secure internet version via the NRPSI website. The internet version is called the Interactive Online Register.

As a subscriber to the National Register each organisation receives both the hard-copy and the CD-Rom version. The CD-Rom is produced six times a year: January, March, May, July, September and November and the hard-copy is produced twice a year in March and September. The internet version will be available 24/7 to all subscribing organisations and will be updated daily.

Each subscription licence is valid for one year from the month the order is received. The National Register is updated throughout the year to include details of the recently registered interpreters, updated contact details of those already listed, together with other amendments which may have been necessary. Towards the end of the subscription period each organisation will receive a reminder that their subscription should be renewed. Also each subscribing organisation is provided with a copy of the Guidelines when working with Interpreters, Code of Conduct and Terms of Engagement.

The Register is available for Public Service Organisations through a licence agreement. There are two forms of licence namely: Standard Licence (for one user on one site) and Bulk Licence – (for use by one public service at a number of different sites).

The 'Hard Copy' of the Register is divided into 3 colour coded sections of Law, Health and Local Government for easy reference. Indexes for each section cross-reference an interpreter according to language, specialism and the area they are based. This is being phased out as more public services have access to the necessary IT.

The CD-Rom and Internet versions are extremely easy and quick to use. The CD-Rom shows very clearly the information which a user would need.

The CD-ROM can be filtered on the following information:

Language, Experience – Law, Health or Local Government, Qualification, County, Town, Postcode, Sex and Status. In addition to this the abstract provides a more detailed description, such as contact details, nationality, and so forth.

The new edition to the National Register is in the form of The Interactive Online Register (IOR) which does exactly the same as the CD-Rom. The IOR is updated daily ensuring that the most up-to-date information is made available; guaranteeing that newly registered interpreter's details will be online within 24 hours of being accepted by the Selection Panel.

After choosing a language the user can then click on various options to define their search. The map splits down into counties so that the user can find an interpreter in their particular region or nearest county. Once the user has defined their search they click on 'Search for an Interpreter' button and a list of names will appear.

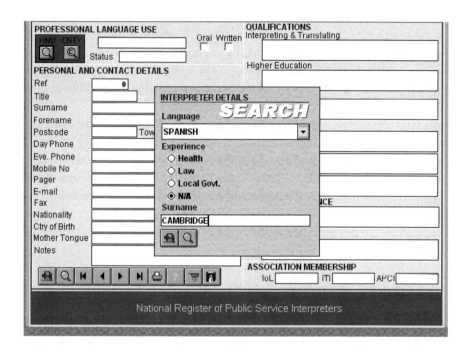

The website has been set up to provide the facility for interpreters to download the application form and accompanying documentation, subscribers to find out more about the interpreting profession and to access the IOR and for each other – interpreters, public services in the UK and other countries to disseminate useful information.

Clearly, in order to provide a professional service, the office processes and procedures have to be clearly defined. Many flowcharts, timetables and documents have been developed to ensure that both interpreters and subscribing organisations are provided with a complete and professional service.

Many issues have arisen over the years between interpreters and the public services. In order that there is a forum for them to relay information the NRPSI published a newsletter twice a year to encourage development and coherent growth for interpreters, and inter-disciplinary approaches to coherent working practices and collaboration, each learning the role and responsibilities of the other and engendering the feeling of working together. A website is now superseding the published newsletter.

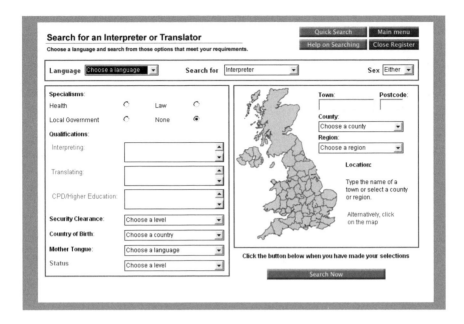

Conclusion

The creation of national professional registers involves an incremental process over time to develop the numbers of public service interpreters needed, and in the range of language combinations and geographical spread required. The NRPSI now has 1,900 registered interpreters in 87 languages with English. This is not yet sufficient to meet the national demand. Accurate calculation of what that demand is, and will be in the future, is impossible because of such factors as unpredictable changing population profiles, second language acquisition and deficiencies in consistent and precise record keeping of the need and employment of interpreters.

Professional recognition by other disciplines, such as medicine and law, is part of the development process. There is already a National Agreement on the part the criminal justice system of England and Wales whereby there is an aim to employ only members of the NRPSI, or the equivalent, which has helped enormously. Although health and other services are lagging behind that, they are beginning to show an interest.

The structures are now in place in the UK through which to grow. It has been interesting to see the broadly similar initiatives developing in other countries. The NRPSI Board are grateful for the generosity of colleagues in sharing their ideas so that we could learn from them. Consideration could be given to whether it would be possible to work towards an international consistency and equivalencies in national registers – which does not mean the same in detail but the same in standards and principles.

References

Corsellis, A. 2000. Turning Good Intentions into Good Practice: Enabling the Public Services to Fulfil their Responsibilities, in Roberts, R.P, , S. Carr, D. Abraham & A. Dufour (eds.) *Critical Link 2: Interpreters in the Community,* 89–99. Amsterdam/Philadelphia: John Benjamins.

From Aequitas to Aequalitas

Establishing standards in legal interpreting and translation in the European Union

Erik Hertog, Ann Corsellis, Kirsten Wolch Rasmussen, Yolanda van den Bosch, Evert-Jan van der Vlis and Heleen Keijzer-Lambooy

The two European Union Grotius projects described below have contributed to establishing standards and international equivalencies in legal interpreting and translation, more specifically regarding selection and training, codes of ethics and conduct and interdisciplinary working arrangements with the legal services. They have also suggested ways for dissemination and implementation of their recommendations. The projects have played a major role in the formulation of EU policy in this area in the form of a proposal for a Framework Decision. The Agis projects are intended to carry the achievements forward.

Introduction

The time is fast approaching when serious consideration should be given to establishing international equivalencies in public service interpreting and translation. International equivalency does not necessarily mean the same but rather common standards of training, assessment and practice, reached through individual national systems and conventions.

An international professional structure based on equivalent standards of legal interpreting and translation would allow, for example:

- qualified legal interpreters and translators (LITs) to work in the two or more countries of their accredited languages
- for those LITs to have similar working arrangements and professional support in countries other than their own

- reliable communication support where matters, such as medical care, involve more than one country
- reliable communication support to facilitate co-operation between organizations in two or more countries e.g. to prevent trafficking of drugs or people.

The projects, described below, focus on the legal systems of the member states of the European Union. The same principles, however, could apply to other countries and indeed to other domains such as medical and social welfare.

There are three broad stages in establishing international equivalencies:

- setting out the standards
- disseminating that information to appropriate people and organisations in other countries
- promoting implementation of those standards on an international basis.

The *Grotius* and *Agis* programmes of the European Commission's DG Justice and Home Affairs have supported three projects to seek equivalent standards for legal interpreting and translation in all member states, in order to meet what is required by the European Convention for the Protection of Human Rights and Fundamental Freedoms (ECHR). The first set out the standards, the second disseminated them and the third is currently developing implementation tools in response to the proposed EU Framework Decision (cf. infra). There is a still a great deal to be done but a sound foundation has been laid.

GROTIUS Project 98/GR/131: Aequitas or setting the standards[1]

The first two-year project (1998–2000) set up a collaborative action proposal between five institutes – all of which had practical experience in the field – in four EU member-states (Belgium, Denmark, Spain and the UK) and sought to establish EU-equivalencies on:

- standards of selection, training and assessment
- standards of ethics, codes of conduct and good practice
- and inter-disciplinary working arrangements between LITs and the legal systems.

The aim was to establish internationally consistent good practice through looking at existing systems, or those under construction, and filling any gaps on the basis

---

1. The information on this project is succinct as it was already reported on at Critical Link 3 (see Corsellis et al. 2003).

of practical experience. At the same time it was recognised that it was necessary that the core standards devised should be strong enough to be responsive to national differences in demands and traditional practices.

It was relatively easy, through long and careful discussion, to reach common agreement about the structure and standards needed. The participants were guided by what was needed for the task and responsibilities involved which they knew, from experience, it was possible to achieve. The headings covered in the project are set out in the flow chart presented at Critical Link 3 (Corsellis et al. 2003: 305) whereas the full text of the report is available in book form (Hertog 2001) as well as on the project's website (www.legalinttrans.info).

GROTIUS project 2001/GRP/015: Aequalitas or disseminating the standards

Dissemination of these standards with a view to encouraging the different EU-countries to implement them has proved quite a challenge. In the context of the increasing need for international collaboration and observance of common professional standards, the actual process of dissemination is actually as vital as its content and outcomes. People and countries, naturally and understandably (though often in the face of logic), are proud of their own institutions, resistant to change and, above all, reluctant to do what anyone else suggests to them. If one adds to that the reluctance of governments and people in almost every country to address the practical needs of those who do not speak their language, one gets some idea of the challenge. There is a saying in English: "you can take a horse to water but you can't make him drink". People, and especially their governments, have to be convinced of the benefits and see routes of implementation that they find feasible, cost-effective and acceptable before they will even begin to put in place common standards.

This dissemination project was the core objective of *Grotius project 2001/ GRP/015* and carried out by interdisciplinary teams of four from Belgium, Denmark and the UK, who had participated of the first project, joined now by The Netherlands and one of the EU (then) accession countries, the Czech Republic.

An incremental dissemination process was devised and after a first preparatory meeting we were joined at the second preparatory seminar by senior legal and language experts from Germany, France, Italy, Spain and Sweden. In between meetings, representatives consulted with their own national professional organisations both to inform them of what was being suggested and to gather their views. The project culminated in a three-day conference attended by legal and LIT-delegates from each EU member state and from the Czech Republic and Poland.

The aims of this project were defined as follows:

- to consult with, and gain insights from selected LIT-representatives of each EU member state on the developments which have been made in establishing equivalent standards in LIT
- to disseminate the achievements of *Grotius project 98/GR/131* to all member and accession countries
- to work together on the development of a quality trajectory, as exemplified in Appendix 1 to *Aequitas* (Hertog *et al*, 2001), both in the member states separately as well as in the EU as a whole, to take the process forward, in ways which achieve common standards while responding to national needs and conventions
- to establish potential collaborations for mutual support in practical development of the standards.

Again, it was recognised, from the outset, that the process of implementation of equivalent standards by different member states would involve different starting points, different approaches and different time-scales. After all, the equivalence of standards envisaged does not necessarily mean the same but rather the identification of common targets, which each state may reach according to their individual systems and conventions. It is anticipated that these can only be achieved in incremental stages, which are carefully planned over a period of time. We are convinced however, that co-ordination between member states would produce quicker and more useful results.

Implementation will further require that the key people in all member states be given the opportunity to go through a process of:

- gaining an understanding of what is being recommended, including the opportunity to challenge it and to suggest improvements
- consulting with the relevant bodies and individuals within their own countries
- reaching a consensus on the main elements, while accommodating any necessary national variations
- establishing which of the recommended activities already exist in their own countries e.g. training programmes for legal interpreters and translators at the level suggested
- planning and managing overtly the necessary changes, which will bring about over time the implementation of any activities not yet addressed, aimed at EU consistency
- making positive use of collaborations and mutual support between member states.

The outcomes of this second *Grotius*-project are also published in print (Hertog 2003) and again made accessible on the project's website (www.legalinttrans. info).

They are grouped under the headings 'Requirements' (an analysis of ECHR and relevant international legislation on LIT), 'Possibilities' (the skills and structures needed in LIT), 'Synthesis' (codes of ethics and professional conduct) and, finally, 'Models for implementation' (quality trajectories of LIT). The outcomes and recommendations of both projects contributed significantly to the EU Commission's consultation process on LIT in the EU and formed the core of the section on interpreting and translation in the Green paper and EU Proposal for a Framework Decision on procedural safeguards in criminal proceedings (see infra).

A quality trajectory example

As said, when disseminating the recommendations of *Grotius* I and II, we were aware that making the EU member states take action would not be an easy task, but various examples show that it actually was not an impossible one. One example – that of The Netherlands – is set out in *Aequalitas* (Van der Vlis 2003), another is the impact the *Grotius* projects have had in Denmark.

Here an interdisciplinary national committee comprising legal practitioners, LITs and LIT-trainers was established, which has created a growing awareness and recognition of the importance of LIT and prompted a variety of actions. Firstly, two members of the Committee (a judge and an LIT-trainer) published an article in a legal journal on interpreting in Danish courts (Bisgaard & Martinsen 2000), pointing out the current weaknesses and suggesting improvements to ensure effective communication in courts whenever a non-Danish speaking person is involved. The Danish project partners also gave a seminar to Danish judges on interdisciplinary conventions and about the qualifications and registration of LITs.

This was followed by a number of initiatives. For example, at the District Court of Aarhus, one saw

- the establishment of an interdisciplinary working party on interpreting, the aim of which is to improve the quality of court interpreting by, among others, improving the working conditions of the interpreters
- the institution of annual meetings between legal practitioners and interpreters attached to the court in order to discuss issues of mutual interest
- the appointment of a judge as contact person for the interpreters attached to the court.

These initiatives were all local in the sense that they were centred around the District Court of Aarhus and the Aarhus School of Business, both represented in the Danish *Grotius* committee.

However, things started to accelerate in 2002. With direct reference to the above-mentioned article, the Danish Court Administration set up a working party with the mandate to identify the problems related to LIT in the Danish courts. In April 2003, this working party presented its report – *Rapport om tolkebistand i retssager* – (Arbejdsgruppen 2003) in which it points out a number of problems – both legal and practical – and offers suggestions as to how to remedy them, some of which imply amendments to the law. The working party has also drawn up guidelines on court interpreting – *Vejledning om tolkning i retten* – aimed at both interpreters and legal practitioners, and a letter of agreement form – *Aftale om tolkning i retten* – to be filled in and signed by the interpreter and the court before each assignment.[2]

This report has cast light on important legal, practical and educational aspects of legal interpreting and it has given rise to a number of initiatives, both by the Court Administration itself, by professional organizations and, last but not least, political parties:

–   the Court Administration has decided henceforth to organize seminars for all Danish judges on how to work with LITs
–   one professional organization of interpreters and translators has organized an interdisciplinary symposium on interpreting in the courtroom and at police stations while another has set up a project concerning the establishment of an electronic register of qualified interpreters
–   two political parties have raised the question of court interpreting in the Danish Parliament and made proposals for actions to be undertaken to improve interpreting and interpreter training in the languages spoken by the largest immigrant and refugee groups.

As can be seen from the above succinct account, the recommendations put forward in the *Grotius* projects can in fact have an important impact on the awareness and development of legal interpreting and translation in a given country, in this case in Denmark. All of the above-mentioned initiatives and proposals have been inspired by the *Grotius* projects and are all in accordance with the fun-

---

2.   Further information at http://www.domstol.dk/HTML/Tolkebistand/Rapport.htm. and http://www.domstol.dk/HTML/Tolkebistand/Vejledning.htm and http://www.domstol.dk/HTML/Tolkebistand/Aftale.htm

damental recommendations, though, of course, adapted to the specific national situation.[3]

Recent legal developments in LIT in the EU

On 19 February 2003, the European Commission presented a *Green Paper on procedural safeguards for suspects and defendants in criminal proceedings*.[4] By means of this Green Paper the Commission aimed to ensure that the rights stipulated in ECHR are not 'theoretical or illusory' but rather 'practical and effective'. Although no discrepancy is seen between the aims of the Convention and its interpretation and monitoring by the European Court of Human Rights, according to the Commission however, differences in the way in which human rights are given practical shape, run the inherent risk that mutual trust is violated, even if the differences do not constitute actual violations of the ECHR.

The European Council of Tampere in 1999 had concluded that the principle of mutual recognition must be regarded as the 'cornerstone of legal collaboration' in the EU. However, mutual recognition is based on mutual trust in the legal systems of the member states. In order to achieve and enhance that mutual trust, it was suggested that a standard set of procedural safeguards for suspects be established in the member states.

The Green Paper focuses on five such aspects of legal protection: the right to legal assistance and the support of an interpreter, the right to translation of relevant documents, the suspect's right to information, the protection of vulnerable groups and consular support. In what follows we shall deal only with the issue of interpreting and translation.

---

3.   Other examples of the impact of *Grotius* on member states are the bills on LIT presently (at the time of writing: early 2005) before the Belgian and Dutch parliaments.

4.   http://europa.eu.int/cgi-bin/eur-lex/udl.pl?GUILANGUAGE=nl&DOCID=503PC0075& LANGUAGE This initiative was in line with earlier ones such as e.g. the Council Framework Decision on the standing of victims in criminal proceedings (15 March 2001); the Framework Decision on the European arrest warrant and the surrender procedures between Member States (13 June 2002); and the Council Directive to improve access to justice in cross-border disputes by establishing minimum common rules relating to legal aid and other financial aspects of civil proceedings (18 November 2002). The Green Paper on Procedural Safeguards itself was prepared for and preceded by an EU Questionnaire and a Consultation Paper.

Assistance of an interpreter or translator in the Green Paper

Chapter 5 of the Green Paper deals with the assistance of a qualified interpreter or translator, so that the suspect is aware what he/she is being charged with and can effectively participate in the procedure. To a large extent this chapter is based on the aforementioned *Grotius* projects. The Commission stipulates that, in the interest of the right to impartial legal proceedings, a formal mechanism must be established to ensure that suspects sufficiently understand the language of the legal proceedings to be able to defend themselves. The Commission emphasizes that the assistance of an interpreter or translator must be free of charge. Therefore, the Commission is of the opinion that member states must

- have a system to train qualified LITs
- have a system for the certification of these LITs
  introduce a registration system that is not unlimited in time, in order to encourage LITs to keep their language skills and knowledge of legal procedures at the required level
- establish a system of continuous professional development allowing LITs to maintain their skills at the required level
- formulate a professional code of ethics and professional guidelines for good working practices, which must be identical or very similar throughout the entire EU
- offer training to judges, public prosecutors and solicitors in order to provide them with a better insight into the role of LITs, allowing them to work more efficiently with LITs.

Response to the Green Paper

During a public Commission hearing on 16 June 2003 it emerged that responses to the Green Paper differed greatly. Human Rights organisations responded positively to the proposal and so did professional associations of solicitors and interpreters and translators. However, the reactions of the member states were mostly negative. Although the member states feel that the focus on safeguards for suspects in criminal proceedings throughout the EU is a positive development, many feel that guaranteeing these rights is primarily a national responsibility. The principle of 'subsidiarity' was invoked again and again as most of the member states do not support the view that it is necessary to give the European Union a coordinating role on this issue. Moreover, a number of member states argued that the ECHR already provides sufficient guarantees and it is therefore not necessary to translate these regulations into detailed European legislation. An additional major point of criticism concerned the financial consequences associated with the implementation of the guidelines in the Green Paper, particularly the issue of the translation of documents and the audio-video recording of interpreted proceedings.

The response of the European Parliament was considerably more positive.[5] Again with regard to the assistance of an LIT, the European Parliament on 6 November 2003 issued a Resolution that EU regulations must ensure that the courts are reminded of their duty to ensure, in accordance with international jurisprudence, that the various parties in the proceeding are able to understand each other (Consideration 8). The Resolution also states (Consideration 9) that common minimum norms must stipulate that, starting from the suspect's (or the accused's) first hearing, free interpretation must be provided during all hearings, so that the suspect is able to understand everything that is being said. In addition, these norms must stipulate that, in the event of a conflict of interests, it may be necessary to deploy two different interpreters or translators, one for the defence and one for the prosecution (or the court, depending on the legal system), and that all documents the suspect needs to understand for an impartial court ruling or the consultation whereof can be useful for the suspect's defence, must be translated. In this respect the Resolution specifically refers to:

- the police report
- the statements made by person(s) reporting an offence or made by witnesses
- the statements made by the suspect/accused, both before police and court authorities
- the charges made by the Public Prosecutions Department and other parties pressing charges
- the court decision which confirms the charges against the accused.

With regard to quality, the Resolution states that each member state must be obliged to introduce a register of LITs. Each member state must also establish a national body that is charged with the certification, registration and permanent professional training of qualified LITs. In this context, the member states must formulate a code of conduct containing professional rules for good working practices and the failure to adhere to this code must result in the loss of certification or expulsion from the profession. In the formulation of this code of conduct, the views of training institutes for translators and interpreters, Ministries of Justice and professional organisations must be taken into account. In this context, the Resolution stresses that member states must provide training so that LITs are familiar with the legal procedures and the terminology of the legal systems in

---

5.   http://europa.eu.int/abc/doc/off/bull/en/200311/p104025.htm

which they work (Considerations 9 and 10). It is interesting that the European Parliament also holds that all legal professionals, including police officers, solicitors, prosecutors and judges, must receive training in working with an interpreter (Consideration 10).

Proposal for a Framework Decision on Procedural Guarantees for Suspects

Following the Green Paper and the ensuing public consultation round, a few days before the enlargement of the EU to twenty-five member states, the European Commission finally presented its proposal for a *Council Framework Decision on certain procedural rights in criminal proceedings* (COM 2004 328 final). A first perusal of this proposal makes it clear that the Commission has considerably adjusted, i.e. *lowered* the high ambitions of the Green Paper. It appears the Commission has been sensitive to the criticism voiced by many of the member states regarding the appropriateness of the Decision as well as its financial and practical implications.

The proposal again focuses on five areas:

– the right to legal assistance and representation by a solicitor
– the right to an interpreter and/or translator, so that the suspect is aware what he has been charged with and understands the proceedings
– suitable protection of suspects who are unable to hear or follow the proceedings as a result of a disability or impairment
– the right to consular assistance for foreign detainees
– written notification of the suspect's rights.

With regard to interpreting and translation, Articles 6, 7, 8, 9 and 16 of the *Proposal* are of particular relevance.

Article 6 instructs member states to guarantee that a suspect who does not have a good command of the language of the proceedings, should be assisted by an interpreter or translator, free of charge, throughout the entire proceedings. According to the Commission this is a *conditio sine qua non* for fair legal proceedings.

The proposal also underlines the fact that this stipulation is not limited to situations whereby the suspect does not have a good command of the language, but also applies to suspects with hearing or speech impairments (Art. 6, par. 3).

Article 7 instructs the member states to take measures to ensure that the foreign suspect receives a free translation of all relevant documents relating to his case. The second paragraph of this article stresses the fact that the solicitor of a foreign suspect can request the translation of such documents.

Article 8 relates to the accuracy of the translation and interpretation. The first paragraph of this article states that the member states must ensure that the LITs that are used are 'sufficiently qualified' to be able to provide accurate translation or interpreting. In addition, the member states must make provisions to ensure that an LIT who is not carrying out his work with the appropriate degree of accuracy is replaced.

Article 9 instructs the member states to have a system in place to record the interpreting on audio or videotape to ensure quality.

Finally, the Commission feels it is important that some form of monitoring is put in place to check the extent to which the member states adhere to these standards. To this effect Article 16 contains a number of detailed obligations relating to the collection of information regarding foreign suspects who do not understand the language of the proceedings.

Minimum standards

Guarantees ensuring fair legal proceedings have already been laid down in a number of international instruments.[6] The Commission's proposal does not aim to establish new rights but rather to monitor adherence to rights that exist pursuant to the ECHR and other instruments in order to enhance the transparency and effectiveness of these instruments and to ensure that they are applied consistently and uniformly throughout the EU. In view of this objective and in the light of the abovementioned criticism of the Green Paper it is understandable that, for now, the Commission elects to establish and implement minimum norms only. But they are, after all, truly minimum rules for effective legal protection which – when it comes down to it – can, in practice, only be obtained after many years of legal battles, as all national legal options must first be exhausted before an appeal can be made to the ECHR. Furthermore, the ECHR only assesses the actions of the authorities of a member state and does not monitor processes at a European level, for instance joint actions by several EU member states such as e.g. *Joint Teams* or *Europol*). This means that the legal protective power of the ECHR remains limited at a European level, even more so because the European Union as such is not a party to the ECHR. It is therefore extremely important that the Commission does

---

6. See Vandenberghe B. "The European Convention on Human Rights: The Right to the Free Assistance of an Interpreter " in Hertog 2003, 53–59, and Vanden Bosch Y. "Adequate legislation to Equal Access to Justice across Language and Culture", ibidem, 61–73.

indeed propose to establish minimum norms for an adequate system of legal protection of suspects.

The proposals – and obligations – concerning the free-of-charge assistance of an interpreter or translator formulated in Articles 6 and 7 are underpinned by Article 6 of the ECHR, and more specifically by the European Court of Human Rights landmark decisions in the cases of *Kamasinski, Cuscani* and *Luedicke Belkacem and Koç v. Germany*.[7] With regard to the accuracy of the interpretation or translation (Art. 8) the Commission agrees with the duty of care as laid down in the case of *Artico v. Italy*, where the Court stipulated that not only is the State obliged to appoint an interpreter or translator, it also has a certain responsibility for the quality of their work. Moreover, in criminal proceedings it is the court that will always need to assess whether an interpreter is needed and, if so, whether the quality of the interpreting is deemed adequate. The court cannot hide behind the ignorance of the defendant or the indifferent attitude of a solicitor, as was demonstrated in the case of *Cuscani v. The United Kingdom*.

However, given the jurisprudence of the ECHR it is disappointing that the Commission does not specifically indicate which standards LITs must meet. The Green Paper suggested imposing an obligation on the member states to make provisions for the training, certification and registration of LITs. In its Proposal the Commission is no longer specific about the minimum quality requirements and how they must be guaranteed. The Commission does, however, introduce the instrument of audio-visual recording of interpretations as a means of monitoring quality as these recordings could obviously be used as evidence in cases of individual complaints or appeal and would also have a cautionary effect on the conduct of interpreters.

But the governments of member states will no doubt once again formulate objections: how to ensure, and at what price, good quality and archiving of these recordings; who is to be given access to these recordings, under what conditions; will solicitors actually make use of and spend time studying these recordings? After all, in most cases the recording will have to be translated if it is to be of use to the solicitor and for this another interpreter or translator must be deployed, which is not only expensive but can also be difficult given the limited availability of interpreters in languages of limited distribution. From the point of view of the foreign suspect, his solicitor and, one must hope, the courts, these objections in no way counterbalance the threat of an unfair conviction and potential miscarriage of justice. Potential miscarriages of justice as a result of inadequate interpreting or translation must never again occur in a European Union that prides itself on being an area of freedom, security and justice. In the same way that all other par-

---

7.   See again Vandenberghe o.c., Vanden Bosch o.c.

ties to the proceedings – police officers, judges, solicitors, bailiffs etc. – can be held responsible in the case of errors, this also applies to LITs. Therefore, one must hope that all member states will ultimately implement audio-visual recording as an essential guarantee for a fair trial and accept Article 9 of the Proposal.

At the time of writing, the European Parliament and the Commission are pursuing their proactive support of the Proposal, whereas the member states are still debating the fundamental issue whether an EU initiative and EU collaboration are actually required in this area and if so, what practical and financial implications the Proposal might entail. For LIT, the latter involves such issues as: does all interpreting have to be free of charge at all stages of criminal proceedings? What does a 'sufficiently qualified' interpreter mean? Who decides on the issue of the translation of 'all relevant' documents? The one Article that at this time of writing seems to stand no chance whatsoever of getting the required unanimous approval of all member states, is the one on the recording of interpreted proceedings. Expectations are therefore that the final version of the Framework Decision will be a further toned down document and a long way from the excellent initial Consultation Document and Green Paper.

The AGIS-project 'Aequilibrium or Instruments for lifting language barriers in intercultural legal proceedings' (JAI/2003/AGIS/048)

The AGIS-programme is a new EU framework initiative for the period of 2003–2007 and serves as a follow-up to the *Grotius* programmes. The focus is similar to the general objective of *Grotius*: implementing legislation and strategies to provide the citizens of the EU with a high level of protection in an environment of freedom, security and justice.

With regard to the role of LITs within the judicial procedures, the European Commission has supported an *Agis-* project entitled 'Instruments for lifting language barriers in intercultural legal proceedings'. It was proposed and coordinated by the Dutch ITV Hogeschool voor Tolken en Vertalen in collaboration with partners from Belgium, the Czech Republic, Denmark, Greece, Poland, Spain and The United Kingdom.

The aims of the project consisted of an international conference, the publication of a collection of position papers, a manual of training materials for LITs and the legal services, a study on sign language interpreting in Europe and the updating and expansion of the *Grotius-Agis* projects website (www.legalinttrans.info).[8]

---

8.   Aequilibrium or Instruments for lifting language barriers in intercultural legal proceedings (ISBN 90-809509-1-2); Working with legal interpreters and translators: Training materials for

The EU-wide conference was held in The Hague in November 2004. Over a hundred participants from various professional backgrounds (judges, prosecutors, attorneys, police officers, policy advisors, translators, interpreters, sign language interpreters, LIT trainers and representatives of professional organisations) from twenty-two member states of the European Union, and from Norway and the United States of America, gathered during three days in the Hague, the judicial capital of the world, to share ideas and constructive criticism on the proposed *Framework Decision* and to exchange best practices in legal interpreting and translation. A major achievement of the conference was that a network was formed that created a better understanding of each other's position concerning safeguards in criminal proceedings, paving the way for equal treatment of suspects and victims, irrespective of language barriers, throughout the EU. In this respect, the conference paid particular attention to the provision of quality sign language interpreting in courtrooms and other legal settings.

Another important part of the conference was devoted to strategies to improve the professionalism of the suppliers of legal translation and interpreting services.

Conclusion

Public service interpreting, including legal interpreting and translation, is gathering a strong momentum and dynamic in response to a global need. Its strength and continuance depend upon looking ahead and working with colleagues on an international basis to reflect upon and plan for the future before it is upon us.

The theme of the Critical Link 4 Conference – professionalisation – is important and apposite at this juncture because it is only through the development and protection of standards that there will be a worthwhile future for LITs or for their services. The negative collusions working against standards are as powerful as they were for the older established professions such as e.g. medicine: governments and public services fearful of having to pay reasonable fees to people with qualifications; unqualified practitioners who fear for their livelihoods; educational establishments who fear they will not have sufficient students if they aim for responsible standards. This unholy trinity of, often unnecessary, fear has hindered and still hinders progress.

The participants in the *Grotius* and *Agis* projects described above would not claim to have yet entirely overcome these obstacles in their own countries but

the legal professions (ISBN 90-809509-3-9); Sign Language Interpreting in Europe (ISBN 90-809509-2-0). Available in print and on the project's website.

they have discovered that, by working together, they have clarified their objectives, learned from one another, found strength in each other, gained the confidence of the legal service practitioners and mapped out strategies for the next phases of professional development.

References

Arbejdsgruppen om tolkebistand i retssager nedsat under Domstolsstyrelsen 2003. *Rapport om tolkebistand i retssager*. Copenhagen.

Bisgaard, O. & Martinsen, B. 2000. "Tolkebistand i retssager". *Ugeskrift for Retsvæsen* 45: 577–582.

Corsellis, A., Hertog, E., Martinsen, B., Ostarhild, E. & Vanden Bosch, Y. 2003. "European Equivalences in Legal Interpreting and Translation". In *Interpreters in the Community: Proceedings of Critical Link 3*, L. Brunette, G. Bastin, I. Hemlin & H. Clarke (eds.), 293–306. Amsterdam: John Benjamins.

Hertog, E. (ed.) 2001. *Aequitas. Access to Justice across Language and Culture in the EU. Grotius Project 98/GR/131*. Antwerp: Lessius Hogeschool.

Hertog, E. (ed.) 2003. *Aequalitas. Equal Access to Justice across Language and Culture in the EU. Grotius project 2001/GRP/015*. Antwerp: Lessius Hogeschool.

Van der Vlis, E. J. 2003. "Implementing a Model: The Dutch Experience". In Hertog 2003, 149–167.

The California Standards for Healthcare Interpreters

Ethical principles, protocols and guidance on roles and intervention

Claudia V. Angelelli, Niels Agger-Gupta, Carola E. Green and Linda Okahara

California Healthcare Interpreting Association, U.S.A.

The California Standards for Healthcare Interpreters: Ethical Principles, Protocols, and Guidance on Roles and Intervention created by the Standards and Certification Committee of the California Healthcare Interpreting Association (CHIA), have been in use in California since fall of 2002. The Standards document breaks new ground in its theoretical grounding in medical ethics, the use of an ethical decision-making model to resolve ethical dilemmas faced by interpreters, the guidance provided on four common medical interpreting roles, and in the extensive feedback process developed by the Association's Standard and Certification committee (S&CC) for validating the Standards by interpreters across California. This article describes the development and validation process, highlights innovative concepts, and reports on the application of the standards in California.

Introduction

According to the 2000 U.S. Census, Californians speak over 224 languages. These demographics challenge all aspects of U.S. society, particularly the delivery of healthcare services. The California Healthcare Interpreting Association (CHIA) is devoted to improving patient health and well-being and increasing equal access to healthcare services by developing and promoting the healthcare interpreter profession, advocating for culturally and linguistically appropriate services, and providing education and training to healthcare professionals. In early 2001, CHIA convened researchers, trainers, and practitioners to build a shared understanding of interpreting standards. The result was the 2002 California Standards for

Healthcare Interpreters: Ethical Principles, Protocols and Guidance on Roles and Intervention (the Standards) published by The California Endowment, designed for interpreters, providers, advocates, administrators and government.

Historical background

In November 1996, interpreters and representatives of California healthcare organizations met to create a support network for healthcare interpreters. The group appointed a governing board, created two chapters – Northern and Southern California – and elected co-chairs. In May 1998, CHIA was officially established as a membership-based nonprofit organization. In February 2000, CHIA received funding from The California Endowment to develop its infrastructure and establish interpreter standards. A Standards and Certification committee (S&CC) (Chun et al. 2002:9) was created in September 2000. The voluntary membership included interpreters, trainers, managers, clinicians, administrators, researchers, and university faculty.

The S&CC first reviewed existing healthcare interpreter standards, training literature, and the literature in related academic fields. Reviewed standards included ASTM Standard F15.34, Components of Quality Language Interpretation Services (2001), Standards for Health Care Interpreting (British Columbia Health Interpreter Standards Initiative, 1996); Code of Ethics for Medical Interpreters and Translators (Stanford Hospital and Clinics, 1985); Medical Interpreting Standards of Practice (Massachusetts Medical Interpreters Association, 1995); Medical Interpreter Code of Ethics in the Interpreter's Handbook (Cross Cultural Health Care Program, 2000.); and Mental Health Interpreting: a Mentored Curriculum (Pollard et al. 1999). The Australian Institute of Interpreters and Translators' (AUSIT) Code of Ethics (1995) were also considered, although not specific to healthcare interpreting.

Framework for the Standards

The Standards are based on the concept that appropriate actions for medical interpreters should be based on principles of medical ethics. Argyris and Schön's concept of "theories-in-use," (1992, 1974:6–12), suggests that people routinely make stereotypical inferences of others' behaviors as a result of their own culturally-learned expectations of 'right' and 'wrong.' This idea closely relates to a social construction theoretical framework of reality as both linguistically and socially constructed through interactions among people; there is no 'objective' existence independent of these interactions (see for example, Angelelli 2004a: 29–33; Berger & Luckman 1966: 152–55; or Pearce 1995: 88–113).

Multiple health beliefs and ethics exist in cultural contexts around the globe, and particularly in California, where families from most of the world's cultures have migrated. The first job for most interpreters in the USA, once they learned to speak English, was as their family's ad-hoc interpreter. Moral principles (or theories-in-use) are inductively derived from moral intuitions about situations and then deductively applied to new situations, according to Beauchamp and Childress (1994: 14–26). Moral intuition is therefore, first and foremost, a cultural concept. Untrained interpreters (using their moral intuition) make attributions of intentionality about their clients in order to expedite their interpreting task. They do this by editing what has been said to some degree, and by making inferences about what "should" be happening. This is problematic in a medical context, since interpreters are not trained clinicians and do not know what the clinician's process or intentionality is in conducting a medical interview or recommending treatment (Flores et al. 2003; Putsch 1985; Jacobs et al. 2004). Since interpreters have a set of experiences and attribution theories from a particular cultural context, it is therefore critical they understand the western bio-medical culture in order to facilitate the clinician's work toward the best health outcomes of the patient. Since medical interpreters interact in the cultural and linguistic social milieu of both patients and clinicians, a solid grounding in both interpreter and medical ethics is essential in healthcare interpreter training.

Validation of the document

The Standards development process involved 21 drafts over 28 months. Throughout this time, the S&CC was committed to a collaborative process, including public review and ongoing feedback. After receiving feedback from readers and viewers the S&CC made modifications when suggestions contributed to a clearer understanding of the standards. The 12th draft of the Standards was used in the focus-group study (Angelelli 2002) and sought to answer the following research question: What are healthcare interpreters' opinions of CHIA's Standards?

To elicit feedback from the primary stakeholders, medical interpreters, CHIA organized four focus groups. Based on the number and location of the three existing and one emerging CHIA chapter (at the time of the study) focus groups were held October-November 2001 in the San Francisco Bay Area, Central Valley, Los Angeles, and San Diego.

Approximately 7 days prior to each focus group, participating interpreters received a package containing an invitation letter, two copies of the consent form,

Table 1. Participants per focus group site

Sites	Number of interpreters	Percentage of CHIA members
Central Valley	13	46%
Los Angeles	13	38%
Bay Area	14	79%
San Diego	13	8%

and the Standards (draft 12). Participants were asked to return a signed copy of the consent form to CHIA and keep the other for their files. The only criterion for participation was 3 years of interpreting experience in a health or health-related setting; CHIA membership was not required. Participating interpreters were recruited from a wide range of local/regional interpreting services departments in local/regional health organizations and community agencies across a wide range of languages, not just Spanish. CHIA's staff facilitated all four focus groups, took notes, and audio-taped each session.

Fifty-three interpreters participated in this study. Thirty nine (72%) were female and fourteen (28%) were male. Of the total of participants, 43% were CHIA members. (Table 1 shows the breakdown of participants and percentage of CHIA members per site).

Participants represented various language combinations; with Spanish being the most frequent across the four sites. The least number of languages spoken by participants was two (e.g. English/Hmong) and the maximum was six (English, Farsi, Hindi, Pashto, Urdu, Dari). In general participants saw the Standards as an important document long overdue in the profession of healthcare interpreting. This was especially noticeable in the wide range of sometimes contradictory actions suggested by participants in response to critical ethical dilemmas. Participants did, however, identify a schism between the ideal situation ruled by the Standards and the reality of their workplaces. Participants hoped both realities could be reconciled once all parties involved in an interpreting encounter became aware of the Standards (Angelelli 2002). For most participants, raising awareness of the Standards would only become possible through sustained education of interpreters, their clients, other healthcare professionals, and administrators. The final document consists of an introduction, three sections and five appendices.

The final version

Ethical principles

The Standards (Chun et al. 2002) are based on six ethical principles governing all aspects of an interpreter's interaction with patients and clinicians. Additionally, the Standards provide guidance for interpreters in situations of conflicting ethical principles. The six ethical principles (ibid: 24–33) are confidentiality, impartiality, respect for individuals and their communities, professionalism and integrity, accuracy and completeness, and cultural responsiveness. *Cultural responsiveness* is defined as a measure of the knowledge, skill and sensitivity of healthcare professionals and their organizations to become aware of the individual and systemic needs of culturally diverse populations, and the subsequent receptivity and openness in developing, implementing and evaluating culturally-appropriate responses to these needs" (ibid: 47). These six principles correspond to general medical ethics as follows: Confidentiality (fidelity, or loyalty to the patient); Impartiality (interpreter autonomy, or independence); Respect for Individual and Community Beliefs (justice and beneficence, or benefit to the patient); Professionalism and Integrity (beneficence, autonomy and fidelity); Accuracy and Completeness (veracity, or truthfulness, and non-maleficence, or doing no harm); and Cultural Responsiveness (beneficence, justice, and fidelity).

Resolving ethical dilemmas

"Dilemmas occur when any action in support of one or more ethical principles conflicts with one or more other ethical principles" (ibid: 9). Without strong ethical training, interpreters fall back on their own experience and cultural context for their sense of "right action" in any particular dilemma. But are the interpreter's instincts and decisions correct from the stand-point of the clinician determining the best health interest of the patient? Additionally, other parties need to understand the interpreter's rationale. The identification of the ethical principle(s) underlying the interpreter's intuition, and the likely consequences of any action (or inaction), are important. The S&CC laid out the following six-step ethical decision-making process:

1. Ask questions to determine whether there is a problem
2. Identify and clearly state the problem, considering and ranking the ethical principles that may apply.
3. Clarify one's personal values as they relate to the problem.

4. Consider different actions with the benefits and risks or consequences for each possible action.
5. Make a decision and carry out the chosen action.
6. Evaluate and reflect on the outcomes of the action and consider what you might do differently next time.

In the Standards (Chun et al. 2002:54), we present an example of an ethical dilemma: "Don't tell the doctor what I just told you!" In this scenario, the patient has requested confidentiality for unsolicited information told to the interpreter, in an understandable attempt by the patient to align (Angelelli 2004 a and b) with the interpreter rather than with the clinician.

The dilemma is that the interpreter does not have the medical knowledge to make an informed decision about telling or not telling the clinician the confided information. Is it critical for the patient's health or safety and therefore important for the physician to know? Could remaining silent about the confided information negatively impact the patient's health and well-being? How will disclosing confided information to the clinician impact the trust between interpreter and patient, and the patient's community? What about the trust between clinician and interpreter if the interpreter withholds information which negatively impacts the patient's health?

In the healthcare setting 'confidentiality' is understood to mean that medically-relevant information about a patient is shared with members of the healthcare 'team' including the interpreter, for the purpose of treatment. However, the same information cannot be shared with others, except for purposes of billing or healthcare operations.

Guidance on interpreter roles and interventions

Multiple terms describing the different interpreter roles are simultaneously in use in interpreter training and in the different academic fields, each with different analogies, connotations and controversies. In early writings about interpreting, the conduit model prevailed (Reddy 1979:284–324). The CHIA Standards, firmly grounded on empirical research, recognize that the interpreter has multiple roles as a party in the patient/clinician interaction in addition to the message converter role portrayed in earlier writings. Some studies suggest that the required "participation" or "intervention" arises because the interpreter may be the only person in the medical encounter able to identify the emergence of potentially critical patient health and safety issues (Kaufert & Koolage 1984; Kaufert & Putsch 1997; Putsch 1985). Other studies, bridging from communication studies, sociology and sociolinguistics, consider interpreters as "co-participants" in the interaction (Roy 2000;

Wadensjö 1998) and look at various instances of the interpreter's agency in typical interactions (Angelelli 2003, 2004 a and b; Metzger 1999).

'Message converter' is the first role discussed in the Standards (Chun et al. 2002: 42). It involves facilitating the flow of the conversation between two parties. The second role of 'message clarifier' includes gaining more information from a speaker to transparently explain a message or concept in an alternate or more easily understood manner to facilitate communication. The third role, 'cultural clarifier', involves transparently confirming and providing cultural information, particularly about cultural health beliefs. *Transparency* is defined in the CHIA glossary as, "The idea that the interpreter keeps both parties in the interpreting session fully informed of what is happening, who is speaking, and what the interpreter is doing. Whenever interpreters intervene by voicing their own thoughts and not the interpreted words of one of their clients, it is critical that they ensure that a) the message is conveyed to all parties and b) everyone is aware that the message originates from the interpreter. The fourth role, 'patient advocate' (ibid: 44) – a prohibited role for the court interpreter – may be required in the healthcare setting to support the health and well-being of the patient.

The American Heritage Dictionary defines 'advocacy' as 'active support.' In the healthcare setting, advocacy is an action taken by an interpreter to further the interests of, or rectify a problem encountered by one of the parties to the interpreting session, usually the patient" (2002: 45). Unlike normal service activities, such as directing the patient to the pharmacy, advocacy might include helping ensure the patient receives an interpreter on their next visit, or identifying the basic right to an interpreter for either the patient or the clinician. CHIA recommends that interpreters intervene as little as necessary to allow the two monolingual interlocutors to resolve their differences once a misunderstanding has been drawn to their attention. But, as stated by Kontrimas (2000: 4), "Interpreters cannot and should not be responsible for everything that everyone does, or doesn't do. But, if they happen to notice something starting to go wrong, it is reasonable to bring it to the attention of someone who can correct it before it becomes a problem, rather than sit back and watch a disaster unfold".

The patient advocate is a demanding role requiring significant experience, judgment, and confidence on the part of the interpreter, and involves potential invasiveness, controversy and risk, both for the patient and for the interpreter. For this reason, the S&CC recommended that patient advocacy be an optional role. The decision to intervene as a patient advocate must be left to the interpreter's judgment as a healthcare professional. This degree of latitude within the scope of a set of standards may be new for interpreters but is not unusual in other professions. Most professionals conduct their work by what Mintzberg describes as the "standardization of skills," where precise directions are unnecessary because training and ethics establish a known set of skills (1993, 1983: 4–6).

Interpreters should learn to use the ethical decision-making process to weigh the potential benefits and risks of assuming the patient advocate role in an ethical dilemma. The ethical decision-making process has a steep learning curve and requires significant practice before it can be ingrained. The learning process, (Mink et al. 1993) moves from 'unconscious incompetence,' through 'conscious incompetence,' to 'conscious competence,' before any skill, including ethical decision-making, can be used with 'unconscious competence'.

Applications of the CHIA Standards to the teaching of medical interpreting

When developing the California Standards for Healthcare Interpreters, CHIA and its S&CC envisioned a broad array of potential applications. These ranged from serving as a reference for practicing interpreters; a knowledge or skills requirement within job descriptions; a basis for performance evaluations; guidelines for training curriculum content; and, potentially, certification or licensure potentially leading to state reimbursement of interpreting services.

When funding CHIA to develop the standards, The California Endowment also provided grants to several organizations to expand cultural and linguistic competence within healthcare. Included was a grant to develop and implement a healthcare interpreter training curriculum. Entitled *Connecting Worlds – Training for Healthcare Interpreters* (Okahara et al. 2004), this training incorporated the Standards and provides a solid introduction to the ethical principles, protocols, and guidance on roles and interventions.

To better understand how the standards have been utilized since their release in September 2002, two of the co-authors of *Connecting Worlds* (Okahara & Nguyen) conducted a small convenience sample survey of healthcare organizations involved with service delivery and advocacy efforts in April–May 2004. The survey was distributed via e-mail to individuals and organizations involved with healthcare interpreting. Thirty-two surveys were returned. Fifty seven percent of the responses indicated that the standards were most commonly used in conjunction with training. Participants in the training events ranged from healthcare interpreters, healthcare administrators and managers, and providers working with interpreters. Twenty nine percent of respondents indicated they incorporate familiarity or knowledge of the standards as a job requirement while 25% replied that they include compliance with the standards as a requirement in their contracts with interpreter agencies or individual interpreters and also used them in their testing efforts. Interestingly, 15% stated that they used the standards to advocate for improved linguistic services both within their own organizations and when advocating for policy changes within the broader healthcare system. Positive comments related to the provision of real-life examples, its comprehensive scope, and easy to read presentation. One respondent was grateful the Standards were available for free! The challenges described by respondents in using the standards included: a) disagreement with descriptions and labels of the interpreter roles, b) questions regarding the optional nature of the patient advocate role, c) the potentially contradictory nature of the ethical principles, particularly in the context of ethical dilemmas, and d) the lack of guidance in how to practically operationalize the standards into activities such as training and interpreter assessment. The challenges mentioned in categories a) through c) are in agreement with the results obtained from the focus groups during the validation study (Angelelli 2002).

An additional example of how the Standards have been incorporated into health policy is from the Los Angeles County Department of Health Services, which requires interpreter adherence to the Standards as part of its own Cultural and Linguistic Competency Standards (Agger-Gupta et al. 2003: 18).

Conclusion

This paper described the S&CC process to develop and validate the CHIA Standards. Innovative concepts were highlighted and implications for training healthcare interpreters were discussed. We believe that as the dialogue on our 'work in progress' continues in the coming years, it will stimulate rethinking and on-going revisions to this document. We hope it continues to serve as a reference to all healthcare professionals and particularly healthcare interpreters.

References

Agger-Gupta, N., Iwataki, M., & Wang, K. (eds.). (2003). *Cultural and Linguistic Competency Standards*. Los Angeles: County of Los Angeles Department of Health Services (Available online: http://www.dhs.co.la.ca.us/odp/standards.htm).

Angelelli, C. (2002). *Focus Group Study on California Standards for Healthcare Interpreters: Proposed Ethical Principles, Protocols and Guidance on Interpreter Interventions and Roles* San Diego: California Healthcare Interpreters Association (CHIA). (Available online: http://www.chia.ws/standards_committee.php#news)

Angelelli, C. (2003) The Visible Collaborator: Interpreter Intervention in Doctor/Patient Encounters. In Melanie Metzger, ed. *From Topic Boundaries to Omission: New Research on Interpretation*. Washington DC: Gallaudet University Press.

Angelelli, C. (2004a) *Medical Interpreting and Cross-cultural Communication*. Cambridge: Cambridge University Press.

Angelelli, C. (2004b) *The Visible Interpreter: a study of community, conference, court interpreters in Canada, Mexico and United States*. John Benjamins: Amsterdam.

Argyris, C., & Schön, D. (1992, 1974). Theory in Practice : Increasing Professional Effectiveness (Jossey Bass Higher and Adult Education Series). San Francisco: Jossey-Bass Publishers.

ASTM. Subcommittee F15.34 of American Society of Testing and Materials. (2000). Standard Guide for Quality Language Interpretation Services (document F2089). Conshohocken, PA.: American Society for Testing and Materials (ASTM).

Australian Institute for Interpreters and Translators (AUSiT). (1995) *AUSiT Code of Ethics*. Victoria, Australia. (Available online at http://www.ausit.org: Australian Institute for Interpreters and Translators (AUSiT)

Beauchamp, T. L., & Childress, J. F. (1994). *Principles of Biomedical Ethics [4th ed.]*. Oxford: Oxford University Press: pp. 14–26.

Berger, P. L., & Luckman, T. (1966). *The Social Construction of Reality: A Treatise in the Sociology of Knowledge*. Toronto: Anchor Books / Doubleday.

Chun, A., Nguyen, E., Agger-Gupta, N., Angelelli, C., Green, C. E., Haffner, L., Mochel, M., Okahara, L., Solís, B., & Tang, G. (2002). *California standards for healthcare interpreters: Ethical principles, protocols and guidance on roles and intervention*. Santa Barbara, California: California Healthcare Interpreters Association (CHIA) and The California Endowment. (Available online: http://www.calendow.org)

Flores, G., Laws, M. B., Mayo, S. J., Zuckerman, B., Abreu, M., Medina, L., et al. (2003). Errors in medical interpretation and their potential clinical consequences in pediatric encounters. *Pediatrics, 111*(1), 6–14.

Jacobs, E.A., Agger-Gupta, N., Chen, A.H., Piotrowski, A., & Hardt, E. (2003). *Language barriers in health care settings: An annotated bibliography of the research literature*. Woodland Hills, California: The California Endowment: pp.1–72. (Available online: http://www.calendow.org)

Kaufert, J. M., & Koolage, W. W. (1984). Role conflict among ‚culture brokers‘: the experience of native Canadian medical interpreters. *Social Science and Medicine, 18*(3), 283–286.

Kaufert, J. M., & Putsch, R. W. I. (1997). Communication through interpreters in healthcare: ethical dilemmas arising from differences in class, culture, language and power. *The Journal of Clinical Ethics, 8*(1), 71–87.

Kontrimas, J. (2000). The trouble with the term "advocacy" *Massachusetts Medical Interpreters Association Newsletter, 3*(Fall), 1–4.

Massachusetts Medical Interpreters Association and Education Development Center, I. M. (1995). *Medical Interpreting Standards of Practice*. Boston: Massachusetts Medical Interpreters Association.

Medical Interpreters: *Interpreter's Handbook – 3rd ed.* (1st Edition – 1996). Seattle, Washington: Cross Cultural Health Care Program of Pacific Medical Clinics.

Metzger, M. (1999). *Sign Language Interpreting: deconstructing the myth of neutrality*. Washington, DC: Gallaudet University Press: pp. 1–9.

Mink, O. G., Esterhuysen, P. W., Mink, B. P., & Owen, K. Q. (1993). *Change At Work: a comprehensive management process for transforming organizations* (1st ed. Vol. 1). San Francisco: Jossey-Bass: pp. 217–222.

Minnesota Interpreter Standards Advisory Committee. (1998). *Bridging the language gap: how to meet the need for interpreters in Minnesota*. Minneapolis, MN: Minnesota Interpreter

Standards Advisory Committee. (Available online: http://www.cce.umn.edu/creditcourses/pti/downloads.html)

Mintzberg, H. (1993, 1983). *Structure in Fives: Designing Effective Organizations*. Englewood Cliffs, NJ: Prentice-Hall, pp.4–6.

Office of Diversity Mount St. Joseph Hospital. (1996). *Health Care Interpreter Standards of Practice*. Vancouver, British Columbia, Canada: Mount St. Joseph Hospital

Okahara, L., Vu, H., Choi, S., Foong, H. L., Hiramine, N. J., Medal, L., Mochel, M., Moore, B., Moua, P., Nakashima, D., Nguyen, E. A., Vizcaino-Stewart, T. & Yang, C. (2004). *Connecting Worlds – Training for Healthcare Interpreters*. San Francisco: The California Endowment. (Available online: http://www.calendow.org)

Pearce, W. B. (1995). A Sailing Guide for Social Constructionists. In W. Leeds-Hurwitz (Ed.), *Social Approaches to Communication*. New York: The Guilford Press: pp. 88–113.

Pollard, R. Q. J., Miraglia, K., Pollard, K., Chapel, S., Elliott, M., & Abernethy, A. (1997). *Mental health interpreting: A mentored curriculum*. Rochester, New York: Department of Psychiatry, University of Rochester. School of Medicine.

Putsch, R. W. I. (1985). Cross-cultural communication: The special case of interpreters in health care. *Journal of the American Medical Association, 254*(23), 3344–3348.

Reddy, M. J. (1979). The conduit metaphor: a case of frame conflict in our language. In A. Ortony (Ed.), *Metaphor and thought* . New York: Cambridge University Press: pp. 284–324.

Roy, C. B. (2000). *Interpreting as a discourse process*. New York: Oxford University Press.

Stanford Hospital and Clinics Interpreter Services Department. (1985). *Code of Ethics for Medical Interpreters and Translators*.Stanford, California: Stanford Hospital and Clinics.

Wadensjö, C. (1998). *Interpreting as interaction*. London & New York: Longman.

PART V

Professional ideology

Food for thought

Professionalisation of interpreting *with* the community

Refining the model

Graham H. Turner

Heriot-Watt University, Edinburgh, United Kingdom

In this paper, I argue for a revised understanding of interpreting as a comprehensively *collaborative* activity. In presenting this case, I focus on the interpreter's role as a weaver-together of narratives and a connector of people. I stress the interpreter's task of working *with* others, i.e. actively bringing them into the process of negotiating meaning, to share triadic communicative events where participants constantly align and re-align themselves in complex kaleidoscopic ways to achieve their collective communicative goals. Building on previous work, I work towards the notion of a *cycle of empowerment*, reinforcing the imperative to work closely with the full range of relevant stakeholders to construct, implement and refine a shared understanding of roles and responsibilities.

Introductory remarks

For well over a decade, it has been clear that that the development of the sign language interpreting profession in the UK – as is true for community interpreting in general – will depend to a considerable extent upon maintaining a mutually supportive, though constructively critical, relationship between service providers and consumers (Pollitt 1991; Scott Gibson 1991). The aspiration of theorising and practically realising the key features of an interpreting profession which will fully meet the needs of both service users and practitioners, embedding in shared understandings of 'good practice' the kind of give-and-take which will enable interpretation of real quality to occur, has been central to the field in various forms for many years.

Models in our field have moved (see Pöchhacker 2004 for an excellent overview) towards a robust understanding that effective 'dialogue interpreting', the prototype for many community or liaison settings, commonly requires an interactive or participatory stance on the part of the practitioner. This has been elegantly theoretised and illuminatingly described with reference to spoken language interpreting (e.g. Berk-Seligson 1990; Wadensjö 1998; Anderson 2002) and sign language interpreting (e.g. Metzger 1999; Roy 2000) alike. The sign language interpreting field has also seen repeated calls for enhanced recognition of Deaf perspectives and increased participation by Deaf people in processes of definition and codification of the interpreter's role and ethical responsibilities (see, for example, Baker-Shenk 1991; Philip 1994; Scott Gibson 1994; Brien et al. 2004).

I have argued in my own work that although Deaf people do have a right to quality interpreting, they also have the responsibility not to take features of that service for granted (Turner 1995a), and that the correlate of this is the 'institutionalised altruism' expected of interpreting practitioners which is a cornerstone of their claim to professional status (Turner 1996). Capturing an appropriate model of the relationship between practitioners and service users within a Code of Ethics is considered crucial to professionalisation, and the absolute value which interpreters placed upon reference to such a Code emerges very clearly from qualitative data gathered in a survey of BSL-English interpreters (Tate & Turner 1997). With reference to particular interpreting settings – especially legal environments – fieldwork focusing on sign language interpreters in action was able to explore the way in which they enacted their understanding of the prescribed role and to critique and offer refinements to its construction (Turner 1995b; Turner & Brown 2001) and the embedding of an enriched appreciation of the interactional complexities of the role within interpreter education (Turner & Harrington 2002; Turner 2005). The impact upon service delivery of the interpreter's perception and construction of their relationship with other 'stakeholders' has steadily developed as a focal issue, drawing upon ethnographic data of sign language interpreting in settings ranging from residential social care to the theatre (Atherton et al. 2002; Turner & Pollitt 2002). It is to this last area and its impact upon professionalisation through the modelling of roles and responsibilities that the present paper now turns.

This paper draws together a number of strands in order to introduce the idea that a revised conception of how the interpreter can work *with* 'primary participants' (PPs) (Wadensjö 1998) may enable us to develop our thinking on the roles we ascribe to interpreters and the kinds of relationships with PPs which will maximise the efficacy of interpreted communication. For me, the notion that the sign language interpreter should be expected always to act as a 'conduit' or machine through whom messages merely pass as through a telephone wire has been robustly challenged and found wanting (Baker-Shenk 1991; Roy 1993; McIntire & Sanderson 1995: which is not to say that it is in all circumstances inappropriate – see Mindess 1999; Pollitt 2000). This paper pushes the re-distribution of responsibilities within the interpreting triad a little further, though, to suggest that it is a legitimate part of the interpreter's professionalism to seek to bring PPs to an overt and active appreciation of the interpretative work – the fine-grained semantic, pragmatic and discoursal navigation and management – in which the practitioner is engaged.

Working with others as meaning-makers

Like many in this field, I like to notice words that are new to me, to be hoarded up like a squirrel with his nuts, and I heard a good one recently which I thought might come in handy. The word was 'confabulation', and it struck me that this was rather an apt description of part of the interpreting task. Is it not true that the interpreter is a kind of weaver-together, a connector of people and their narratives, telling their stories *with* them and enabling them to tell stories *with* each other, knowing them so that they may know each other? This is part of the story that interpreters and interpreting theorists have been seeking to develop over the last decade or so: that *making meaning is a co-operative venture.*

For me, the idea that language is absolutely and always a social process, in which meaning derives from interaction *between people* rather than from either the words or the utterer, is absolutely fundamental. Each participant in talk 'projects' their understanding, their vision or their story about the universe through their contributions to talk and interlocutors seek to arrive at a shared image or notion of the world. The more focused the outcome, the greater the mutual understanding achieved (see Le Page & Tabouret-Keller 1985).

In everyday monolingual talk, this is typically an unspoken process: we do not tend to say *"When you offer me an 'ice-cream', I understand you to mean a frozen, traditionally cream-based, highly-sweetened confection, often served in my country in a crisp, dry, conical wafer – and yes, I'd like a large one, please!"* There is a difference, of course, generated by the presence of the interpreter who is "actively articulating her understanding for every turn at talk" (Hewitt 2003: 4). This means that the interpreter enacts the task of 're-projecting' what each participant independently generates, and aims to enable both participants to share a perception of the co-constructed image.

Shaping shared interaction

The idea of the interpreter as a 'confabulator' therefore seems to offer an opportunity to review our understanding of the nature of the co-participation undertaken by interpreters and PPs within the interactional triad. In what kinds of ways can we see the principle of collaborative meaning-making being translated into practical applications by interpreters seeking to co-operate with consumers in the search for effective interpreted exchanges? In what ways is the interpreter already understood as a 'co-worker'? I would highlight three elements. Firstly, the interpreter must share the floor in working *with* other people in a genuinely triadic communicative event – the communicative *pas de trois* described by Cecilia Wadensjö (1998) in her pioneering analysis. Danielle-Claude Bélanger (2003) has subsequently pointed out the extent to which different combinations of the triad align and re-align themselves in a talk-event and how sensitive the interpreter needs to be over this. Secondly, the interpreter must work *with* the nature of the processes in which one is engaged: when educating, engage in an educational process; when in court, getting inside legal processes; and so on. The process of educating, job interviewing or making legal judgements is part of what the interpreter is seeking to convey, i.e. she is participating in delivering that *process*. And thirdly, the interpreter works *with* insights from scholarship, creatively inhabiting them and renewing them for our purposes: for instance, Kyra Pollitt and colleagues have recently produced (Pollitt et al. 2005) some elegant reflections on telephone interpreting using sign languages which draw upon unexpected sources to begin to suggest how, talk-event by talk-event, we need to re-create the interpreter's participation-style and discourses to maximise primary participants' sense that they are talking *with* – rather than past! – one another.

Thinking about how interpreters work *with* others certainly helps to foreground a co-participatory or triadic model of interpreting. There clearly has been a late 20th century 'turn' towards a model of the interpreter as a co-ordinator and negotiator of meanings in a three-way interaction (Mason 1999, 2000), but there is progress yet to be made in pushing at our understanding of how triadic, multi-layered, interpreted interactions work.

In particular, as Cynthia Roy put it more than a decade ago:

> While descriptions and standards of ethical practice extensively, sometimes exhaustively, list what interpreters should *not* do, they seldom, if ever, explain what interpreters *can* do, that is, explain what 'flexible' means. Consequently, no one really knows where to draw the line on the involvement of the interpreter (Roy 1993: 134).

For me, it is Roy, again (1989: 265), who pinpointed what we seek to figure out: "[W]hen interpreters are used, they are part of the interaction naturally. The point is not their neutrality but rather what is or can be their participation in the event". We are still trying to figure this out in detail: *what can be their participation?*

Exploring lateral thinking

How *does* the interpreter actively 'project' her understanding of every turn at talk and what does that imply for our analyses and therefore for our teaching? We know, as Roy (2004) put it more recently, that "people act in concert with each other" – meaning is in the shared space between them – so how do interlocutors get meaning there and how can we find it there? In order to explore these questions, I think we will need more research that continues to apply insights from outside of our immediate spheres of reference with as much sophistication as Roy herself did in her own initial analyses (Roy 1989) of the interpreting triad. This will be hard, for it requires gigantic leaps of the imagination and real conceptual invigoration to see new connections, but there is evidence of such innovative theoretical links being both forged and applied to interpreter education.

To illustrate the illumination that may be derived from a little lateral thinking, let me suggest an analogy I find rather intriguing. I listened to a discussion about the making of documentary films recently and was struck that the idea of the 'invisibility' of the interpreter is akin to that of the documentary-maker producing 'fly-on-the-wall' documentaries. Both are considered *passé* at the leading edge. Audiences just do not buy the idea that the film-crew's presence has no effect on the behaviour of the film's subjects. So what alternatives have *they* come up with, and can we learn anything from them?

If you are a documentary-maker, you can, at one extreme, act in a relatively invasive, overtly challenging fashion, catching people on their door-step and winding them up with 'in-your-face' questions. Or, at the other, you can seek to blend wholly into the background, to be lost in the scenery, so that your presence passes almost unnoticed. Between these extremes, you might back off, ask questions with no apparent agenda and give subjects room to 'expose themselves', so to speak, simply by talking unguardedly – here you may still be asking them questions, but at least the idea is that you seek to do so as far as possible as a 'naturalised' element of the environment. Whatever the strategy is, documentary-makers argue that you can work either fairly or exploitatively using any approach: it is not the *approach* that defines whether the story is being elaborated, 'brought out' or simply observed, but the integrity of the producer. To have integrity in this context certainly means not to cheat, manipulate or wilfully misrepresent, but also *not to hide your influence on the process and the product, opting rather to acknowledge your strategy overtly.*

So if you are an interpreter trying to get some inspiration for progressive interactional strategies by watching the approach of documentary-makers, how might you borrow ways to acknowledge your visibility and active participation and get co-participants to recognise and engage with the active re-casting of meaning that you are undertaking?

1. '*Opening titles*': You might explain your approach as part of the title sequence, i.e. before the interpreting assignment proper begins.
2. '*Direct to camera asides*': This might be akin to what Kyra Pollitt and Tina Little (2003:68) have described as "annotated interpreting", i.e. providing a live self-commentary, where necessary, to explain one's own interpreting decisions.
3. '*Interactive functions*': Are interpreting consumers always encouraged – as the BBC's digital channel adverts suggest – to 'press the red button' when they want elucidation, thus suspending the on-screen action while they review or explore a particular element in more depth? Do interpreters always encourage interpreting consumers to take this kind of control?
4. '*Split-screen format*': Documentary-makers sometimes use this to show what is happening from a different angle – for instance, one might use it to show what is happening behind the camera, to show the interviewer and what is over their shoulder. The parallel technique might be to have two interpreters simultaneously producing different text-tracks in different languages.
5. '*Checkout our website*': Documentaries nowadays all seem to end with this kind of offer; so perhaps we might imagine in the future seeing "*if you missed something in this conversation or want further information and links to other related or background material to help you understand the provision of this interpretation more fully, check-out* www.todaysinterpretation.com"
6. '*Aftercare helplines*': In the same way, following the style of modern documentaries, we can imagine seeing the message "*if you have been affected by or would welcome further clarification on any of the issues in this interpretation… just call 0800-TERP-RE-CAP. Helplines are open from 0.900–18.00h*".

Any of these might actually be applicable. It is the lateral thinking, the world of possibilities already framed in some other context, familiar to consumers and ripe for adaptation, which is provocative.

Developing knowingness

Beyond any of these, though, what the best contemporary documentary-makers have done has been to work on and with audiences over time to develop our *knowing* awareness of what is going on beneath, behind and beyond what appears on screen. When the interviewer raises an eyebrow, though his or her voice remains carefully modulated, we readily notice both the eyebrow and the blissful unawareness of it shown by the interviewee. The unspoken interpretative work that goes into the programmes we watch is well understood by sophisticated modern audiences. (We are no longer afraid, like early cinema news-reel audiences, of being run over by the train as it bears down upon the screen! We largely, though tacitly, understand the grammar of programme-construction.) The same is perhaps the optimum strategy for interpreting development: working with co-participants over time *so that they know what the interpreters are up to* and are complicit in it.

Crucially, all of the notions (1–6) above are strategies for working *with* co-participants; that is, they recognise and respond to the recognition that 'the truth' of the documentary's story or of the meaning of words interpreted is not simply 'out there'. The image and the viewers, knowledge and the knowers, the meaning and the 'meaners', are *interdependent*. What we have here in documentary-making is partly a familiar recognition that the observer cannot be absent from defining the behaviour observed, and in interpreting, that the interpreter's input partly defines the talk-in-interaction that unfolds. But it is more than that.

What the above list of parallels with documentary-making works towards is pushing *beyond* our understanding that interpreting takes place through a triadic relationship between the interpreter and the interpretees, and trying to draw the latter into an *active appreciation* of what the interpreter is doing, so that they, too, are consciously active *in the interpretation process itself*. In other words, the ideas in 1–6 above are ways of bringing to consciousness, acknowledging, making transparent, the influence of the documentary-maker (or, by analogy, the interpreter), in such a way as to enable the consumer to be aware of it and thus to react 'knowingly' and not 'naively'.

Working with others to produce the circumstances for real interpreting

In part, my suggestion that we try to bring PPs into the interpreting process is done in an attempt to 'de-mystify' the field. As researchers, teachers and practitioners, we cannot do too much, in my view, to draw others into sharing our understandings of interpreting and co-creating with us better understandings for the future. I think we do need to keep pushing ourselves to imagine how better we can work with others to produce the circumstances in which effective interpreting can occur.

During the past year, we have certainly been very much aware of this issue in the field of sign language interpreting in the UK. We live, as the saying has it, in interesting times. After 20 years of frustratingly slow but steady and apparently co-operative professionalisation, one consumer group has begun openly to criticise the edifice painstakingly built so far. The British Deaf Association has recently launched its own proposals for an alternative system of standards, training, qualifications and regulation for British Sign Language/English interpreters. I do not propose to examine the options here: what this illustrates, though, is the tireless work which needs to go on in order to get all stakeholders to lead each other to a *shared* vision of professional interpreting. Appropriate ways, it is argued, have not been found for Deaf people to be meaningfully involved as consumer representatives; as trainers; as regulators; as researchers; as service managers; and, above all – since I increasingly think that this 'core' experience of the job is the key to a full understanding of what it means – as *practitioners* and thus as 'professional reflectors' on interpreting.

Co-production and empowerment

All of this is intended to suggest a slight shift in thinking about how to make interpreting work. One might signify that shift by enlisting the term 'co-production'. This is an idea usually related to generating equal partnerships between professionals and clients in the areas of welfare programmes, education, policing and health: finding practical and often surprising ways in which professionals can transform their relationships with clients. Public services designed like this would have a different focus from that with which we in the UK are familiar, with different targets and working styles.

Professionals have been accused of creating a dependency of a particularly corrosive kind which convinces their clients that the latter have nothing worthwhile to offer. Thinking in terms of co-production in the professions turns matters somewhat on their head by stressing the *interdependence* of service users and practitioners. Interpreters, I have suggested, would benefit from working with clients who are active collaborators in the face-to-face interpreting process. In the same way, active collaboration in developing the environment for interpreting (training, regulation and the rest) should be a target.

Our aim has to be, I think, for a *cycle of empowerment*: from research to education to management to practice to reflection to regulation (see Turner 2005). Research and scholarship gather and generate knowledge and ideas upon which good practice can be built: the educational curriculum presents and interprets this material: institutional structures are designed to facilitate the same ideas of good practice: interpreters are guided in the practical application of the theory: as practitioners, they undertake reflection which not only enriches their ongoing practice but is in itself a form of analytical scholarship that can and does give rise to innovation and insight with which to re-commence the cycle: and the whole is subjected to regulatory attention representing the interests of all stakeholders. The empowerment cycle is thus one which behaves as continuously self-regenerating. And the process requires a state of permanent dialogue: at all stages in the cycle, information and ideas need to flow both into the process and out of it.

Conclusions

Here is where all of this takes me. The kind of interpreting I want, if I am ever in a police cell or on an operating table in some far corner of a foreign country, is the kind that arises from this kind of richly collaborative ground, where principles for working with others to co-create good practice have been understood and implemented.

To capture the point, I find myself wanting to speak, by analogy with the field of physics, of 'quantum interpreting'. Fundamental to quantum physics is the notion that the nature of phenomena only exists in the act of our knowing about them: and I want to suggest that, ultimately, effective interpreting is similarly embedded or instantiated within our collective awareness, our co-construction, of the task.

A classic statement of the core idea I am after can be found, for scholars of physics, in the famous problem of Schrödinger's cat, which goes something like this. Take one cat, put it in a closed box. The cat is in the box, it is understood, but is it alive or deceased? To know this, to be able accurately to describe its state of being, we have to open the box. Its nature is unknowable without undertaking the act of looking. It is our looking which 'defines' its state of being. The key to this conceptual step is in acknowledging the *interdependence* of process, perceiver and product. The interpreter's output is the cat in the box; it is only with the active 'uptake' or appreciation of it by the PPs that it is fully 'made real' as effective communication. This key point significantly extends, in my view, the analysis presented in earlier work (Harrington & Turner 2001) of what it means to engage in 'real interpreting'. After all that I have discussed in this paper about the range of factors which, to my mind, inform quality interpreting, I arrive at the notion of 'quantum interpreting' as a shorthand term to try and capture something of this sense of reflexivity, this necessarily *knowing* relationship, this interdependent relationship *of knowing* between the interpreter, the interpreters, the act of interpreting and that which is interpreted.

There is in all of this discussion repeated use made of a certain prefix. I have been discussing collaboration, co-construction, co-participation, co-production and co-operation. Not so long ago, for sign language interpreters, the significance of the prefix 'co' was quite different. Professionalisation then (see Pollitt 1997 and Cokely 2005 for a critique) was supposed to be all about being businesslike – interpreting as a profession that was hard-nosed, uptight, pin-striped and commodified for the market-place. Interpreters expected themselves to be detached to the point of untouchability and unreachability. The alternative use of 'co', though, as I have stressed, points us along a different track, to its roots as a signifier of doing things *with* others. Achieving effective mediated communication through the practice of interpreting is something no individual can do alone. In this paper, I have tried to suggest a further development in the way we conceive of the contributions to interpreted communication made by the co-participants in such activity, and a corresponding shift in our thinking about professionalisation.

References

Anderson, R. B. W. 2002. "Perspectives On The Role Of Interpreter". [Originally published in 1976 in R. W. Brislin (ed.) *Translation: Applications and Research*. Gardner Press: New York. 208–228.] In *The Interpreting Studies Reader*, F. Pцchhacker & M. Shlesinger (eds), 209–217. London: Routledge.

Atherton, M., Gregg, A., Harrington, F. J., Quinn, G., Traynor, N. & Turner, G. H. 2001. *Addressing Communication Disadvantage: Deaf people with Minimal Language Skills*. Preston: University of Central Lancashire/Deafway.

Baker-Shenk, C. 1991. "The interpreter: Machine, advocate, or ally?" In *Expanding Horizons: Proceedings of the 1991 RID Convention*, 120–140. Silver Spring MD: RID Publications.

Bélanger, D.-C. 2003. Les differentes figures d'interaction en interpretation de dialogue. In *The Critical Link 3: Interpreters in the Community*, L. Brunette, G. Bastin, I. Hemlin & H. Clarke (eds), 51–66. Amsterdam: John Benjamins.

Berk-Seligson, S. 1990. *The Bilingual Courtroom: Court Interpreters in the Judicial Process*. Chicago: Chicago University Press.

Brien, D, Brown, R. & Collins, J. 2004. "Some recommendations regarding the provision and organisation of British Sign Language/English interpreters in England, Scotland and Wales." *Deaf Worlds: International Journal of Deaf Studies* 20 (1): 6–60.

Cokely, D. 2005. "Shifting positionality: A critical examination of the turning point in the relationship of interpreters and the deaf community." In *Sign Language Interpreting and Interpreter Education: Directions for Research and Practice*, M. Marschark, R. Peterson & E. A. Winston (eds), 3–28. Oxford: Oxford University Press.

Harrington, F. J. & Turner, G. H. 2001. *Interpreting interpreting: Studies and reflections on sign language interpreting*. Coleford, Gloucestershire: Douglas McLean.

Hewitt, G. 2003. "Hidden shifts: Interpreter influence on meaning construction in group psychotherapy". University of Central Lancashire, unpublished ms.

Le Page, R. B. & Tabouret-Keller, A. 1985. *Acts of Identity: Creole-based Approaches to Language and Ethnicity*. Cambridge: Cambridge University Press.

Mason, I. 1999. "Introduction." *The Translator* 5 (2): 147–160.

Mason, I. 2000. "Models and Methods in Dialogue Interpreting Research." In *Intercultural Faultlines: Research Models in Translation Studies 1 – Textual and Cognitive Aspects*, M. Olohan (ed), 215–231. Manchester: St. Jerome.

McIntire, M. & Sanderson, G. 1995. "Who's in charge here? Perceptions of empowerment and role in the interpreting setting." *Journal of Interpretation* 7 (1): 99–114.

Metzger, M. 1999. *Sign Language Interpreting: Deconstructing the myth of neutrality*. Washington, DC: Gallaudet University Press.

Mindess, A. 1999. *Reading between the signs: Intercultural communication for sign language interpreters*. Yarmouth, Maine: Intercultural Press.

Philip, M. J. 1994. "Professionalism: From which cultural perspective?" Paper presented at *1st Issues in Interpreting* conference, Durham, England.

Pöchhacker, F. 2004. *Introducing Interpreting Studies*. London: Routledge.

Pollitt, K. 1991. "Rational responses." *Signpost* 4 (2): 24.

Pollitt, K. 1997. "The state we're in: Some thoughts on professionalisation, professionalism and practice among the UK's sign language interpreters." *Deaf Worlds: International Journal of Deaf Studies* 13 (3): 21–26.

Pollitt, K. 2000. "On babies, bathwater and approaches to interpreting". *Deaf Worlds: International Journal of Deaf Studies* 16 (2): 16–24.

Pollitt, K. & Haddon, C. (with the interpreting team of the University of Central Lancashire) 2005. "Cold calling: Retraining interpreters in the art of telephone interpreting." In *Advances in Teaching Sign Language Interpreters*, C. B. Roy (ed), 187–210. Washington, DC: Gallaudet University Press.

Pollitt, K. & Little, T. 2003. "Beyond the courtroom: Legal interpreting in child protection". In *Traducteurs et interprètes certifiés et judiciaires: Droits, devoirs et besoins*. E. de la Fuente (ed), 61–78. Paris: UNESCO/Fédération Internationale des Traducteurs.

Roy, C. B.1989. *A Sociolinguistic Analysis of the Interpreter is Role in the Turn Exchanges of an Interpreted Event*. Unpublished dissertation. Washington DC: Georgetown University, University Microfilms DAO64793.

Roy, C. B. 1993. "The Problem with Definitions, Descriptions and the Role Metaphors of Interpreters." *Journal of Interpretation* 6 (1): 127–154.

Roy, C. B. 2000. *Interpreting as a Discourse Process*. Oxford: Oxford University Press.

Roy, C. B. 2004. "Discourse and the role of the interpreter." Paper presented at NTID/USA National Science Foundation *Educational Interpreting and Interpreter Education: From Research to Practice* research workshop, New Orleans, USA.

Scott Gibson, L. 1991. "Sign language interpreting: An emerging profession." In *Constructing Deafness*, S. Gregory & G. Hartley (eds), 253–258. London/Milton Keynes: Pinter Publishers in association with the Open University.

Scott Gibson, L. 1994. "Open to interpretation: The cult of professionalism." Paper presented at *1st Issues in Interpreting* conference, Durham, England.

Tate, G. & Turner, G. H. 1997. "The Code and the Culture: Sign Language Interpreting – In Search of the New Breed's Ethics." *Deaf Worlds: International Journal of Deaf Studies* 13 (3): 27–34.

Turner, G. H. 1995a. "Rights and Responsibilities: The relationship between Deaf people and interpreters." *Deafness, the journal of the sociology of deafness* 11 (3): 4–8.

Turner, G. H. 1995b. "The bilingual, bimodal courtroom: A first glance." *Journal of Interpretation* 7 (1): 3–33.

Turner, G. H. 1996. "Regulation and Responsibility: The relationship between interpreters and Deaf people." *Deaf Worlds: International Journal of Deaf Studies* 12 (1): 1–7.

Turner, G. H. 2005. "Toward real interpreting." In *Sign Language Interpreting and Interpreter Education: Directions for Research and Practice*, M. Marschark, R. Peterson & E.A. Winston (eds), 29–56. Oxford: Oxford University Press.

Turner, G. H. & Brown, R. K. 2001. "Interaction and the role of the interpreter in court." In *Interpreting interpreting: Studies and reflections on sign language interpreting*, F. J. Harrington & G. H. Turner, 152–167. Coleford, Gloucestershire: Douglas McLean.

Turner, G. H. & Harrington, F. J. 2002. "The Campaign for Real Interpreting." *Deaf Worlds: International Journal of Deaf Studies* 18 (2): 69–72.

Turner, G. H. & Pollitt, K. 2002. "Community interpreting meets literary translation: English-BSL interpreting in the theatre." *The Translator* 8 (1): 25–48.

Wadensjö, C. 1998. *Interpreting as Interaction*. London: Longman.

"Why bother?"

Institutionalization, interpreter decisions, and power relations

Stephanie Jo Kent
University of Massachusetts Amherst, USA

This paper presents a case for the re-enactment of power relations when mac-rosocial, organizational structure influences interpersonal communication. A microsocial effect of the professionalization of community interpreting (ASL/English) is examined through two cultural discourses about the interpreter's role and a theoretical application of Goffman's notion of footing. Management of the communication process by interpreters has become a deeply meaning-ful and potent site of cultural struggle because of an institutional structuring of professional ambiguity regarding impartiality. This ambiguity has produced conditions under which evaluating the interpreter's performance of role be-comes a microsocial necessity – a site for the exercise of individual and cultural agency.

Introduction

Professionalization, as Mette Rudvin asserts, is not an innocent activity (2004). Her critique intends to expose and challenge inherent cultural biases in the con-cept and process of professionalizing. To organize as a profession is to deliber-ately enter politics and the culture wars. Inevitably, organizing will have a range of anticipated and unpredictable effects. An ironic outcome of professionalizing community interpreters who work between American Sign Language (ASL) and spoken English in the U.S. is that interpreters have become a focal target for Deaf criticism of audist behaviors and practices.[1] This phenomena bears out Rudvin's

---

1.   Capitalization of Deaf is intentional to emphasize the linguistic and cultural social group; when the lower-case "deaf" is used, it refers to audiological loss and encompasses whom sign language interpreters might serve, many of whom are not members of Deaf culture.

claim that professionalization of community interpreting will influence the formation and enactment of identity (2004).

At the macrosocial level, professionalization will interact with and participate in patterns of educational policy, language shift,[2] and linguistic human rights. Interpreters and minority or lesser-used language speakers need to be aware of the dual and simultaneous effects of professionalization within both the macrosocial structure (legally and politically) and at the level of microsocial interaction (the relationships) among and between interpreters and interlocutors (those communicating with each other through an interpreter). The historical conditions and felt experience of inequality can be too easily reproduced, albeit unintentionally, if the link between organizational structuring (policies, guidelines, codes of ethics, etc.) and actual hands-on implementation is not considered in a careful and deliberate manner.

In attending my first Critical Link conference, I was struck by the regard given by conference planners and participants to sign language interpreters because of our relatively high degree of professionalization.[3] Being accepted as a peer alongside spoken language interpreters was refreshing because, in my experience, this is rather unusual. This is due, at least partly, to residual prejudice that denies ASL full linguistic status on a par with foreign spoken languages. My pleasure at the welcome in Stockholm was tainted, however, by doubt as to the pragmatics of the accompanying ... professional envy? Specifically, is the professionalization of sign language interpretation in the US a heuristic model or a bad example?

Many of the outcomes of the professionalization of sign language interpretation could not have been predicted at its inception forty years ago.[4] There is much to celebrate in terms of increased accessibility and opportunities for deaf people. However, with the lessons of the past and the dilemmas of the present available for scrutiny, we can anticipate at least some of the ways in which certain strategies for professionalization might unfold over time with both good and ill effects. By thinking deeply about the functions and desired outcomes of professionalization, interpreters may be able to minimize collusion with systemic oppression. Collu-

---

2. J. Crawford uses this term to refer to "permanent changes in language use that result in the survival of some languages and the disappearance of others" (Santos 2001:602).

3. I am using "sign language interpretation" to encompass a variety of communicative methods including invented codes to represent English in a visual/gestural form. I am using ASL/English interpretation to refer specifically to interpretation between spoken English and ASL as the indigenous language of the culturally Deaf in the United States. The argument presented here is specific to the latter.

4. American Sign Language/English interpretation was first institutionalized in the late 1960's with the establishment of the Registry of Interpreters for the Deaf (RID).

sion should not be understood as deliberate prejudice or discrimination. People, in general, do not question their own logic because ideology encourages us not to suspect ourselves. This lack of self-scrutiny is one of the factors that can lead to, for example, what Skutnabb-Kangas (2000:665) describes as "irrational language policies which result in linguistic and cultural genocide and in prevention of linguistic rights".[5]

First, a clarification. Professionalization is a process of institutionalization more than it is a process of producing uniform practices. In other words, the reason to pursue professionalization is to establish a macrosocial structure (an institution) that can negotiate with other institutional structures, such as governments, courts, businesses, schools, and social service providers. Standardization of practice is only one of the possible outcomes of professionalization: it is neither an inherent nor automatic characteristic of becoming institutionalized.

However, the professionalization process *will* introduce, confirm and reject ways of thinking about practitioners (interpreters) and those who use our services (interlocutors) by establishing certain boundaries for the co-construction and co-enactment of identity. This will be illustrated by a meta-dialogue between (non-deaf) ASL/English interpreters and members of the American Deaf community. The dialogue is described as "meta" because comments from different conversations are juxtaposed to illustrate an argument concerning decisions made by interpreters to manage communication processes during interpretation.

In direct (not interpreted) interaction, practical decisions about whose turn it is, whether or not to interrupt, and other relational decisions happen routinely and are rarely noticed. With the addition of an interpreter, these particular decisions can become a deeply meaningful and potent site of cultural struggle. These decisions must be framed by some kind of logic that guides expectations about when, where, and how to negotiate the relationships that are an inherent and integral component of any communication. This is the logic of role. How role is envisioned and codified undergirds all questions and concerns about professionalization as a process of institutionalization. Rudvin makes this point when she asserts, "professionalism is defined by role" (2004:5). The image or concept of role will become a socializing force (whether one wishes it or not) upon interpreters (current and future) and all interlocutors with whom we come in contact – be they dominant or lesser-used/minority language users.

---

5.   Quoted in Handsfield, Lara J. (2002) Teaching agency and double agents: Reconceptualizing linguistic genocide in education.

The role of the ASL/English interpreter

Non-linguistic decision-making is a commonsense way of referring to those decisions interpreters make which are less about conveying the meaning of produced or implied language, and more about the dynamics and relationships between the people in the interpreted event. The most common examples involve interpreters' interrupting to clarify or manage turn-taking. Curiously, despite agreeing that an interpreter ought to ask for explanation, repetition, and more deliberate pacing if they do not understand or can not keep up, Deaf individuals often criticize interpreters for doing exactly these things.

What generates this contradiction? Interpreters are being evaluated based upon their performance of a professional role. Judgment may include an assessment of how (or whether) the interpreter managed the convergence of the two cultures and their respective ways-of-being in a manner that is deemed acceptable or appropriate by interlocutors. In my experience, members of the dominant language group rarely question the interpreter's competence, while members of the minority language group often provide spontaneous natural criticism. Such criticism, however, is widely divergent.

Different Deaf people, for instance, sometimes express opposite, mutually exclusive opinions about whether, when, or how an interpreter should attempt to manage the practical aspects of the communication process. A close analysis of multiple instances of this natural criticism (generated in videotaped, open-ended interviews about what Deaf interlocutors do and do not like about what interpreters do) allowed the identification of some interesting patterns, centrally the use of three key symbols: "INTERRUPT", "DISRUPT" and "TAKEOVER" (Kent, in progress).[6] A key symbol is a particular term or short phrase that signals the presence of a culturally-specific experience or perception. Key symbols are identified by frequency of use, potency, and prominence (Carbaugh 1989).

One statement of natural criticism using each key symbol was selected from the (2001) taped interviews with Deaf users of interpreting services and shown to forty-seven participants of an interpreter development workshop (in 2004). An additional statement regarding the scope of meaning of the key simbol, "TAKEOVER", was also shown. Interpreters wrote down their responses immediately after viewing each statement. The written comments were then examined for patterns and categorized by emergent themes. The first column of Table 1 contains translations of the three selected Deaf criticisms and the explanation proved for "TAKEOVER". The second column provides an example of a common interpreter

---

6. The standard convention for glossing ASL signs is to use capital letters.

reaction and its categorization by theme: distancing, personalizing, or problem-solving.

An example[7]

Patterns that are evident in spontaneous, naturally-produced American Deaf criticism of ASL/English interpreters are that it is directed at the interpreter (not, for instance, the group-as-a-whole or non-deaf interlocutors) because of decisions about group dynamics that compromise the enactment of cultural identity. The criticism tends to be accompanied by emotion, which may be expressed verbally (through a specific lexical item) or non-verbally (via expression and affect), and is usually not provided directly to the interpreter involved but rather to a third party.

Each statement of Deaf criticism elicited all three types of reaction; however only four examples are provided here, one reaction to each Deaf critique. Most interpreters in this sample reacted by distancing or personalizing. Distancing reactions often indicate the criticism must not be directed at oneself but is either intended for "other interpreters" or is a result of the Deaf person's own "issues". A response indicating distance could also be a generalized reaction to the pressure of the entire interpreting situation. Personalizing reactions assume the individual interpreter is guilty and directly responsible for the criticized behavior. A smaller percentage of the interpreters in this sample responded by problem-solving. Problem-solvers may be reacting defensively out of a personal need to fix, prevent or avoid the criticism without addressing its root causes (many of the comments indicate this), or from a proactive desire to understand the dynamics and conditions in all their complexity so that appropriate bicultural solutions can be created (there is some evidence of this as well). The first and second examples in Table 1 are categorized as distancing, the third as personalizing, and the fourth as problem-solving.

Seventy-five percent of the non-deaf interpreter responses include at least one labeled emotion. The range of emotions is broad: frustrated, challenged, uncomfortable, concerned, anxious, guilty, upset, stressed, empathetic, overwhelmed, uncertain, helpless, hopeless, scared, angry, confused, defensive, self-critical, embarrassed, unappreciated, useless, disappointed, and bewildered. Emotion is also present in almost 100% of spontaneously-produced Deaf criticism. Such consistently high levels of emotion within both groups' discourses clearly indicate the

---

7. This paper presents only a summary. A longer, more detailed report is in progress.

Table 1.

Deaf Interlocutor's Statement*	Interpreter's Reaction
"I've had interpreters completely INTER-RUPT a meeting. They'll say, 'I'm lost! Two people are talking at the same time! I'm lost!' I really don't like it. It's very disruptive for me."	"Sometimes I think 'Yeah I get your point.' Other times I think, 'Damn, you try it then'... Nobody's happy...and I'm stuck in the mid-dle...like we're 'playing nice' [until] it gets sticky – then it's the interpreter's fault." *Distancing response*
"If I'm being interrupted frequently, for exam-ple, I know I'm not in my culture <u>at all.</u> I know it! If the communication process is erratic and disjointed; I'm in your culture, not mine."	"The interpreter is taking the anger or confu-sion – the deaf person gives this anger and confusion to the one who is communicating for them." *Distancing response*
"I was watching everything quite smooth-ly, then the back-up interpreter suddenly launched into an explanation! They TOOK OVER with a rapid explanation then sat back, done. It was so visually jarring for me, I didn't like it at all. I can't stand that!"	"[This] bothers me, because it is my job to facilitate communication and [the reason] I am working [in this] situation. It somewhat makes me feel like why bother." *Personalizing response*
"That sign, TAKEOVER...is not superficial. It's very serious. It's taking someone's power, their space, and their respect all at the same time: wrenching it away."	"I would like to see an example...is it subtle (in terms of the whole group) or can it just be seen/felt by the deaf person? Is the inter-preter aware of it? Is it an enabling issue? It make[s] me feel sick – I would never want someone deaf/hearing/hard-of-hearing to feel that!" *Problem-solving response*

* Translations of the original ASL by the author.

high-stakes nature of practical decision-making about the relational component of the communication process.

Footing

Goffman's concept of footing provides a theoretical framework for understand-ing the relevance of these decisions. As he explains "a change in footing implies a change in the alignment we take up to ourselves and the others present as ex-pressed in the way we manage the production or reception of an utterance" (Goff-man 1981: 128). This happens when interpreters shift from conveying language-based meaning to negotiating practical aspects of the communication process. Specifically, the alignment of the interpreter to the interlocutor(s) shifts from a stance of facilitating linguistic understanding to a stance that acknowledges the relationships embedded in the communication process.

In other words, "a change in our footing is another way of talking about a change in our frame for events" (ibid.: 128). Something must occur to require a change in the frame – a change in the logic of role. Interpreters routinely shift footing, because of "complex social reasons" upon which they "act instinctively" (Roy 2000: 89). Interpreters develop strategies for interjecting, for knowing when to ask for clarification or not, for mediating the time difference produced by the act of interpreting, and for managing the turn-taking process (to name a few). Interpreters alter alignment because we intuit that the frame for the event has shifted between, for example, colleagues engaging a mutually-understood task to a manifestation of cultural difference with potentially oppressive implications. The change in the frame requires a shift in role, which is justified by a shift in the logic of role. The logic entails a decision about how the overall communicative process can proceed most smoothly.

The trigger for Deaf criticism could be these shifts in footing, which, from their vantage point in the moment, may occur inexplicably and without warning. Interpreters' general defensiveness to Deaf criticism may be because unconsidered shifts in footing are likely sites for the unconscious enactment of subtle forms of oppression. At this point in the research, it is premature to do more than speculate, however the significant presence of emotion does suggest this is an area that may yield important new understandings about interpreting.

If we consider these two discourses as cultural, as being rooted in particular experiences of social identity such as being Deaf and being non-deaf or " hearing", then we can imagine the dialogue constructed here as part of a larger discourse about power relations. In fact, while not mutually exclusive (Deaf persons can be professionals, and all hearing people are not professionals), the emotion-laden pattern in these two discourses can perhaps be best understood as an exchange of Deaf criticism and *professional* response. While Deaf individuals seek to enact their cultural identity through fluent use of ASL and a smooth flow of communication, interpreters are seeking to perform a professional role conceived as separate from their cultural identity.

A theme in much of the naturally-produced Deaf criticism is a sense of loss of power, of the inability to represent oneself in the way one prefers. Could this be because, at least sometimes, the assumptions informing interpreters' professional intuitions about the need to shift footing reinforce Deaf minority status? At the very least, I suggest that these shifts implicate the question of impartiality, because when ASL/English interpreters shift frames from interpreting the communication to mediating the cross-cultural relationships, we receive the most vigorous and consistent criticism. In other words, interlocutors may well wonder whose side we are on. To put these microsocial interactions in perspective and understand whether or not they represent larger issues of social justice, we have to consider the historical context.

Institutional and cultural context

The late 1980's and early 1990's were an exciting time for Deaf Education in the U.S. with the ascendancy of the Bilingual/Bicultural (BiBi) movement at The Learning Center in Framingham, Massachusetts and The Indiana School for the Deaf in Indianapolis, Indiana. Deaf culture and Deaf pride were riding the momentum of the successful 1988 "Deaf President Now" movement at Gallaudet University (which installed the first deaf president in the institution's 130-year history); this energy was also felt within the interpreting profession. A series of *Allies* conferences was organized by activists in which interpreters and Deaf interlocutors met to discuss ways of improving professional interactions.[8] Ideological debates within The Registry of Interpreters for the Deaf (RID) at this time centered around whether or not to privilege American Sign Language and interpretation between ASL and spoken English as the core professional activity of members, or to maintain the inherited range between the culturally Deaf and those deaf persons preferring transliteration of one or more of the invented sign systems and manual codes for English that continue to permeate the larger deaf and hard-of-hearing community. Frustration with the measurement of qualifications, and a stalemate within RID, led The National Association of the Deaf (NAD) to design and implement its own autonomous screening and testing process for interpreter credentialing.

These meaningful and positive attempts at institutional change have taken new forms or faded. What was driving the need for change? What was "wrong" with the professionalization of sign language interpretation that inspired both grassroots (*Allies*) and institutional (NAD) attempts to effect change within and upon the institutionalized, professional body (RID)?

Perhaps it goes without saying that the members of the professional interpreting organization (RID) are overwhelmingly not Deaf. In other words, professionalization is a process that further institutionalizes the privilege of members of the dominant language group by granting them the authority of a professional credential. Additionally, professionalization is a raced, gendered, and classed

---

8. The first Allies conference occurred as a track at the RID Region 1 Conference in Philadelphia (1992). Four followed in Concord, NH (1995, 1997, 1998, 1999), and then two occurred in 2000: one in New Haven, CT and the other just outside of New York City.

endeavor. The members of RID are predominately white, female, have attained various levels of academic status, and operate (generally) from the assumptions of the middle class.[9] Because RID has positioned itself, macrosocially, as "the only national, professional organization that represents the needs and concerns of interpreters,"[10] minority language speakers (in this instance, the Deaf) experience – and resist! – minimization of their views and opinions through both formal (collective) and informal (individual) means. Resistance is a cultural mode that the Deaf community has utilized for centuries; it has deep implications for the performance of identity. The limited success of formal, organized methods of collective resistance means that empowerment must continue to manifest on the individual, interpersonal, microsocial level.

If we agree that the discursive data shared above, of non-deaf interpreters and Deaf interlocutors, composes distinct discourses that embody and enact cultural differences, then we can also perceive the power relations between members of privileged and disadvantaged linguistic groups. The two (opposed?) ways of talking about the same thing (role performance) demonstrates a power-imbalance that pervades the interpreting process. The disparity is brought into view by the disagreement regarding what the interpreter ought and ought not to do – what our proper role is – in situations of relational ambiguity. This is the macrosocial-microsocial juncture: institutionalized, professional ambiguity about role is exacerbated in moments of interpersonal, intercultural distress.

Discussion

Rudvin argues that the conflation between opinions about the interpreter's role and ambiguities inherent in the concept of 'professionalism' influences understandings of role, codes of conduct, and interacting with interlocutors. The discourse analysis summarized here supports her argument. The difficulty RID has encountered in developing and providing guidelines for resolving the tension between the communicative and relational elements of the interpretation process contributes to, and may even instigate, certain forms of identity performances between Deaf interlocutors and interpreters at the interactional level.

RID's Code of Professional Conduct (adopted in 2005 to replace the previous Code of Ethics) was developed jointly with the National Association of the Deaf. It addresses this relational component with tenet 4.2: "Interpreters recognize the

---

9. The author is an example of this profile.

10. Online document, "About RID".

right of consumers to make informed decisions. Choices could include but are not limited to, selection of interpreter, seating arrangements, and interpreting dynamics."[11] As a remedy for audism, this locates resistance at the smallest scale possible, between the deaf individual and the interpreter, instead of focusing on the development and dissemination of bicultural communication norms. Such a code may exacerbate current tensions because it eliminates impartiality by insisting that interpreters deliberately and intentionally privilege Deaf interlocutors.

As a macrosocial structure, this professional code produces the conditions under which the evaluation of role based on interpreters' on-the-job performance becomes a microsocial *necessity*. The code establishes the interpreter's professional performance as a site for the exercise of Deaf individual and cultural agency. This is a mission beyond the task and purpose of most interpreted situations. On the surface, in terms of intention, such mechanisms are crucial as a check-and-balance of the power relation. However, in a subtle and undermining way, institutionalizing *this particular site* of power struggle may ironically serve to reinforce the status and identities of Deaf individuals as disadvantaged victims and interpreters as privileged rescuers who must work "on behalf" of deaf empowerment.

Conclusion

Professionalizing community interpreting requires an ideological framework that takes into account the representational desires and communicative goals of minority and non-dominant interlocutors while also enabling the interpreter to proactively engage with linguistic and cultural differences as these occur. The parameters of the professional role, the rights and responsibilities it embodies, must be ethically adaptable to the cultural and social identities of all participating interlocutors as well as responsive to institutional claims structuring each specific situation. In order for institutionalization's negative (oppressive) socialization effects to be minimized and its positive (empowering) aspects to be maximized, the power relations identified by Skutnabb-Kangas (2000) as the core issue in language policies must be addressed at the highest levels and earliest stages or, the evidence suggests, power struggles will pervade the interpreting process itself. This is a serious dilemma for which there are few precedents.

Issues concerning the practical management of communication are familiar to anyone involved with the field of community interpreting. This research attempts to identify the reasons why some instances of interpreter decision-making invite criticism and others do not. There is some evidence that it may not be *what*

---

11. Online document, "RID Code of Professional Conduct" (Adopted July 2005).

interpreters do, as much as *how* we do it. Both considerations point directly to role definition and performance, and these questions return us to the macrosocial structure provided by the institutionalizing process of professionalization. A comparison of discourse practices between practitioners and interlocutors highlights the interpreter's role as a site for the negotiation of power relations.

Professional community interpreting organizations must struggle through the thorny issues of impartiality and accountability, because the failure to do so pushes issues of power relations to the level of microsocial enactment. It is not surprising that the Deaf community continues to advocate, as individuals and through their national association, for more participation in the professionalization process. It could be taken as discouraging that after forty years and honorable efforts by many of the best and brightest practitioners, instructors, and users of sign language interpreting that the profession has yet to define the most desirable conditions for effective cross-language communication. However, this speaks more to the influence of gaps in planning and implementation than it does to ill intent. There has been progress, and this will continue. The legacy of the issue can, however, lead one to wonder whether anything can make a difference.

"Why bother?" asked one of the participants in this study. Indeed, with the potential for misunderstanding and hurt feelings, it would be prudent to hesitate before engaging such potential volatility. The alternative, however, is despair, apathy and repetition. It is always hard to enact change against precedent; however new attempts at professionalization can benefit from collective hindsight, just as internal change is sought within established organizations such as RID, as evidenced by the new and highly visible partnership with the NAD.

An intriguing approach to the definition of role has been proposed by both Rudvin (2004) and Elghezouani (this volume). They propose that the enactment of role should be governed by the ultimate goal of the communicative event. This strategy would (theoretically) eliminate the question of impartiality by transferring the interpreter's primary accountability from the interlocutors to the institutional context. There are, no doubt, risks associated with this strategy which will have to be anticipated, experienced, and addressed as they unpredictably emerge. Yet it does offer an alternative model for the interpreter's role that has the potential to avoid the insidious reinforcement of linguistic and cultural oppression still painfully rife within the field of sign language interpreting in the U.S.

References

Carbaugh, D. 1989. *Talking American: Cultural discourses on Donahue*. Norwood, NJ: Ablex Publishing Corporation.

Crawford, J. 2000. *At war with diversity: U.S. language policy in an age of anxiety*. Clevedon, Eng: Multilingual Matters.

Crawford, J. 2002. *Obituary: The Bilingual Education Act*. http://ourworld.compuserve.com/homepages/JWCRAWFORD/T7obit.htm Retrieved online 9 August 2004.

Elghezouani, A. 2007. "Professionalisation of interpreters: The case of mental health care" (In this volume).

Goffman, E. 1981. *Forms of talk*. Philadelphia: University of Pennsylvania Press.

Handsfield, L. J. 2002. "Teaching agency and double agents: Reconceptualizing linguistic genocide in education." *Harvard Educational Review* 72 (4): 542–561.

RID. – *About RID*. http://www.rid.org/about.html Retrieved online 29 August 2004.

RID Code of Professional Conduct (Adopted July 2005) http://www.rid.org/coe.html Retrieved online 18 September 2006.

Rudvin, M. 2004. "Professionalism" and contradictions in the interpreter's role. Paper presented at Critical Link IV, 20–23 May, Stockholm.

Roy, C. B. 2000. *Interpreting as a discourse process*. New York: Oxford University Press.

Santos, M. G. 2001. "At war with diversity: U.S. language policy in an age of anxiety." *Harvard Educational Review* 71 (3): 602–605.

Skutnabb-Kangas, T. 2000. *Linguistic genocide in education – or worldwide diversity and human rights?* Mahwah, NJ: Lawrence Erlbaum.

The interpreter as advocate

Malaysian court interpreting
as a case in point

Zubaidah Ibrahim

University of Malaya, Kuala Lumpur, Malaysia

The principle of impartiality is one of the foundations of interpreter ethics. To privilege or penalize either side in an exchange is commonly judged to be professional malpractice and, although this is recognized, in reality it is not an easy goal to achieve. This paper provides evidence that, in many Malaysian courts, the principle is regularly flouted by interpreters who are permitted to act as advocates. The study raises a question of professional ethics which deserves the careful thought of interpreters at international level. Is there a universal and internationally applicable set of ethical principles or are such principles variable across time and space and mediated by cultural relativity? And how should the profession respond to such a situation?

Introduction

The principle of impartiality is one of the foundations of interpreter ethics in the courtroom as well as in other settings. Privileging or penalising either side in an exchange is commonly judged to be professional malpractice. The ethical standards and responsibilities of the court interpreter include the requirement to "... remain impartial, and [...] confine himself or herself to the role of interpreting" (González et al. 1991:475) and to avoid undue contact with witnesses, attorneys, and defendants (Code of Professional Responsibility, Administrative Office of the United States courts in González et al. 1991:585).

Similarly, Colin and Morris (1999:148) advise interpreters to ensure that they do not appear to be prejudiced by "avoiding unnecessary discussion with counsel, parties, criminal defendants, witnesses or other interested parties inside or outside the courtroom in order to observe impartiality". The Australian Institute of Interpreters and Translators' (AUSIT) Code of Ethics is equally clear on the question of impartiality and neutrality, stating that "the court interpreter shall at all times be neutral and impartial and shall not allow his/her personal attitudes or opinions to impinge upon the performance of his/her duties" (Article 4).

This paper sets the issue of professional ethics in the context of the Malaysian justice system and, in particular, in the situation of the interpreter who is required to interpret for an unrepresented defendant and, as a result, may have his or her neutrality compromised by acting more as an advocate than an interpreter.

The discussion is the third in the series which highlights a number of salient findings (Ibrahim & Bell 2003; Ibrahim 2004) of a longitudinal study which started in 1997.[1] The study aims to gain an understanding of the nature of the court interpreting system in Malaysia: who the interpreters are, what their training and remuneration is, the extent to which the system is working efficiently and effectively, and, if there are deficiencies, what evidence can be obtained on which planning for the improvement of the provision can be based.

Methodology and data collection

The overall research is underpinned by both hard and soft data deriving from a multi-method approach, which incorporates both qualitative and quantitative techniques. The bulk of the soft data consists of 70 interviews conducted with senior members of the police, the Bar Council, court registrars, magistrates and judges, and interpreters. Twelve of these interviews were audio recorded and have been fully transcribed but the remainder are represented by informal notes taken by the interviewer at the time.

Additional data was obtained from informal observations of verbal and non-verbal exchanges between participants in the trial process. Since video and audio recording is not permitted in the Malaysian courtroom, these transcripts had to be made in real time by the researcher and, inevitably, lack the detail and reliability required for discourse analysis and an ethnographic study. However, their purpose was more to enhance understanding of the system and the perceptions of the role players in the system than to obtain hard data.

Quantitative data derives from the responses to two nationwide surveys: the first on the interpreters themselves in 1998 in which 471 out of 566 (82%) responded; the second in 2000 on the administrators and judges in which 152 court registrars, magistrates and sessions court judges out of 292 (52%) responded.

---

1.   The study began in 1997–1998 with funding from the University of Malaya, it was then continued as a PhD research, at the University of Malaya from 1999 to 2002.

Interpreters in the Malaysian court

In many parts of the world, for example Australia and the UK, interpreters work as individuals and on a part-time basis (Hale 2004; Chesters 2003). In the Malaysian system of justice, in contrast, interpreters are part of the civil service and are placed under the overall administration of the Public Service Department, recruited on a basis similar to any other civil servant, given a salary scheme appropriate to their level of qualification, and are generally expected to do much more than interpret (Ibrahim & Bell 2003).

Only when languages other than English and Malaysian languages (of Malay, Chinese and Indian speech communities) are involved, will freelance and outside parties (often embassy staff) be called upon to be a linguistic intermediary. However, even in these cases, the resident interpreter would still be there to assist in the trial in other areas which will be highlighted later in the paper.

As an officer of the court, the resident interpreter deals with all parties present in the court, civil and criminal i.e. the Bench, the prosecution, defence lawyers, the clerks, witnesses, defendants, litigants.

Although criminal and civil trials follow essentially the same general process, there are clear distinctions between them, as each has a set of procedures of its own and the interpreter has to be aware of these. For example, all criminal cases (except where juveniles or matters of national security are involved) and the majority of civil cases are held in open court (to which the public are admitted) and conducted mainly through the process of spoken debate and question-answer exchanges but, in civil cases, in addition to trials in open court, hearings are also held privately in chambers, and much greater emphasis is placed on written documents.

On the basis of my observations as a researcher, and of what my informants say about their practice, it can be suggested that interpreters are involved in three clear stages of communication with other involved individuals: pre-session (before the court is in session), in open court (during the hearing), and post-session (after the hearing).

Before the court is in session, the interpreter registers the cases reported for the day; ensures that all parties are ready to proceed with the trials, confirms the presence of the witnesses and defendants by communicating with defence lawyers and prosecutors and fixes the dates for mention. In addition, in civil cases, (s)he ensures that all relevant documents are ready for the court: Writ of Summons, Affidavit of Service, Memos of Appearance, Statement of Defence, Bundle of Documents – Agreed and Non-Agreed; and Notification of Trial.

During the trial, the interpreter communicates with prosecutors, defence counsels, witnesses, defendants, and the Bench. (S)he is expected to announce the case; establish the identity of the accused and witnesses; read the charge and ask for the plea; interpret; record exhibits; and assist in formulating a plea in mitigation.

After a trial is over, the interpreter deals with the staff of the court office, the police and the respondents. (S)he is expected to collect the notes and files to be handed over to the court's secretary to be typed, fill in the bail bonds, warrants of commitment if the accused is not able to pay the fine(s) imposed; and assist with the signing of bail bonds. In civil cases, (s)he often explains the judgement (the sum demanded by the plaintiff) and recommends taking legal advice, if the respondent disputes it.

The interpreter's responsibilities in any particular case are only considered ended when the hearing is over, notes of proceedings are typed and documented and the file is closed and sent to the Registry for safe keeping. (Ibrahim 2002; Ibrahim & Bell 2003: 216–217).

Interpreter as advocate

The issue of the interpreter acting as advocate arises from the frequency of hearings in which defendants are unrepresented.

While defendants in the sessions courts are invariably represented, the reverse is the case in the Magistrates' court.[2] Frequently, in addition to the normal feelings of nervousness and confusion, the unrepresented defendant faces the challenge of attempting to put his/her own case and cross-examine prosecution witnesses: the sophisticated and complex activities of the trained legal professional. It is in this situation that the interpreter is sometimes called upon to "help": not only to interpret, but to provide procedural advice to defendants, which merges into advocacy.

The advocacy role is not a recent development but one which can be traced back to colonial practice. It was well-established 20 years ago when it was documented in the first study of court interpreting in Malaysia (Teo 1984), a former court interpreter (now a Public Prosecutor) who gathered data for the study from interviews with judges, magistrates, assistant registrars, retired senior interpreters and serving interpreters in Kuala Lumpur and Johor Bahru. His findings confirm his own experience as an interpreter: that the Malaysian court interpreter is far

---

2. This was borne out during three weeks' observation of some 30 cases: 100% representation in the sessions court and only 8% in the magistrates'. Many unrepresented accused cannot afford to engage a lawyer but do not qualify for the Legal Aid available from the government or the Bar Council or are simply not aware or not informed of the provision.

more than an interpreter. (S)he is, among other things, a bilingual intermediary, clerk of the court, and advocate to unrepresented accused, receives little or no training and is not paid appropriately for the responsibilities (s)he carries.

There are many examples of interpreters regularly taking on an advocacy role. Three stand out as particularly significant:

- Coaching
- Directing
- Providing an "interpretation"

Coaching the unrepresented defendant

Interpreters regularly coach unrepresented defendants on the content and wording of questions, during cross-examinations and in responses to the counsel. When a magistrate allows a defendant to question a witness, (s)he often does not know what question to ask and how to word it appropriately and, therefore, is not in the position to take advantage of the opportunity. According to senior interpreters, the normal practice in cases in which the defendant is unrepresented is for the interpreter to assist the defendant in formulating the questions and responses in ways that are acceptable to the court. During cross-examination, for example, the interpreter normally rephrases what was said into the formulaic phraseology of the court: "I put it to you that ..." or "Is it not true that ....?"

This is precisely the kind of assistance recommended in an early report by the Law Society in the UK:

> [the clerk of the court] .... should regard himself as *being under a duty to help* by translating the statement into question form...This *departure from the ordinary rules of the adversary procedure* is especially *justified* when the defendant cannot grasp the difference between asking questions and making a statement. (Samuels 1971: 40. Emphasis added by the writer)

Several points stand out here: (1) the UK justices' clerk is *required* to perform this service; (2) and even though it puts him/her in the position of an advocate, this is justifiable when (3) the defendant is at a linguistic disadvantage.

However, whereas in the UK, the clerk of the court is legally qualified, in Malaysia the interpreter is not.[3] And yet (s)he is allowed to take the role of the clerk of the court. In the year 2000 I conducted an extensive interview with a retired senior Malaysian interpreter who said the following:

---

3. The entry qualification is school certificate (see Ibrahim & Bell 2003).

> There are times when the accused or defendants are not represented by lawyers. The tradition is the interpreter must assist the accused in asking questions of the witness in the form of cross-examination. He must help the accused because very often these illiterate (sic)[4] accused persons or defendants do not know how to cross-examine... (Ibrahim 2002).

The same interpreter, who is also involved in in-house training for the judicial department, gave the following account of one aspect of the job of an interpreter:

> As soon as the case is called, the accused will go into the box. The prosecuting officer will just handle the charge sheet. The interpreter must know what he should do. He takes the charge sheet, verifies the name of the accused with the charge sheet, he goes near the accused, confirm again are you so and so, residing in such and such a place. Is this your Identity Card, identity card number yes? Now you are charged in respect of a criminal case: this is the charge and now I'm going to read the charge. Then he reads the charge. After reading the charge, "Do you understand the charge? Yes, is there any problem in understanding me? Right, now what is your plea?" The accused blink, "What do you mean what is my plea," "It means, you have heard the charge, now do you admit that you committed that offence or you do not admit," "No, no, no, you see before I say that, I want to tell you what actually happened," "No, you cannot give any qualification, you either plead guilty or you don't plead guilty. I'm not forcing you to plead guilty and you don't have to" (Ibrahim 2002).

The above shows clearly that the Malaysian interpreter engages in advising the unrepresented accused. In this particular instance, i.e. asking for and recording a plea, it was found that interpreters, lawyers and judges consider the practice to be normal and justify it by analogy (made by another senior interpreter in the study) with the paramedic who, having observed a doctor carrying out a particular procedure, has acquired equal facility to that of the doctor.

Directing the witness/defendant/accused

This is advocacy which goes beyond merely suggesting appropriate words to a defendant, to proposing arguments and strategies. For example, when the unrepresented defendant is found guilty, the magistrate will ask, "Do you have anything to say?" The defendant usually does not know what to say and usually accepts the sentence. In most cases observed by the writer, the interpreter advises the ac-

---

4. It must be pointed out that the majority of those brought to the magistrate courts are usually uneducated and unfamiliar with courts procedures, hence the interpreter's use of the word "illiterate".

cused on how to present a plea in mitigation. The accused will be asked about his personal, financial or domestic circumstances: if he is a first time offender; if he is married with children; if he is supporting aged parents; if he is a student; if he is repentant and promises to turn over a new leaf. The interpreter will then suggest a form of mitigation and, on the basis of this, the Bench decides whether to be lenient or not. This is the normal practice, which the Bench not only accepts but expects. Interpreters tend to give the defendant a formula, which is used whatever the crime and this can lead to inappropriate wording such as (in a rape case observed by the researcher) "I promise to co-operate with the police and not to do it again". An extreme example of direction occurred in the same rape trial. The interpreter – without the knowledge of the Bench – persuaded the unrepresented accused to change his plea from not guilty to guilty, since the interpreter considered that, given the weight of evidence against the accused, he stood no chance of an acquittal. The advice was based on the fact that the victim (a teenage girl), who the defendant was accused of having raped, had given birth to a child and the forensic evidence (which the interpreter had seen) showed conclusively that the accused was the father.

Providing an "interpretation" rather than a "translation"

Typical examples of providing an interpretation are (a) when the interpreter came up with one word for the judge when the witness gave quite a lengthy response to a question, and (b) when the interpreter gave a different version such as "Was weapon A used in the fight?" instead of "Can you tell us which weapon was used in the fight; A or B?" (Teo 1984: 114).

Judges and lawyers often lament the fact that Malaysian interpreters "interpret" instead of "translate" what was stated by a witness. A senior High Court judge expresses his disapproval in the following:

> That's what they do which is wrong. They should not, I always tell them, you just interpret what they say, whether it's right or wrong, to the point or not to the point, that is not their [the interpreter's] problem (Ibrahim 2002).

The above however, seems to be in direct contradiction to the first two instances, i.e. the interpreter is given the mandate and in fact is expected to perform duties which put them in the position of advisor, however, in so far as being a linguistic intermediary is concerned, Malaysian judges are almost unanimous in their objection to interpreters giving other than literal interpretation.

Discussion and conclusion

The Bench is quite comfortable in accepting the practice that interpreters take on the role of clerk of the court and thus the advocacy role as referred to above. However, in the matter of interpreting, opinions are divided. While some junior magistrates, who depend on senior and knowledgeable interpreters, welcome the assistance of the interpreter in helping the court to be more efficient and to save time, the senior judges, see the use of discretion by the interpreter as an example of usurping the role of the judge and thus insist that the interpreter "translate" everything the witness says without adding, omitting, summarising, editing or changing anything. In the eyes of the Bench, "interpretation" is the prerogative of the Judiciary.

In other words, at one end of the scale the interpreter is an involved servant of the court assisting the Bench or even as a recognised and accepted surrogate for the advocate in the case of a defendant who is handling his or her own defence or mitigation. At the other end of the scale, (s)he is viewed solely as a non-participating, passive channel through which information is conveyed to the court.

One may well ask how is it that the Malaysian court interpreting system has ended up in this way? The findings suggest that the practice was started during the British colonial times, as a way to cope with the shortage of staff and to dispense trials in a competent manner. However, over the years, no real improvement was made to the system by the authorities. It therefore seems to be a fine example of an ad hoc measure being a permanent feature of the system.

In Malaysia at present, just as it was more than fifty years ago, apart from a short course instructing the interpreters on court procedures, there is no formal training and no special entry requirement except a school certificate and a credit pass in the language concerned. Interpreters' behaviour is dictated by their superiors, and the senior interpreters before them. If the existing set up is to be justified, there is an argument for the interpreters to be trained as paralegals as well, as otherwise they run the risk of intruding into a profession in which they are not qualified.

It may seem that what is being described in Malaysia is typical of the emerging stages of the profession of interpreter. In the absence of a definite set of guidelines, those acting as interpreters do what they think they should do as general helpers. However, the Malaysian case is exceptional in the sense that what may actually be considered advocacy is listed in their range of duties. In fact the range of duties expected of the resident interpreter is so wide that there is confusion among the interpreters as to what (s)he can and cannot, should, and should not, do. It is not uncommon that due to this, conflict arises between the Bench and the senior interpreter.

The term *court interpreter* in Malaysia is therefore a misnomer: as in every trial they must be there, not necessarily to interpret, but to assist in a trial. It is not surprising that there is a perpetual shortage of interpreters in Malaysian courts, as senior ones retire and new ones either resign after a short period or do not come forward at all. Although the issue of interpreter shortage is acknowledged to be a serious problem, it has yet to be recognised by the authorities that the reason for the difficulty in recruiting new interpreters and retaining existing ones is the confusion between what the interpreter and the clerk of the court does.

References

Chesters, R. 2003. "The Diploma in Public Service Interpreting". *The Critical Link* 1.1. 7

Colin, J. & Morris, R 1996. *Interpreters in the Legal Process*. Winchester: Waterside Press.

Criminal Procedure Code 1997. *(F.M.S. Cap 6) Laws of Malaysia as of January 1997* Kuala Lumpur: International Law Book Services.

González, R.D., Vásquez, V.F. and Mikkelson, H. 1991. *Fundamentals in Court Interpretation: Theory, Policy and Practice*. Durham, North Carolina: Carolina University Press.

Hale, S. 2004. *The Discourse of Court Interpreting: Discourse Practices of the Law, the Witness, and the Interpreter*, Philadelphia: John Benjamins.

Samuels, A. 1971. *The Unrepresented Defendant in Magistrates' Courts* London: Steven & Sons.

Teo Say Eng. 1984. "The role of interpreters in Malaysian courts". *Unpublished Research Paper*. Kuala Lumpur: Faculty of Law, University of Malaya.

Ibrahim, Z. 2002. *Court Interpreting in Malaysia in Relation to Language Planning and Policy*. Unpublished PhD Thesis. Kuala Lumpur: University of Malaya.

Ibrahim, Z. 2004. "Clash of Perceptions in the Malaysian Court". In *Language, Linguistics and the Real World: Language Practices in the Workplace*. In Ibrahim Z. et al. (eds). Kuala Lumpur: University of Malaya Press.

Ibrahim, Z. & Bell, R. T. 2003. "Court interpreting: Malaysian Perspectives". *The Critical Link* 3. 211–222. Amsterdam: John Benjamins.

Professionalisation of interpreters
The case of mental health care

Abdelhak Elghezouani
Appartenances, Lausanne, Switzerland

In this paper I suggest that the professionalisation of interpreters in mental health care must be linked to the specific functions they have in their role as mediators and consequently to the identities they assume in this context. The involvement of a linguistic intermediary, a third person, brings additional complexity and plurality of frames to a setting that ordinarily includes two persons. Professionalisation, to my mind, implies sorting out and determining more precisely which function (or functions) the interpreter can have and will have in this kind of setting. In other words, professionalisation will concern the real functions and the desired functions of the linguistic intermediary.

The paper distinguishes between four ways of viewing the role of interpreter, suggesting one of these – that of a culture and language broker more than that of a mere translator – to be developed for mental health care encounters specifically.

Introduction

Should the professionalisation of the community interpreters be justified only by the improvement of their formal status? Wouldn't it be more appropriate to conceive of professionalisation as emerging from and being based on the various definitions of the professional mandate? How then could we visualise this professionalisation in the context of mental health care? I believe that the professionalisation of the mental health interpreter is intricately linked to the functions and to the goals of therapeutic encounters, and the socio-verbal complexity of these communicative events.

It is for this reason that I believe that before asserting the professionalisation of the community interpreter, we should look at the range of settings where interpreters are employed and the multiple functions that interpreters may have in various situations. Consequently, professionalisation would have to be based on the real, as well as the desired functions of the interpreter within a given setting, taking into account the nature and purpose of the situation and the aims of the participants.

Some preliminary assumptions

I shall begin with some appreciations and several personal convictions, concerning the mental health care encounter as a specific case in point:

–   In intercultural situations, psychological assistance is limited by "blind spots" (Fr: *tâches aveugles*) (Sironi 2004: 3), which cause suffering; it may even be or become pathogenetic, harmful, and, in all cases, it can perpetuate a relationships of domination and alienation.
–   In institutional intercultural situations, the social relations are asymmetrical and always in favour of the representatives of the host society, or the institutional representative. Such an imbalance does not help the non-native client, for a real expression of his needs and may cause parasitic movements of *capture* (Eng: catching, draining) and *contre-capture* (de Jonckheere & Bercher 2003: 85).
–   There is an absolute need for interpreters in mental health care. However, the social conditions and lack of professional training for community interpreters means that they are not automatically assuming a well defined responsibility in the mental health care encounter.
–   I believe that the professionalisation of mental health interpreters should be based on their interactional and verbal functions as well as on their specific status and responsibility in mental health care encounters.

What does bilingual mental health care mean?

In the practice of trans-cultural, intercultural or bilingual psychotherapy, the translator is imposed upon by the situation. Sybille de Pury's, in her book *Traité du malentendu* ("Treated by misunderstandings") talks about the interpreter as a sort of partner, indicating that this situation allows the interpreter to assume a double role: that of translator and that of provider of cultural information. "Whereas the translator repeats, in this type of situation, the interpreter speaks [for himself][1]" (de Pury 1998: 24).

---

1.   Translated from French by the author.

How then can we account for and recognize this socio-verbal dynamic activity? It can be very genuine, very creative but it is also very atypical in relation to the theoretical, institutional, interactional and interpersonal framework where it takes place. To my knowledge, few efforts have been made to describe the practice of interpreters within the field of mental health care.[2]

The initial question has become: 'is culturally competent mental health care (moreover bilingual) really possible'? Answers to this query could follow two tracks: If it is possible, then why and how? If we take it for granted that mental health care *can* be carried out in bilingual encounters, then what is the role of the interpreter? As Bot and Wadensjö (2004) suggests in their article on interpreter-mediated treatment of traumatized asylum seekers: "It already happens, so it is worth exploring and explaining" (2004: 356).

Combining theoretical approaches

Discursive psychotherapy (the verbal cure) is based, *inter alia*, on verbal interactions in which knowledge is exposed, questioned and deconstructed, where problems are identified and ways of resolving them co-created, proposed and/or applied (Grossen 1992). All protagonists are starting from their own positions, have each their own knowledge and interests and are working towards the co-construction of a new interpersonal and social reality.

In addition, the product of a linguistic mediation is never the same as the result of a direct experience put into words, in which productions are reactions to former productions. It would be naive to believe that the participants of a conversation mediated by an interpreter are not conscious of the fact that they are committed to a specific and unique form of communication. If this awareness is not compensated or balanced by another force, this might lead to a form of alienation and inadequacy among the participants.

A descriptive and operational model should then be able to represent and analyse the triangular exchanges including the interpreter, the professional and the client. Moreover, such an analysis should make it possible to highlight the capacity of the interpreter to influence and to be influenced by the verbal and the non-verbal productions and interactions. Such a model can in no way satisfy itself with the "conduit metaphor" (Roy 1989: 102) considering the interpreters as passive and as mere extensions of those whose speech they translate.

---

2. A recent exception is however Hanneke Bot's Ph.D. dissertation "Dialogue Interpreting in Mental Health" from 2005.

From a sociological and an interactional perspective, the triad created by the patient, the professional and the interpreter appears as a social encounter and a social communicative event where individuals are enacting certain social roles by semantico-pragmatic productions. On the one hand, the study of these dynamics can be undertaken neither without theoretical concepts relating to the triad as a social system, nor without theoretical tools allowing for the study of interpreting in mental health care. On the other hand, it has to take into consideration the very specific nature of the bilingual mental health care encounter, to regard these types of settings as an empirical field in its own right.

The interpreter as a partner

Following these statements drawn from various fields, I believe that the social, the interactional and the interpersonal functions of the interpreters on the one hand, and their verbal, linguistic and cultural functions on the other hand, should be combined in order to provide an original and creative basis to the status of the interpreter as a partner in the bilingual mental health care encounter; a partner assuming an authentically active and creative role in the zone of contact, in the zones of friction and at the time of the *capture* and *contre capture* (de Jonckheere & Bercher 2003: 85). It is for this reason that we can assume that the functions of the interpreter are closely linked to the intentions of the setting generally, as well as to the intentions of each principal protagonist. The function brings to mind Katan's (1999) cultural mediator (in contrast to a traditional translator). Seen as a cultural mediator following Katan, the interpreter would be expected to "understand and create frames" (1999: 125).

Following this, I find it useful to analyse and model the role and the socio-verbal behaviours of the interpreter applying a more interactive and a more goal-oriented approach. In doing so, I can rely upon investigations showing how the participation framework (Goffman 1981, quoted in Wadensjö 1998: 86) allows several status of participation and flexibility and diversity, according for example to whether the interpreter is involved in one form of interaction or another and will assume/will be attributed, with one communication role or another. Such a frame of analysis is appealing because it draws on a structural level and introduces a sociolinguistic point of view.

One can use anthropological and sociological theories to discuss the various functions of the intermediary, making a distinction, for example between the simple messenger and the intermediate carrying a larger mandate. One can also distinguish between the middleman and the mediator whose function is to contribute to the resolution of the conflict whereas the function of the first is to facilitate the communication between the parties. Applying the perspective of medical anthropology, Kaufert and Koolage (1984: 125–126), assumed that the interpreter played a central social role between the indigenous patient and the doctor in a Canadian context. In addition, one can easily consider as significant that in a relationship where there is a great social and cultural difference, in addition to the linguistic barrier, the work of interpreter will act out on different levels: the global situation, the conversational framework and the purpose of the encounter. Hence, the interpreter in a mental health care encounter cannot be limited to the role of speaker without his own words. They must invest and be invested in the role of a highly involved interlocutor as this type of situation, the triadic socio-verbal interaction, can vary according to rules of a triad subjected to movements, explicit or implicit, conscious or unconscious, which involve varied configurations, coalitions, etc. (Putsch 1985: 3346).

Towards a new paradigm (some empirical and theoretical foundations)

Personal experiences from the field

As a psychologist and as an interpreter I have experience of working in an outpatient psychiatric consultation centre for immigrants. My field of work and of study is thus mental health care for refugees and asylum seekers. These people come from various areas of conflict and the studies concerning their mental health coincide on three essential points:

– a great number of refugees suffer from the consequence of trauma which occurred in their country of origin,
– their escape was in itself traumatic,
– their problems are by far not over when they reach their destination.

A holistic, non-medical approach (social needs and social resources)

For all these reasons, one has to take a holistic view on how this kind of psychosocial need and distress is responded to. An initial factor relates to the psychological distress of members of the communities of refugees, which is worsened by the fact that many of them "feel reluctant to use services of assistance based and designed formally on psychology, psychiatry, psychopathology and psychotherapy, in other words, any approach known as clinical" (Watters 2003: 3). This means that this kind of assistance, based on the classic clinical approach – which defines their suffering and normal reactions to intense stress as so-called mental health disorders – cannot be anything but based on a pseudo adequacy. A second factor is that these psychiatric definitions of their problems and the care provided to them does not fit their expectations, rather it stigmatises them. A third factor is that their unsatisfied social needs have direct implications on their well being.

The field of psychosocial interventions in complex mental health situations is still characterised by a lack of consensus, or at times, by an eclecticism of conceptualisations of goals, strategies and practices. However, I consider it important to take an integrative and socio-centred approach, implying a specific position of interpreters in bilingual mental health care.

Four models of the interpreter's function

In order to schematise and to illustrate the topic, I have defined four possible positions of an interpreter appointed to assist in mental health care between immigrants and therapists.

The first of these positions seems to be the most traditional, the one in which the interpreter is seen as "a linguistic conduit" (Roy 1989:102), a non-person whose social role, communication contract and linguistic or verbal contract are limited to the translation of the received or heard statements of the two principal protagonists. The status of a non-person given to the interpreter in this kind of setting involves a relatively 'direct' relationship between the patient and the therapist, reducing accordingly the transitional area of negotiation and increasing the zones of friction.

The second position of the interpreter includes all the elements of the first category plus, a new function for the interpreter, namely a role of a cultural information provider.

The third position takes place in a design of psychotherapeutic encounter that could be called a bi-centred bilingual psychotherapy; i.e. a psychotherapy with two psychotherapists, one of them sharing the same mother tongue as the client and playing alternatively the role of interpreter as described by Piret (1991).

The fourth position is the one I want to promote because it appears to be the only one allowing the avoidance of asymmetry, of too much focusing on psychiatric categories and concepts, and of sanctioning only "literal" interpreting of client and therapist discourse. Moreover, this fourth position presupposes a bilingual mental health encounter that is close to a social work setting. It leaves room for the interpreters' interactional, cultural and verbal expertise, making it possible for them to become a real "bridge" (Fr: *pont*) (Métraux & Alvir 1995:22) as they can fully play their role of explainer, clarifier and go-between during negotiations.

Conceptions of the therapeutic setting

In my view, the real and essential needs of traumatised refugees challenge both the attitudes and the accepted manner of working in the provision of mental health care to these specific clients. Their need for recognition as victims and as requiring 'repair' is at the forefront of the scene. Unfortunately, the existing models of professional intervention in mental health care were not designed for these specific needs.

In my experience, many refugees do not at once conceive of their problems and suffering in terms of mental health, even if they may do so later. Moreover, they are encountering pressing practical difficulties that also may have significant effect on their mental health. Weine (2001) suggests tackling this situation with a "new ethnology". He writes: "Paradigms of cultural competence only based on the recognition of the cultural difference are not sufficient to take into account subtleties and the importance of the intercultural interactions between refugees and mental health services. On the contrary, the paradigms inspired by what could be considered as a new ethnology which highlight the fact to which great extent cultures act upon and influence one another should contribute to the conception and the design of mental health services" (Weine 2001: 1214).

Knowledge about community interpreting in the field of mental health remains meagre until now. Research based on socio-linguistics, however, contributes to modify the framework of observations, of descriptions as well as the theoretical models devoted to the study of the contents and the interactions found in the communicative events mediated by interpreters in mental health encounters. It appears that the significant processes in these situations, and in particular, the role and the actions of the interpreter, should be understood as social and interpersonal actions, having a therapeutic and healing function. Finally, it should not be neglected that interpreting is a human activity, implying an interpersonal involvement from which novel, mutual, social and mental constructions may arise.

A new communication contract

Roy describes the mental health interpreter in the following way: "The community interpreter is not only qualified in relation to the two languages used during the intercultural mental health encounter, but also by his/her knowledge of the social condition, manners of speaking, and of communication management strategies" (Roy 1999: 265).

This general description, largely based on conversation studies, suggests a new conception of the role and action of the interpreter in mental health care. This would involve a new communication contract between the client and the professional. The zone of interaction between the protagonists could be conceived as a "contact zone" rather than a "war zone" (Weine 2001:1214), with all protagonists acting at the same hierarchical level, having their own conceptions, their own experiences and their own expertise. This does not imply denying the specialisation, the particularity of their respective roles or functions. Rather, as the healing and the helping intention is commonly shared, there would be a functional working division, and maybe even disagreements among the protagonists acting together in the "contact zone" as a "place of exchange, interweaving and negotiating between two or more worlds" (Weine 2001:1216).

The creation of a new mental health care setting

Gilliard and Hauswirth argue that "a health problem should not only be determined by the presence of a threat for survival and/or by the presence of a symptom, but also by the inhibition of the creative potentialities of the individual and the community, the impossibility of giving meaning to the lived experiences, and the paralysis of the capacity to conceive projects"[3] (Gilliard & Hauswirth 1996:15). In considering the health problems of the immigrant, we also must keep in mind that he/she is not an isolated entity, but often belongs to a Diaspora within the hosting society. Moreover health is not only individual, it is also a community matter and health "is built by keeping the values of the community of origin and by integrating to them new values of the hosting society and, last but not the least, by building new projects"[4] (Gilliard & Hauswirth 1996:16).

To my mind, one can assume that the interpreter will represent the *worlds* and the *beings* or the *creatures* that are brought into play on the psychodramatic stage of the therapeutic session; stand for those located outside or inside the patient, making these figures present through the character of the interpreter.

These ideas of the role and the functions of the interpreters-mediators, on their contribution in the ritual, the dramatic setting and design, obviously refer to an ethno-psychiatry inspired mental health care encounter. An ethno-psychiatric approach to mental health care implies focusing on cultural and verbal elements (active objects), on community, collective, trans-generational elements (alliances, filiations and memberships), on anthropological subjects (theories of misfortune, order and disorder, active principles, etc.), and on interactional activities (reduction of asymmetry, clarification and interpretation of the rough facts, clarification

---

3. Translated from French by the author.

4. Translated from French by the author.

of contrasts). In such a design and such a device, the professionals (the therapist and the interpreter) and the client stage and act out (reflexive dimension) in a dramaturgy and a scenography (dynamic dimension) which evokes, calls upon and gives space for expression to all the figures and the objects taking part in the drama (structural dimension) affecting the patient. This design would enable the establishment of new bridges between the patient's past, present and future time and between past, present and future others (redistributive and transformative dimensions).

The text of the drama, which expresses itself by the symptoms and the misfortune, under the principle of fate and repetition, is threaded in the new context of the therapeutic *scene* and its actors; a scene nourished by original memberships and belongings of the patient formed by the figures, the words and the objects brought together and animated by each protagonist, including the patient, in an active and deliberate scenography and a staging, sufficiently solemn, intimate and authentic to guarantee its function of *passage* and metamorphosis.

In what I here refer to as the fourth position, the interpreter would play a role of mediator and actor, represent the original group and the original world of the patient. The therapist would be the principal interlocutor as he/she brings and guarantees the active and creative dialogue between the patient and the various figures implied in his/her drama and his/her cure.

All protagonists are then playing a scenario following a therapeutic stage design, a storyboard and a script where roles and functions, characters, objects and words are those chosen for their active past, present and future influence.

Conclusion

In my opinion, the professionalisation of the interpreter performing in mental health encounters should be based on the institutionally defined intentions and goals of the mental health care encounter, and on the needs of the non-native patients. Such a definition is far from readily made, and (still) has to be designed in the coming years. This definition will give place to a necessary multiplicity and diversity of conceptions and solutions. My intention is to conduct further studies on this issue.

In this paper, I have followed several lines of thought while attempting to define a general model:

–   models of mental health care with refugees and asylum seekers, must imply a
    definition of the status of the interpreters, related to their functions and role

in the various settings designed for the purpose of bilingual mental health care;

- over all, I assume that the sharing by the professionals of a common and unique working conception in this type of social, communicative, and mental health care event is the only ethical and technical framework possible ensuring an original and efficient bilingual mental health care encounter;

- I have tried to go beyond and to illustrate the "pas de trois" (Wadensjö 1998) model by claiming that the mental health care encounter should be a real dramaturgic play where verbal, social and therapeutic roles are equally distributed between the therapist, the patient and the interpreter for the purpose of healing;

- I am convinced that it would be very helpful for further studies of interpreter-mediated mental health care to draw on sociolinguistics, and all close domains, and also on ethno-psychiatry and all culturally informed approaches;

- I also believe that the role of interpreter in mental health care extends far beyond bridging a linguistic gap, in that interpreting is instrumental in enabling patients to bridge the past with the present and with a realistic future; bridging the text of their problems with the past context of the roots of this problem and with a new healing context; bridging the gap between here and there, between themselves and past, present and future significant others.

References

Bot, H. & Wadensjö, C. 2004 "The Presence of a Third Party: A Dialogical View on Interpreter-Assisted Treatment", in J.P. Wilson & Boris Drozdek (eds.) *Broken Spirits: The treatment of asylum seekers and refugees with PTSD*, 355–378. Brunner Routledge Press: New York.

Gilliard, D. & Hauswirth, M. 1996. *Appartenances. Projet pour un centre de consultations*. Lausanne: Unpublished manuscript.

Grossen, M. 1992. Intersubjectivité et négociation de la demande lors d'un entretien thérapeutique. In M. Grossen et A.-N. Perret-Clermont (eds.). *La construction de l'espace thérapeutique*, 165–192. Paris et Neuchâtel : Delachaux et Niestlé.

de Jonckheere, C. & Bercher, D. 2003. *La question de l'altérité dans l'accueil psychosocial des migrants*. Geneva : IES Editions.

Katan, D. 1999. *Translating cultures. An introduction for translators, Interpreters and mediators*. Manchester: St Jerome Publishing.

Kaufert, J. M. & Koolage, W. W. 1984. "Role conflict among culture brokers": The experience of native Canadian medical interpreters. *Social Science Medecine*, Vol. 18, No 3, 283–286.

Métraux, J. C. & Alvir, S. 1995. "L'interprète: traducteur, médiateur culturel ou co-thérapeute?". In *Interdialogos* (Neuchâtel) 1995, No 2, 22–26.

Piret, B. 1991. *Paroles sans frontières. La psychothérapie avec interprète est-elle possible?*, available at http://www.psy-desir.com

de Pury, S. 1998: *Traité du malentendu*. Théorie et pratique de la méditation interculturelle en situation clinique. Préface de Tobie Nathan. Collection 'Les empêcheurs de tourner en rond'. Paris : Synthélabo.

Putsch R. W. 1985. "Cross-cultural communication". *Journal of the American medical Association*, Dec 20, Vol. 254, No 23, 3344–3348.

Roy, C. 1989. *A sociolinguistic analysis of the interpreter's role in the turn exchange of an interpreted event*. Unpublished PhD dissertation. Georgetown University. Washington D.C.

Roy, C. 1993. "A sociolinguistic analysis of the interpreter's role in simultaneous talk in interpreted interaction". *Multilingua*, 12(4), 341–363.

Sironi, F. 2003. "Maltraitance théorique et enjeux contemporains de la psychologie clinique". *Pratiques psychologiques*, No 4, 3–13.

Wadensjö, C. 1998. *Interpreting as interaction*. London and New York: Addison Wesley Longman.

Watters, C. 2003. "The need for understanding", in *Health Matters*, issue 39, winter 99/00.www.healthmatters.or.uk

Weine, S. 2001. "From war zone to contact zone: Culture and Refugees Mental Health Services". *MsJAMA-Essay* , Vol. 285, March 7, 2001, 1214.

Professional stocks of interactional knowledge in the interpreter's profession

Satu Leinonen
University of Tampere, Finland

In this article I will present the concept of stocks of interactional knowledge (SIKs) developed by Peräkylä and Vehviläinen (2003) and discuss the respective knowledge about interaction in the interpreter's profession. I will then look at the role ideology that can be derived from a code of professional ethics for court interpreters. In conclusion I will make some suggestions considering the SIKs and the ethical rules as a conceptualising tool for the professionalisation of interpreting in the community.

Introduction: Role ideology in the profession of interpreters

In many professions there are professional ethics to be adhered to. On the Internet one can easily find codes for journalists, doctors, lawyers, social workers, psychologists, teachers, researchers and clergymen, to name but a few. What is common for these professions is that the actual work is conducted by means of language; it is the tool in these professions. The ethical rules can be seen as specifications to the general ethics in professional activities; they define the ethics of professional performance. Behind the rules and codes lies a particular understanding of communication models, language usage and interaction. The rules and codes are normative and prescriptive, and they build an ideal image of the profession. The ethical rules and codes of conduct for the practitioners in part construct the professional role of an interpreter, too. In recent years the role ideology of (community) interpreters has been the subject of redefinition, since the growing body of research results (e.g. Wadensjö 1998, Krouglov 1999, Inghilleri 2003, Apfelbaum 2004, Hale 2004) indicates clearly that the norms applied so far cannot necessarily be achieved or adhered to in practice.

In this article I will first present the concept of professional stocks of interactional knowledge (SIKs) and secondly sketch the possible SIKs of a (court) interpreter by deconstructing the codes of professional ethics for court interpreters laid down by the Finnish Association of Translators and Interpreters (SKTL). However, I will concentrate only on sequences of the Code that comment on (interactional) issues relevant for the SIKs.

Professional stocks of interactional knowledge

In what follows I will shortly summarize the main ideas of professional stocks of interactional knowledge. The Finnish conversation analysts Peräkylä and Vehviläinen write about the new, articulated awareness of questions pertaining to social interaction in many professions with normative models and theories or quasi-theories about interaction that are part of the knowledge base of the profession. These models can be found in professional texts, in training manuals and in written and spoken instructions delivered in the context of professional training or supervision. The authors call these models and theories "stocks of interactional knowledge" (SIKs) (Peräkylä & Vehviläinen 2003: 729–730).

By SIKs, the authors (ibid.: 730) mean organized knowledge (theories or conceptual models) concerning interaction that is shared by particular professions or practitioners. SIKs contain normative and descriptive elements, and they vary in conceptual clarity and sophistication. Some SIKs involve full-blown theories, whereas others involve models or concepts of a less comprehensive type. SIKs can be classified along the following two dimensions:

Degree of detail in terms of interaction

There are detailed SIKs, which offer detailed and extensive descriptions and prescriptions concerning the interaction between professionals and clients. The descriptions and prescriptions concern such things as the ways in which the professionals ask questions and deliver other interventions to the clients, as in Family Systems Therapy, for example. There are also less detailed SIKs, which offer only patchy descriptions and prescriptions; this type of an SIK does not involve detailed descriptions concerning the ways in which certain concepts or ideals can be realized in actual interaction (Peräkylä & Vehviläinen 2003: 730–731).

Degree of penetration into practice

Some SIKs are constitutive to particular professional practices; the professional practice in question is dependent on the SIK and would not exist without it. For example, psychoanalytical practice is thoroughly structured with reference to the theoretical ideas of the respective SIKs – ideas such as '"free association" and "interpretation". But there are also contingent SIKs, that involve maxims and ideals relevant and consequential only occasionally in actual interaction. An example can be provided with the idea of patient-centredness; the professional practices of medicine are not fully dependent of this idea, for a medical consultation can be accomplished without any reference to the idea of patient-centredness (Peräkylä & Vehviläinen 2003:731).

The code of ethical rules for court interpreters in Finland

SIKs can thus be found in professional texts and in written and spoken instructions for the profession in question. When it comes to interpreters and translators, in addition to research reports there are handbooks and course books on interpreting in various settings, many of them focusing on the field of court interpreting (González et al. 1991; Edwards 1995; Colin & Morris 1996; Mikkelson 2000; Hale 2004). The ethical rules and Codes of Conduct are laid down by the professional organizations of translators and interpreters for their practicing members. There are cultural differences and different emphases in them, and they vary in length, scope and depth, as can be seen in a selection of the Codes in Phelan (2001:39–58). Most of the Codes consist of two sections: a set of best practices and a set of professional ethics. The professional standards are laid down in the first part, and in the second part these standards are explicated for practice. The rules and codes are written for the professionals themselves to be understood as advice or tips to follow. They also function as information about the interpreter's profession for those outside the profession, such as the parties involved in a court case.

The Finnish Association of Translators and Interpreters (SKTL) was founded in 1955 and has from the start as one of its objectives to promote compliance with international recommendations concerning different fields in interpreting. In 1994, the organisation published a Code for Interpreters (The Finnish Association of Translators and Interpreters 1994), which includes guidelines that can be applied to many different fields in interpreting. With the steady increase of immigrants and refugees in Finland and the growing need for qualified community and court interpreters, the organisation saw the need for guidelines specifically addressing these kinds of interpreters. Hence, in 2001, SKTL, in cooperation with other institutions in the field (such as the Association of Sign Language Interpreters, interpreter services, etc.) laid down the Code of professional ethics for Court Interpreters (The Finnish Association of Translators and Interpreters 2001a). In 2002, SKTL published a Code of ethics for community interpreters (The Finnish Association of Translators and Interpreters 2002). The fundamental guidelines are the same in both Codes: the requirements of neutrality and impartiality in the daily practice are the smallest common denominator. The rules obviously do not have a legal status. Breaking the code does not lead to legal sanctions. But in the event of this happening, the professional organisation can take measures, such as dismissing a member. It is worth noting here that this would not prevent the dismissed member from practising the interpreter's profession in Finland, because the title "interpreter" is not legally protected or subject to a licence.

The Finnish *Code of professional ethics for court interpreters* (The Finnish Association of Translators and Interpreters 2001a) consists of a set of eight actual rules, and of a section that sets out recommendations for the interpreting assignment as a whole (The Finnish Association of Translators and Interpreters 2001b). (These texts in English also exist in an official Finnish version).

The Finnish guidelines are more or less identical with the rules laid down and adopted by the Committee for Legal Translators and Court Interpreters of the International Federation of Translators (FIT) (in, e.g., Mikkelson 2000:96–99). Due to the limited space I will discuss the rules and recommendations in detail only where relevant for the SIKs.

In the following, excerpts are drawn from two of SKTL's documents (The Finnish Association of Translators and Interpreters 2001a and 2001b) here referred to as "2001a" (the code) and "2001b" (the recommendations).

The introduction to the rules is an attempt to define the function of an interpreter in the court.

> *The term court interpreter in this code of ethics refers to professional interpreters working in courts of law, including sign language interpreters. The function of the court interpreter in the court session is to render the proceedings accurately and reliably. The court interpreter has a crucial role in ensuring a fair trial. Through the practice of his/her profession, he/she contributes to the upholding of basic rights and in particular to the principle of equal treatment in front of law. His/her work may affect the lives and rights of others. Therefore he/she shall adhere to this code of ethics in his/her work (2001a).*

The requirement of accurate and reliable interpretation is understandably one of the leading ideals in the interpreter's profession; one could hardly be pleading for the opposite. But what exactly can be called accurate and reliable? If an interpreter succeeds in rendering the substantive content of a proceeding, but omits all tiny characteristics of talk like hesitations, tacklings, re-starts etc., the function of which is to create a particular tone for the turn of talk, can the interpretation then be called accurate and reliable? Hale (2004:243) ends up defining accuracy as comprising faithfulness of content and manner of speech. One way of reading this definition is to see the connection between the form and the function of speaking. Now, bearing in mind how complex the structure of talk is, one can ask whether it would be at all possible for the interpreter to render all the tokens that make up the manner of the speech: if the interpreter tried to imitate the hesitation markers or re-starts as produced in the original, would there be a risk that these phenomena in the interpreter's turn would be seen as stemming from the interpreter and not as a faithful imitation of the original manner of the speech? Of course, an interpreter has the possibility to mark uncertainty, for example, through lexical choices, but we may ask whether the result could still be called faithful or neutral.

The role of the interpreter is further described as being crucial in ensuring a fair trial, and in contributing to the upholding of basic rights, as is also pointed out by Mikkelson (2000: 48). Hale puts it clearly: "Such a task is extremely difficult, if not impossible" (Hale 2004: 8). As if these requirements were not enough, the next sentence states that the work of an interpreter may affect the lives and rights of others. To my mind this is quite a serious requirement for a profession – all the more so as it is not defined more closely here. In her conclusions Hale (2004: 243) finds it feasible to assume that the work of an interpreter may also influence or alter the outcome of the court case. What about the basic rights then? Or the fair trial? Or neutrality and impartiality?

> *Article 2 Disqualification*
> *The court interpreter shall be deemed disqualified and shall not accept an assignment if performance of it were to place him/her in a conflict of interest that might endanger the objectivity of the interpretation* (2001a).

Again the objectivity of the interpretation is raised to a central position in constructing the role of the interpreter in these ethical rules. It is important to ensure objectivity in advance, and sometimes it is undoubtedly possible. An interpreting assignment, however, is a phenomenon that is talked into being, and objectivity can very well be endangered even during interpreting. Since interaction is "born" on a turn-by-turn basis, one can never know in advance what is really going happen next. Objectivity can be endangered simply by the interpreter choosing a verb, a noun or an adjective that functions in a different way than the lexical choices in the original and leads interaction in a different direction than would have been the case if the primary interlocutors had shared a language of communication.

> *Article 5 Impartiality and neutrality*
> *The court interpreter shall at all times be impartial and neutral. He/she shall not allow his/her personal attitudes or opinions to influence the performance of his/her assignment* (2001a).

Neutrality and impartiality are the ideological home ground upon which the professions of interpreters and translator have been building for ages. According to this article, there seems to be an understanding that only clearly expressed personal attitudes or opinions can endanger impartiality and neutrality. Neutrality is always neutrality in reference to something and therefore a relative concept. In the interpreter's and translator's profession, the requirement is understandable in terms of their position as a man or a woman in the middle. One could hardly allow them to be partial and not neutral. This leads us to the underlying model of communication: that it is possible for communication to be neutral and impartial, which again reveals the corresponding role model for the interpreter: that of a translating machine or a black box between the primary interlocutors. But where exactly do we find these concepts in the actual practice of interpreted interaction? When could an interpreter's performance be classified as neutral and impartial? Even though these norms can be justified by seemingly incontestable (theoretical) grounds, the professional codes contain no indication of how they could be achieved in a real-life situation. I would like to suggest that the notions of neutrality and impartiality can be described twofold: the macro dimension consisting of such things as behaving and dressing appropriately, not making faces, treating all parties concerned equally and respectfully, or the like, and the micro dimension consisting of actual use of language at the lexical, sentential and pragmatic levels (Hale 2004: 8, 12, 238). The micro level is, then, the more important one because it is exactly here that the requirements of impartiality and neutrality should, by necessity, come into being (Wadensjö 1998: 283–284).

> *Article 6 Professional skill*
> *The court interpreter shall only accept assignments for which he/she possesses the requisite knowledge and skill. The court interpreter shall be responsible for the correctness of his/her interpretation and shall correct any mistakes that he/she makes (2001a).*

Here the interpreter is declared responsible for the correctness of his/her work, but correctness is not defined. Is a correct interpretation identical with the above-mentioned concepts of accuracy and reliability? Is the interpreter or his/her clients always able to notice the interpreter's mistakes? I would again like to suggest that there are two dimensions here: the obvious, manifest mistakes at the lexical and substantive level, and the more interesting level of minute mistakes at the pragmatic level. What exactly can be called a mistake in interpreter's performance? What about mistakes made by the primary participants? In conversation analytical terms the repair organisation is one of the basic organisatory types in face-to-face interaction and of importance in constructing the shared understanding. (Schegloff, Jefferson & Sacks 1977). Here a mistake can be something said by mistake or said incorrectly that must be repaired for the sake of faithfulness, but the actual point is: to what extent does the repairing action have an effect on the unfolding interaction? However, if an interpreter is not aware of the possible effect of repairing but thinks that all self-repairs of, say, the witness, can be omitted in the interpretation because irrelevant or redundant *for the interpreter,* can the interpreter's performance still be seen as accurate and reliable? Or the other way around, what about the interpreter constantly repairing him/herself because of poor concentration or insufficient language skills; would this not hamper the understanding of the manner of the primary participant's speech?

> *Article 7 Professional development*
> *The court interpreter shall interact with his/her colleagues, develop his/her professional skills and act in a way that stands the profession in good stead* (2001a).

> *Article 8 Breach of the code of ethics*
> *This code of ethics has been drawn up by the Finnish Association of Translators and Interpreters, the Finnish Union of Translators, the Finnish Association of the Deaf and the Association of Finnish Sign Language Interpreters. Should there be reasonable grounds to suspect that the court interpreter has intentionally breached this code of ethics, he/she shall be granted the opportunity to be heard by the association or professional organisation to which he/she belongs with a view to establishing the possible reasons. Should the court interpreter be found to have acted in contravention of this code of professional ethics, each organisation shall take measures in accordance with the rules applying to its members* (2001a).

The first of these two articles holds the notion of a professional whose skills are never perfected but who needs continuous further education and training. The obligation of professionality is revealed in the last sentence – could it be understood to say that acting against or not in line with the ethical rules would not be of advantage to the profession? Another question is, however, whether the ethical rules on the whole can be adhered to in the actual practice within the structural possibilities of conversation.

The latter article states that if someone has *intentionally* breached the code of ethics, certain measures may be taken. But what about unintended breaches or "hidden" ones; are they somehow more legitimate or not so serious? When considering the complexity of the understanding process in interpreter-mediated encounters, one also has to remember the transient character of talk. If an interpreted encounter is not recorded, there exists no reliable evidence for tracing suspected mistakes by any of the interactants.

Recommendations for court interpreting

The Finnish Association of Translators and Interpreters has published a number of recommendations meant to explain the above set of rules. The recommendations (here referred to as "2001b") have the following introduction:

> The role of the interpreter in the court is strictly that of communicator. The purpose of these recommendations is to guarantee the most favourable conditions for communication and ensure that the co-operation between the interpreter and the other parties functions as smoothly as possible (2001b).

The role of the interpreter is thus defined as a communicator with a huge burden of responsibility, as stated in the Code (see p. 4), but no further definition is given. The further articles concern the acceptance of and preparing for the assignment. The section on performing an assignment contains advice on agreeing the interpreting mode to be used, on a suitable seating position for the interpreter, on proper conduct towards all parties, etc. But then it gets interesting:

> 3.3 The interpreter is an impartial participant in the court session whose function is to render the proceedings accurately and reliably. The interpreter shall refrain from taking sides with the matters being dealt with by the court (2001b).

Again the requirement of impartiality seems to be fulfilled through accuracy, reliability and refraining from taking sides regarding the issue. This is understandable – but the same question can be repeated here: how is this done? Is an interpreter not taking sides with every utterance he/she delivers through the very choice of certain verbs, nouns, question forms, intonation, and so on? Gile (1995: 29) speaks about rotating side-taking because the interpreter's loyalty shifts from one to the other, according to the turns taken by the primary participants.

> 3.4 The interpreter shall speak in the first person (e.g. not "He said that he left the shop", but "I left the shop") (2001b).

Whom does this recommendation serve, when no grounds are given for either form of speaking? Is the first person the best choice on every occasion? Bearing the interpreter's role ideology in mind, perhaps by recommending that the interpreter speak in the first person, he/she is given the obligation to act as the voice of others, and the illusion will be created that the interpreter is an invisible, impartial and neutral mediator between the primary participants who could then, in a way, be speaking directly with each other. This is what Gile (1995: 29) means by the sender-loyalty principle: as long as the interpreter speaks in the first person, he or she is obliged to adopt the sender-loyalty principle. Nevertheless, this illusion cannot hide the fact that even if mediating someone's thoughts and messages the interpreter, by necessity, has to do it with his/her own words. The decision to choose a certain utterance rests with the interpreter alone. Speaking in the third person could perhaps be understood as speaking *on behalf* of the others, making the presence and influence of the third person, the interpreter, clear and visible. The use of the third person could perhaps challenge the notions of impartiality and neutrality – and therefore also the accuracy and reliability of the interpretation. As Gile (ibid.) continues, interpreting in third person relieves the interpreter of the sender-loyalty. But I would like to claim that even when choosing the first-person format, the interpreter only gives the primary interlocutors the illusion of participating in direct interaction, as they would do if they had a common language. The interpreter's first person functions as a referent to the previous speaker; and if the interpreter needs to intervene by herself to ask a clarifying question to ensure her own understanding, for example, the participation status of the interpreter momentarily changes to the speaking self instead of a "referring self". So to choose one of the speaking forms does have an effect on the participation framework (Goffman 1981) in the interpreted encounter, and is therefore not without consequences. The recommendation could be explicated by giving the reasons for the adoption of either form. Interpreting in the first person is not always the most suitable form, either. In an encounter with more than just two primary interlocutors it might be better to choose the third person in order to differentiate between the source speakers.

> *3.5 The interpreter shall observe the reactions of the persons for whom he/she is interpreting to ensure that they have understood what the interpreter has said* (2001b).

These recommendations consider the interpreter to be responsible for ensuring the understanding of the participants. How can the interpreter be sure of that? And what is basically meant by *observing* the others' reactions? Understanding or misunderstanding is not necessarily evident right away; or simulating one or the other can very well be intentional in the course of human interaction.

> *3.6 So as to ensure the accuracy and reliability of the interpretation, the interpreter shall interrupt the speaker if he/she speaks unclearly or at unreasonable length. If the interpreter does not understand what the speaker means the interpreter shall request clarification. [...]* (2001b)

These recommendations are, once again, understandable in that they underline the coordination of the "technical" side of the interpreter's performance with the actions of others. An interpreter's memorizing capacity is restricted and an overload can lead to complex consequences in the court session. The conversational structures also play a role here: the above recommendation gives the interpreter the right to interrupt the others. This can affect the dynamics of the conversation; the primary interlocutors do not have the possibility to react directly to the respective turns. The longer the turns, the longer the time a questioner has to wait, for example, for the answer to arrive in the interpreter's turn. One has also to bear in mind that such things as speaking unclearly can be intentional and everyone experiences them occurring in interaction. Tokens such as tacklings, re-starts, silences or reformulations can be signs of uncertainty, lying, hiding the truth etc., and therefore of essential importance for the course of the interaction at hand: a police officer can miss relevant information, for example, when an interpreter produces a logical, coherent version of an ambiguous original. According to Hale (2004:8) those who speak through an interpreter have a right to express their message in whatever way they like and to expect it to remain unaltered in the process. So is a clear and sense-making interpretation of an intentionally unclear utterance accurate and reliable? It seems to me that professional ideology considers interaction and talk to be invariably clear, coherent and logical, which is very far away from the reality in face-to-face interaction.

In conclusion it may be stated that the Finnish professional codes for court interpreters are norms *for the interpreter*, taking the form of permissions of what she can and may do and restrictions of what she cannot or must not do. The norms are written in the imperative mood and for most of them, no grounds are given. When examining the Codes from the conversation analytical point of view, it becomes clear that the Codes are not based on knowledge about conversational systematics and interactional structures. A structured, detailed model for interaction cannot be extracted from the Codes and they do not capture the complexities of practice very well, not least for the reason that the institutional and ideological requirements of language usage and communication in the court setting have been left out of account.

Stocks of interactional knowledge in the profession of interpreters

Having conducted a simple text analysis of the Finnish ethical rules I will now try to sketch possible SIKs for the interpreter's profession against the background of the ethical rules and the parameters outlined by Peräkylä & Vehviläinen in their article (2003). It seems to me that the concept of interaction underlying the Finnish rules is that of impartial and neutral communication conducted through an interpreter. Looking at the *degree of detail in terms of interaction* (see p. 228 above), one can easily see that the SIKs in the interpreter's ethical rules are not very detailed or extensive. Normative descriptions and prescriptions are given about accuracy, reliability, neutrality and objectivity, but no hints or advice about how they can be realized in actual practice, where do they come into being or how could the conforming to the rules be ensured. The concept of interaction is not described explicitly. It seems evident that the ethical rules are not at all based on conversational systematics. Interpreting is conducted by the means of talk and by the regularities of human interaction, and whether these enable or restrict the application of the rules does not appear to be taken into account.

Considering the second dimension, the *degree of penetration into practice* (see p. 228), it seems that the SIKs in the interpreter's professional rules are contingent rather than constitutive, for an interpreted encounter can be accomplished without any reference to the ideology constituted. The basic guidelines remain mysterious, implicit, vague and hidden. Or are they self-evident and taken for granted, or paradoxical myths (Metzger 1999)? There seems to be a wide gap between professional ideology and appropriate practice. Wadensjö (2004: 109) argues that the link between certain instructions and certain communicative behaviour can be methodologically hard to establish. Indeed it is easier to prove the opposite; how a missing link is produced, as has been shown in the works of Krouglov (1999) and Hale (2004). Wadensjö further states (ibid.: 120) that professional ideology needs to be distinguished from professional practice because the Codes of Ethics cannot work as a list or as a description of everything that could be expected of an encounter assisted by professional interpreters. I agree with Wadensjö in that a list of every possible outcome of the interpreter's solutions cannot be included in the Codes of Ethics – and if we attempted it, we might end up protecting ourselves paranoidally against everything. However, I am not convinced that distinguishing professional ideology and practice would bring us any further. To my mind practice needs to be supported by a corresponding ideology. I would like to suggest that by developing the concept of the SIKs in interpreter's profession, we could diminish the gap between the professional ideology and practice, and the above-mentioned degrees of interactional details and penetration into practice would become more articulated. As is argued by Wadensjö (2004: 119), the survival of the "myth" of the interpreter's role must probably be explained by the fact that in the background lurks a layperson's understanding of what interpreting is all about. The Codes would gain in substance and professional ideology would become closer to the practice, if they reckoned with the setting they are meant to be applied in and the systematics of conversation through which the whole encounter is put into action.

In their article Peräkylä and Vehviläinen aim to explore further the possibility of a dialogue between conversation analysis and the SIKs. They propose that conversation analytical findings may 1) falsify or correct assumptions that are part of an SIK, 2) provide a more detailed picture of practices that are described in an SIK, 3) add a new dimension to the understanding of practices described by an SIK and 4) provide the description of practices that are not provided by a very abstract or general SIK (Peräkylä & Vehviläinen 2003:731–732). Through the works of Wadensjö and Hale, for example, it has become obvious that an interpreter-mediated conversation is structurally far more complex than is given to understand by the professional ideology and Codes of Ethics. If the findings of empirical interpreting studies could enrich our knowledge about interpreting as a conversational phenomenon along the lines suggested by Peräkylä and Vehviläinen, we would be a good bit further on our way to professional interpreting in the community. And vice versa, empirical research outcomes would provide new information to the field of conversation studies, too, since a bilingual conversation through an interpreter has not been explored there either.

Conclusion

To draw parallels with interpreting studies, there are works of the representatives of what is called the interactionist approach, for instance Wadensjö (1998), Roy (2000) and Apfelbaum (2004), who have shown the inseparable interplay between all participants in an interpreter-mediated encounter. The research outcome sheds light on the interactive phenomenon of interpreting in practice, and reveals the fact that ideals given in normative prescriptions are sometimes impossible to achieve or contradictory in themselves. As pointed out especially by Linell (1997) and Wadensjö (1998, 2004), interpreting studies and practice seem to start out from a monological understanding of language and communication, even if this is not expressly stated and the professional ideology claims the opposite. A similar view can be read in Inghilleri (2003), who focuses on investigating the norms in interpreting. In spite of the growing number of empirical studies in IS, a dialogical understanding still does not prevail in the field. Rudvin (2002) suggests that since the illusory character of the positivist "equality" paradigm is proven, this very fact should lead the IS research community to question the neutrality paradigm as well.

The theme of the Critical Link 4 was "Professionalisation of interpreting in the community". If it is the common aim of the conference community to promote the professionalisation of community interpreting as a whole, then I would like to claim that this requires professional knowledge and a conceptualisation of the very basics of communicating in ordinary and institutional conversation, interaction, understanding and language usage in all that. In order to achieve this, those researching interpreting and those educating (community) interpreters do have an important role, as they should raise awareness about these matters among trainee and student interpreters. Is it a mark of a true professional to uphold the prevailing ideals and norms without ever questioning them or not to pay any attention to thinking about the grounds and reasons for them? Given the particular role of the interpreter and the burden of responsibility laid on him, the knowledge on the specific format of interpreter-mediated communication should also be professional in nature and not based on everyday thinking or too simplistic. The professional codes and the norms constructing them could be better defined if they consisted of three building blocks: 1) the requirements for interpreting performance, 2) the specific conversational structure of an interpreter-mediated encounter and 3) the institutional requirements of each setting and its language usage.

It has not been my aim to show that everybody before me was wrong or to claim that the whole role ideology or the ideals of impartiality and neutrality should be changed – but I do think they should be better defined. My aim was to look at the interpreter's role from the point of a new angle, that provided by the SIKs, and to see if something new could be gained to enrich and complement the knowledge about the profession of interpreters and the specific communication mode that is conducted via an interpreter. A process of professionalisation is also under way in interpreter training and in research, the latter only slowly gaining a more sound status among translation studies. The more we know and the more we share what we know, the better the theoretical ideas can meet the practical requirements and vice versa, and the more tools we as interpreters would have at hand while practicing our profession, walking the tightrope between impartiality and neutrality.

References

Apfelbaum, B. 2004. *Gesprächsdynamik in Dolmetsch-Interaktionen in Situationen internationaler Fachkommunikation.* Radolfzell. Verlag für Gesprächsforschung. http://www.verlag-gespraechsforschung.de/apfelbaum.htm

Gile, D. 1995. *Basic concepts and models for interpreter and translator training.* Amsterdam/ Philadelphia: John Benjamins.

Goffman, E. 1981. *Forms of talk.* Oxford: Basil Blackwell.

González, R., Vásquez, V. & Mikkelson, H. 1991. *Fundamentals of court interpretation: Theory, policy and practice.* Durham, North Carolina: Carolina University Press.

Hale, S. 2004. *The discourse of court interpreting.* Amsterdam/Philadelphia: John Benjamins.

Inghilleri, M. 2003. "Habitus, field and discourse. Interpreting as a socially situated activity." *Target* 15:2, 243–268.

Krouglov, A. 1999. "Police interpreting: Politeness and Sociocultural Context." *The Translator* 5:2, 285–302.

Linell, P. 1997. "Interpreting as communication." In: *Conference interpreting: current trends in research*. Edited by Y. Gambier, D. Gile & Ch. Taylor, 49–67. Amsterdam/Philadelphia: John Benjamins.

Metzger, M. 1999. *Sign language interpreting. Deconstructing the myth of neutrality*. Washington D.C.: Gallaudet University Press.

Mikkelson, H. 2000. *Introduction to court interpreting*. Manchester: St. Jerome.

Peräkylä, A. & Vehviläinen, S. 2003. "Conversation analysis and the professional stocks of interactional knowledge." *Discourse and Society* 14:6, 727–750.

Phelan, M. 2001. *The interpreter's resource*. Multilingual Matters, Clevedon.

Roy, C. 2000. *Interpreting as a discourse process*. New York and Oxford: Oxford University Press.

Rudvin, M. 2002. "How neutral is "neutral"? Issues in interaction and participation in community interpreting." *Perspectives on Interpreting*. Edited by G. Garzone, P. Mead & M. Viezzi, 217–233. Biblioteca della Scuola Superiore di Lingua Moderne per Interpreti e Traduttori. Forli.

Schegloff, E., Jefferson, G. & Sacks, H. 1977. "The preference for self-correction in the organisation of repair in conversation." *Language* 53, 361–382.

The Finnish Association of Translators and Interpreters (1994) (Fi: *Suomen kääntäjien ja tulkkien liitto*, SKTL): Tulkin ammattisäännöstö. Available at http://www.sktl.net/pdf/tulksaan.pdf

The Finnish Association of Translators and Interpreters (2001a) (Fi: *Suomen kääntäjien ja tulkkien liitto*, SKTL) <http://www.sktl.net/kotisivu/pdf/code.pdf>. Code of Professional Ethics for Court Interpreters. Available at http://www.sktl.net/kotisivu/oiktulk.htm

The Finnish Association of Translators and Interpreters (2001b) Recommendations for Court Interpreting. Available at http://www.sktl.net/kotisivu/oiktulk.htm

The Finnish Association of Translators and Interpreters (2002) Asioimistulkin ammattisäännöstö. Available at http://www.sktl.net/pdf/asioimistulkin.pdf

Wadensjö, C. 1998. *Interpreting as interaction*. London and New York: Longman.

Wadensjö, C. 2004. "Dialogue interpreting. A monologising practice in a dialogically organised world". *Target* 16:1, 105–124.

Aristotelian ethics and modern professional interpreting

Patrick Kermit

Norwegian University of Science and Technology, Trondheim, Norway

When codes of ethics for interpreters identify what a *good* interpreter should do, this often implies a dual understanding of the term 'good'. In one sense, good involves the question of usefulness. In a second sense, good has something to do with the concept of morality. On the basis of Aristotelian ethics, I discuss the element of unity between these two concepts, trying to show that neither of them should be abandoned. Together with the modern concepts of power and trust, Aristotelian ethics provides us with analytical tools to guide us in our everyday struggle as professionals.

Introduction

In this article I will discuss some issues related to professional ethics for interpreters. In doing so, my main concern is to address the question of what *good* interpreters ought to do. At the same time, I want to explore the relation between this question and the more general one of what it is interpreters do. I will demonstrate the necessity of looking at these two questions in close relation to one another using Aristotelian ethics. More precisely, I will explore how, in the context of interpreting, the concept *good* can be used in two distinct senses. In the first sense, *good* involves the question of *usefulness*. In the second sense, *good* has something to do with the concept of *morality*. I will discuss the element of unity between these two concepts.

Through interviews with interpreters, I have gathered a number of descriptions of various problems occurring in situations where two or more people are trying to communicate through an interpreter. One of these stories will serve as an example. What I want is to form a theoretical description of some important aspects concerning professional ethics for interpreters. Using examples in this manner means applying a method Annemarie Mol (2000: 10) has labelled *empiri-*

cal philosophy. She describes this as a practice where you "mobilize situations that have occurred, at some point, somewhere, to do theoretical work" (ibid: 10).

Using Aristotelian ethics as a ground for modern theories of professional ethics has been done in the case of a number of other professions. Here, I especially rely on the works undertaken both in the area of medicine and education (Hofmann 2002 and Gustavsson 1998).

The concept good in the first sense

As an academic discipline, ethics is concerned with the question of right actions. The word *good* occurs, for instance, when you ask what distinguishes good deeds from bad ones. Making a broad statement, one could say ethics is about how one ought to be.

Already in 300 B.C., the philosopher Aristotle debated the meaning of the concept *good*, and it may still be interesting to take a closer look at some of the answers he argued for. Aristotle, in establishing a foundational concept, stated "[T]he function of a harper is to play the harp," and "that of a good harper is to play the harp well" (Aristoteles 1996: 9[1]).

This might sound naïve, but it is really an acute observation. Aristotle points out that at least a part of the concept *good* has to do with our sense of something being optimalized and suitable. When I, going on a fishing trip, show my companion my new knife and say that it is really good, he will automatically expect it to be sharp, balanced and lie well in my hand even when it's wet. In short, a good knife should be "well fitted for its intended use" (Haga 1992: 10).

The same principle is equally applicable to a professional interpreter. Good interpreters are well suited for their intended purpose. If we elaborate on what it means to be "well suited," then reaching consensus is fairly easy.

Many codes of ethical behaviour for interpreters[2] share the same three basic principles:

- Discretion and confidentiality
- Neutrality and reluctance towards carrying out other tasks apart from interpreting
- All that is said should be translated accurately

---

1. This is a Norwegian translation. The English quotations in this article are taken from the English translation of the Greek original, published on the Internet (Aristotle 2006).

2. I do not pretend to know all existing codes of ethics for interpreters. This statement is based on what I found searching through the Internet and searching available literature.

Using the Aristotelian reasoning mentioned earlier and comparing the interpreter with a tool, it is easy to explain why these three principles are common among interpreters. They are the result of a reflection on what can be referred to as the idea or even the myth of *the interpreter as the invisible professional* (cf. e.g. Venuti 1995; Metzger 1999; Katan & Straniero Sergio 2001; Angelelli 2004).

As an interpreter engaged in situations where you are physically facing your clients, there is no feedback more rewarding than when one of them says afterwards: "What you just did was fantastic! I almost forgot you were there!" Interpreters are seldom granted the pleasure of hearing these words themselves though they tend to pretend that someone else has heard them at some time.

It is important to emphasise that this idea of *invisibility* should not be interpreted literally. There are already too many interpreters believing good professional behaviour consists of trying to merge with the white wall. This is of course impossible and a dangerous idea. Hence, it is important to remember that the use of the idea of invisibility is metaphorical. However it is more important to understand how this metaphor says something about how interpreting is carried out *at its best*. (Aristoteles 1996:9) If someone almost forgets that the interpreter is there, this person experiences an interpreter able to make his or her clients feel that they are communicating as if they shared the same language without the interpreter.

If one of the basic principles listed above is violated by the interpreter, the illusion one might have of being able to communicate, as if one shared a common language, would most certainly be destroyed. The possibility of experiencing such a genuine contact with your dialogue partner is seriously threatened if 1) you don't trust the interpreter's confidentiality, 2) the interpreter offers his or her own opinions during the conversation, 3) the interpreter simultaneously carries out other tasks and 4) if the interpreter doesn't translate everything that is said.

It is no wonder that different codes of ethics for interpreters share these common principles. The codes seem to cover some of the most important aspects of the interpreter's *modus operandi,* but the question still remains: Do these principles address the basic question of ethics?

The concept good in the second sense

Ethics deal with the great and important issues of life: Whether you are allowed to tell a lie or not, if you can justify hurting someone's feelings or if you are allowed to use another person as a means and not an end.

If we compare the average code of ethics for interpreters with codes of ethics developed among other groups of professionals like nurses, social workers, teachers and so on, we will discover a sharp contrast. Instead of issues of functionality, the codes of the other professions focus on the very nature in which their professions are exercised.

These codes speak about respect for the individual and address his or her human rights. They promise that the professional will use an empathic approach toward the people who depend on the professional. Last but not least, these codes prohibit the abuse of power by the professional.

Power is a strange word, and many interpreters will describe themselves as professionals with little or no opportunity to exert power. Nothing could be further from the truth.

When I use the concept *power*, I have to emphasize that this word is used in a narrow sense. The German sociologist Max Weber (2000) makes a distinction between what he, in German, named *Macht* and *Herrschaft*. The latter concept, which can be translated *control* or *dominion*, designates the legal use of power. Having this legal opportunity to exert power is always a part of what it means to be a professional. This is a part of our every day experience.

There are, for instance, very few people whom I would allow to put their fingers into my mouth. If someone I didn't know did this, I would most certainly consider it offensive. There is, on the other hand, one person who is automatically allowed, even though I really barely know her, and that is my dentist. When I lie in her chair, I am willing to suffer treatments, which no one else may put me through. There is absolutely no way I can control what she is doing. She is in control, and I simply have to trust her, even though I don't know if she is trustworthy. I certainly am running a risk in making myself so vulnerable. However I visit her every year because, after all, she is a trained dentist. By attending her company on a regular basis, I hope to avoid the more severe consequences, like a toothache or cavity.

This example illustrates an important lesson about the needs of those relying on the interpreter's services.

First of all, interpreters should accept that no one calls upon them out of joy and desire. Most people would probably prefer to communicate directly with each other if they could.

Secondly, when clients accept that they have to trust the interpreter and subordinate to his or her dominion, the clients' most important hope and desire will be that the interpreter doesn't exert power in a way that could be harmful. Only after that will the client start worrying about the interpreter's skills in language and translation.

Here, the word *good* has another sense than the prior concept of something well fitted for its intended use. Here, *good* addresses something more solely ethical, not limited to one's deeds as interpreters, but to one's deeds as responsible individuals. Both are of importance, and it is possible to elaborate further on a theoretical basis on the difference and the relation between these two meanings of the concept *good*. Aristotle offers his aid. In his ethical works he distinguishes between what he calls *poiesis* and *praxis* (Skirbekk 1987: 130).

Poiesis and praxis

Poiesis describes an act as a means to accomplish an end, where this end is something different from the act itself. For professional interpreters, an example of such an act would be when they apply a strict rule of confidentiality so the clients can get the feeling they communicate as if they shared the same language. Confidentiality is a means to obtain an end, the necessary feeling of privacy. That is experiencing *good* interpreting in the first sense.

Praxis describes an act that is both a means and an end. This might sound strange, but it is a part of our every day experience. Acts of friendship or kindness would not be considered truly friendly or kind if the person carrying them out had ulterior motives, for instance, to gain an advantage or to benefit from the acts in one way or another. For professional interpreters, an example of such an act would be when they apply a strict rule of confidentiality as a means to prevent abuse of the professional dominion, abuse that could harm and offend the client. That is experiencing *good* interpreting in the second sense.

It is no accident that both examples are drawn from the same principle, the principle of confidentiality. By this, I hope to demonstrate what distinguishes professional ethics from every day morality.

The heart of the matter is as follows: Professional ethics must describe the professional both in terms of *poiesis* and *praxis*.

Interpreters, who are *good* only in the first sense, will be insensitive to the many challenges facing them, as they meet people who depend on the choices they make on the clients' behalf.

Interpreters, who are *good* only in the second sense, will most certainly be a disappointment to the people depending on them. Worse, these interpreters will violate the trust the clients have to show the professionals, because the clients have no other choices. The interpreter's morality will not compensate or make up for his or her incompetence.

In other words, in order to be a good interpreter, one has to do what interpreters do, and at its best we may add. In addition one has to carry out the acts which are themselves both means and ends.

For interpreters, as for most other professions, professional ethics is a necessary supplement to the morality we apply to our lives. The fundamental condition in all professional ethics is that the professional never exerts their power in a way that violates the client's trust. Secondly, the best way the professional redeems the trust shown by the client, is by proving her- or himself to be an expert, as in our case an interpreter at their best.

Strangely enough, it then becomes a moral challenge to be *good* in the first sense if one want to be *good* in the second sense.

Possible dilemmas

When it comes to what one would actually do in a given situation, this only offers specific guidance to a limited extent. There are many examples showing how the two notions of *good* would seem to contradict each other. The following example address such contradictions:

> You are interpreting between an old man belonging to a linguistic minority and a doctor speaking the language of the majority. The doctor explains the results of a biopsy and states that the tumour is a benign one. You know the equivalent term of "benign" in the minority language, but here the term is uncommon and not the word a doctor would normally use, except between colleagues. You choose to use it anyway, telling yourself the importance of equivalent translation. You want to give the patient the same opportunity of asking for an explanation, as a person who didn't need an interpreter would have. The patient, unfortunately, asks no questions, but his attitude convinces you that he didn't understand. You leave the doctor's office together and have barely closed the door before the patient turns to you. "Please," he says, "you have to let me know! Do I have cancer or don't I?"

Situations like this are usually highly complex. This normally implies showing cautiousness in not being too dogmatic in making judgements. However, in order to analyse the dilemma in play, I will outline three possible stereotypical responses to the patient's question:

1) The extreme instrumentalist's response would be "Sorry, I am your interpreter not your doctor, so I can't answer your question." Even if one put this in a slightly more polite way, one would still give priority to the principles derived from the concept *good* in the first sense, mostly ignoring the second sense. Some have tried to defend this response by claiming it to be a means to a pedagogical end. Even old men have to learn what to expect from their interpreter. This is most likely not a sufficient defence for such behaviour.

2) A more "concerned" instrumentalist's response could be "Sorry, as your interpreter I find it incorrect to answer you (so many things were said in there and I am not sure I remember it all…). If you want it, I will gladly walk you back to the doctor, so that you can ask him again, through me."

Here, the interpreter clearly recognizes the urgent need for an answer. This shows more concern for being *good* in the second sense, but the means proposed may be problematic. Doing as the interpreter proposes means forcing the man to admit something he didn't want to admit in the first place: his lack of understanding. In addition, a more practical evaluation of the proposed procedure points out the obvious obstacles. What if the doctor is no longer available, and what if the patient decides living in uncertainty is preferable to the humiliation of admitting ignorance?

3) You can simply answer, "The doctor said your tumour wasn't a dangerous type, which means you don't have cancer."[3] This answer isn't *good* in the first sense mentioned here but is *good* in the second. It is on the other hand not sufficient to rely on one's *goodness* in the second sense, if one cannot repay the client's trust by being good also in the first. By this reply, the interpreter ceases to be an interpreter and takes on a different role.

The outlined alternative 1 and 2 both mean risking offending the old man, thus overlooking his obvious vulnerability. In strict ethical terms, the third alternative then seems to be the only defendable one. Being *good* in the first sense hardly can have ethical priority. The dilemma is that response 3 means a *de facto* termination of the role as an interpreter, implying that another, more actively helping role is taken on. Hence, none of the three outlined responses should be that of an interpreter combining both notions of *good*.

The dilemma is not easily solved. Trying to be *good* in both of the above mentioned senses certainly means wanting to help the people depending on one's service. At the same time, however, the interpreter does not want to take on a similar role as a nurse or a social worker. Helping others is an outspoken part of having the professional role of these latter two. Nurses and social workers are professional 'helpers', representing an official body and at the same time they have a mandate to side with the person in the need of help. The interpreter's dilemma consists in being obliged to assist without siding with anyone.

It is important to realise potential inconsistencies in interpreters' conceptions of their professional ethics. Dilemmas, as the above mentioned, do not necessarily call for drastic changes in the average code of ethics for interpreters around the world, but they might force interpreters to reflect on their everyday practices with more nuances.

---

3.   The answer is medically speaking not a correct one, but it is anyhow an appropriate answer to the man's question provided that the benign tumour isn't located in a region where it can cause additional harm, or have other harmful side effects.

The realization that being *good* in the first sense is an important part of what it is to be *good* in the second sense represents a genuine ethical realization of great importance for any professional. In the field of professional ethics for doctors, Jonsen (1990) puts it this way: "I'd rather have a competent bastard do my surgery, than a bumbling humanist" (quotation from Hofmann 2002: 144).

The core insight is that the value of benevolence is limited if the professional is unable to perform well or *good* in the first sense. Still, this notion of *good* might be elaborated further.

In the above example, the interpreter's *linguistic skills* are excellent but inadequate in avoiding an ethically challenging situation. The expectation that these skills are sufficient, provided they are excellent enough, might be unrealistic. The interpreter realised that *benign* wasn't understood, something the doctor didn't. The interpreter was able to understand the patient in a way the doctor couldn't. This is often the case when people communicate through an interpreter. To understand another person means a lot more than recognizing the words this person utters.

The focal point of these analyses is slightly changed here. Instead of focusing on the interpreter's response outside the doctor's office, another question can be asked. Would the skilled interpreter, combining the two notions of *good* perfectly, more easily avoid getting into the situation described above? In the example, the interpreter chose to interpret "benign" in a way that was *good* only in the first sense. The interpreter was sensible enough to realize that the term chosen might not be recognized but still used it. Maybe, here, the true ethical challenges facing an interpreter are revealed: Being *good* in both senses means being able to combine skill and morality. In our case, this literally means to deliver good work, not in terms of each single word we choose but *seen as a whole*. Then, part of the answer to our dilemma lies in the small "tricks of the trade" the wise professional knows how to handle. Interpreters in similar situations have asked for explanation, leaving it unanswered who needed them. It might also be perfectly defendable to offer an explication without asking. If one would easily translate the English expression "Number 10" with something equivalent to "the residence of the British Prime Minister," an interpreter should be able to defend the translation of *benign* in a similar way.

Conclusion

In the end, this discussion touches on important Aristotelian concepts. Trying to solve what seemed to be a dilemma in the above example, the importance of taking all things into considerations as a whole becomes clear. Interpreters cannot consider their task to be a number of different subordinated tasks. Only when focusing on the end (*telos*) of our task as a whole, are we able to be really *good* (Aristoteles 1996: 5).

In the struggle to achieve this, the Aristotelian concept *wisdom* (*phronesis*) becomes relevant. Aristotle described *wisdom* as the ultimate intellectual virtue. For Aristotle, wisdom is nourished both from what one knows theoretically/scientifically (*episteme*) and practically/artistically (*techne*) (Hoffman 2002: 137ff. and Gustavsson 1998: 54ff). When it comes to the question of doing the right thing, *wisdom* transcends what can be explicated as *rules* or *codes*. The teleological aspect calls for consistency and unity. The interpreter's challenge is not to carry out some deeds *good* in the first sense and other deeds *good* in the second sense. All the deeds of the interpreter should combine the two notions of *good*.

References

Angelelli, C. 2004. *Medical Interpreting and Cross Cultural Communication*. Cambridge: Cambridge University Press.

Aristotle 2006. *Nicomachean Ethics*. ed. H. Rackham. (English) (Aristot. Nic. Eth.) (cited November 10th, 2006). Available at: http://www.perseus.tufts.edu

Aristoteles 1996. *Etikk (den nikomakiske etikk)*. Oslo: Gyldendal.

Gustavsson, B. 1998. *Dannelse i vor tid : om dannelsens muligheder og vilkår i det moderne samfund*. Århus: Klim.

Haga, Aa. 1992. *Ein huvudmotsetnad i moderne etikk*. Arbeidsnotat TMW-senteret [Working paper], Oslo University.

Hofmann, B. 2002. "Medicine as practical wisdom (phronesis)", in *Poiesis Praxis 1*, 135–149.

Jonsen, A. R. 1990. *The new medicine and the old ethics*. Cambridge, MA: Harvard University Press.

Katan, David & Francesco Straniero-Sergio 2001. "Look who is Talking: The Ethics of Entertainment and Talkshow Interpreting", in Pym (ed.) *The Return to Ethics, Special Issue of The Translator*, Volume 7/2: 2001, 213–237.

Metzger, M. 1999. *Sign Language Interpreting: Deconstructing the Myth of Neutrality*. Washington D.C.: Gallaudet University Press.

Mol, A. 2000. "What diagnostic devices do: The case of blood sugar measurement", in *Theoretical medicine and bioethics* 21: 9–22.

Skirbekk, G. 1987. *Filosofihistorie I*. Bergen: Universitetsforlaget.

Venuti, L. 1995. *The translator's invisibility: a history of translation*. London: Routledge.

Weber, M. 2000. *Makt og byråkrati: essays om politikk og klasse, samfunnsforskning og verdier*. Oslo: Gyldendal.

PART VI

Improving and assessing professional skills

Training initiatives and programmes

Formative assessment

Using peer and self-assessment in interpreter training

Yvonne Fowler
City College Birmingham, United Kingdom

This paper considers the viability and desirability of three aspects of formative assessment: peer assessment, self-assessment and evaluation, and their importance in the training of the professional interpreter. Even experienced student interpreters are often unaware of omissions, additions and misunderstandings in their own performances. When asked to assess themselves or each other, they frequently lack the analytical tools to be able to carry out such exercises. This paper is informed by educational practice in order to validate the use of these forms of assessment, and it demonstrates how student interpreters can use them to increase the amount of feedback they receive as they become professionals.

Definitions

Assessment, whether formative or summative, is an attempt to measure the extent to which learners meet a range of specified criteria known as assessment criteria. *Formative assessment*, according to Sadler (1989: 120) "is concerned with how judgments about the quality of student assessments (performances, pieces or works) can be used to shape and improve the student's competence by short-circuiting the randomness and inefficiency of trial-and-error learning".

The tutor, who may also be responsible for devising the criteria, may carry out the assessment. Alternatively the students can practice on each other, using student-devised criteria (peer assessment) and upon themselves (self-assessment). Peer and self-assessment are often explored together, as peer assessment is considered by Bostock (2000: 1) to help self-assessment. According to Brown, Rust and Gibbs (1994) "peer and self-assessment help students develop the ability to make judgments, a necessary skill for study and professional life".

Feedback is an essential part of formative assessment. Ramaprasad (1983:4) defines feedback as "information about the gap between the actual level and the reference level of a system parameter which is used to alter the gap in some way". Ramaprasad goes on to emphasise that "information about the gap between actual and reference levels is considered as feedback *only when it is used to alter the gap*".

On the other hand, summative assessment, according to Sadler (1989:120), "is concerned with summing up or summarizing the achievement status of a student and is geared towards reporting at the end of a course of study especially for purposes of certification. It is essentially passive and does not normally have immediate impact on learning".

Although summative assessment may be necessary to accredit the skills of the interpreter at the end of the course, it is primarily through formative assessment that the interpreter develops her competence. As Helge Niska (1998) puts it, "I don't think any test can be a substitute for proper training, nor is testing *per se* a remedy for a lack of interpreters. Tests don't produce interpreters; proper education does".

Self-evaluation refers to the expression of feelings and opinions of the student about the learning process. The purpose of self-evaluation is to reflect analytically on one's practice as a professional. Students at City College are asked to provide an evaluation of their response to everything they do, whether it is an interpreting, sight translation, written translation or any other assignment. The evaluation can be verbal or written. For a variety of reasons, some students find this process very difficult. It may be an activity that is alien to the educational systems of other countries, and which feels new and strange; students with low self-esteem or those who feel insecure can find it threatening; complacent students who lack self-awareness regard it as a public admission of failure. However, it is crucial for a tutor to be able to monitor evaluations so that there is clear evidence of development and reflection in the interpreter. If the student is to develop good self-evaluation and assessment skills this requires explicit training by the tutor, and assessment criteria must be devised to guide students. This explicit training should be integral to the course.

Why peer and self-assessment are crucial in professional interpreter training

Once interpreters have finished their training, they will probably be quite isolated throughout their professional lives. There are a few institutions in the UK that support practicing public service interpreters and enable them to link up with one another. But relatively few public service interpreters belong to these, and few can afford conference fees to continue their professional development. Local networks of public service interpreters are also few and far between. Monitoring of the interpreter, therefore, will very likely be left to the interpreter herself, and if that interpreter is not self-aware, and has neither the skills to be able to assess and evaluate her own performance nor those to take action to improve upon weaknesses, the Service User will suffer to a greater or lesser degree. Bruner (1966) maintains that "the tutor must correct a learner in a fashion that eventually makes it possible for the learner to take over the correcting function himself, otherwise the result of instruction is to create a form of mastery that is contingent on the continual presence of the teacher".

Sadler (1989: 121) echoes this:

> the indispensable conditions for improvement are that the student comes to hold a concept of quality roughly similar to that held by the teacher, is able to monitor continuously the quality of what is being produced *during the act of production itself,* and has a repertoire of alternative moves or strategies from which to draw at any given point. In other words, students have to be able to judge the quality of what they are producing and be able to regulate what they are doing during the doing of it.

Thus peer and self-assessment in interpreter training should foster good professional habits in the interpreter.

Black and Wiliam (1998: 6) argue that peer and self-assessment are essential components of formative assessment, and maintain that training in these techniques can be given from the age of 5. They regard the most successful tutor feedback as comprising three essential elements: recognition of the desired goal, evidence of the present position, and some indication from the tutor as to how to close the gap between the two. However, they believe that the amount of feedback that students receive can be increased through the use of peer and self-assessment.

Stephen Bostock (2000: 2) examines peer assessment and concludes that it "encourages students to believe that they are part of a community of scholarship. In peer assessment we invite students to take part in a key aspect of Higher Education: making critical judgements on the work of others".

Preparation for peer and self-assessment

1. Trainees must have a basic understanding of the interpreting process before they begin to practice peer assessment in class. They need to understand how concepts and ideas, rather than words, are transferred from one language to

the other. They also need to analyse the relationship between the interpreter, Service Provider and Service User in the interpreted interview and consider the effects of different models of interpreting, as well as focus in detail on various Codes of Practice for the interpreter. Other practical aspects such as interventions must also be investigated and understood, as well as training in note-taking.

2. Some trainees may not have had any previous experience of using assessment criteria, so will benefit from having had experience of applying tutor-devised assessment criteria to their work before starting to devise their own, or before applying their own assessment criteria to someone else's work. Making the tutor devised criteria explicit and sharing them with the students before they undertake a piece of work means that they have a benchmark by which to measure their own work. They are able to refer to the criteria and tailor their own work to them.

3. Trainees need to be briefed about how to receive and give oral and written feedback to their peers. There is always the temptation for students to focus on the negative, rather than the positive, aspects of an interpreter's production. Trainees should be in the position of welcoming feedback about their work, and they will learn not to do so if they suspect that their peers will dwell upon their mistakes. If criticism can be couched in positive terms, then mistakes can be seen as an opportunity rather than a failure.

4. Trainees need training in the skill of assessing both themselves and each other. They must understand the rationale of peer and self-assessment. They will also require training in how to write assessment criteria and practice in applying them to their own or their peers' work.

Peer and self- assessment in interpreted role-plays

Assessment is an activity that is usually carried out by tutors. If this is the only feedback the students obtain, their opportunities for learning will be fewer. In peer assessment, students themselves are being asked to assume and internalise the role of the tutor. However, unless students are clear about what the learning goal is, say Black and Wiliam (1998:6), they will not be able to assess themselves or give feedback to others. It seems important, then, to make any teacher-devised assessment criteria explicit to the students, so that they clearly perceive the rationale of the task and can tailor their work to those elements in the criteria. All of these activities can lead towards the autonomy of the learner and the reflective thinking so essential in an interpreter.

Students need a great deal of practice in observing their peers as they interpret if they are to learn from one another. In general, the more opportunities for observation of interpreted role-plays they have, the more they will learn. When students have had experience in debriefing their peers, their ability to assess themselves is greatly improved. Again, proficiency in peer assessment leads to skilled self-assessment.

To facilitate this process a clearly structured observation sheet is needed so that students know which aspects of interpreter behaviour they are to observe and which criteria they are to use. Even those who do not understand the foreign language being spoken will be able to make comments about very obvious aspects of the interpreted interaction, for example:

- Was the dialect/language of the Service User matched with that of the interpreter?
- Were introductions and statements of intent properly made?
- Did the statement of intent contain all the elements indicated in the Code of Practice?
- Were interventions handled according to the Code?
- What effect did each intervention have on the interaction between the service user and the service provider?
- Did the interpreter cope with long utterances?
- Were names, numbers and place names noted down?
- Were rejoinders interpreted?
- Was direct speech used throughout?

Naturally students who are part of the same language group as the interpreter can comment on linguistic aspects of the performance.

Feedback procedures

There should be a clear structure for giving feedback after an interpreting role-play has been completed. It is the trainee herself who should be asked first about her own performance. Peers should then be invited to give feedback, using the set of criteria provided. In situations where Service Providers participate in the role-play, their feedback should be next. The tutor can add comments and summarise what has already been said, adding a final positive note. The advantage of this system is that the trainee has the opportunity to gather feedback about her own performance from a range of different sources, all of whom may have a different perspective. As each assessor comments on a different aspect of the performance, the trainee's awareness of her own behaviour as an interpreter is heightened, and a genuine and informed dialogue about the interpreter's performance can take place.

Although these aspects of interpreting may seem very basic, trainee interpreters who have little knowledge of the subject find it very challenging to gather evidence under all these headings through observation. Videoing students' performances and making videos available to the student in question is the best way of encouraging self-awareness and critical thinking in the student. Whether videos are used or not, all students are expected to write up their observations and evaluate them in the form of an assignment. Grades are awarded according to the degree of observational skill, the positive language in which their observations are couched, the degree of analysis applied, and the accuracy of their references to the interpreter's Code of Practice. The exercise accrues status due to the fact that the observation is set as an assignment.

Students' evaluations of peer and self-assessment in interpreting

When students were asked to evaluate peer and self-assessment as learning techniques, they demonstrated that they were well on the way to critical self-analysis. Some focused on the difficulty of presenting feedback, while others noticed that watching peers helped them to learn the Code of Practice. Still others used other students as role models. Here are some of their comments:

- Finding the right way to present criticism when the points I wanted to make were negative ones, was a challenge... As we got to know each other better and we were no longer strangers, it became a lot easier.

- Writing up the role-play assessment was extremely valuable in as much as it made me concentrate on every part of the interpreter's introduction and the Code of Practice deeper [sic] than I had before, and from that moment on I practically knew it by heart... It reinforced my capacity to appreciate what others do and gain more from self-criticism...

- I attempted to look at myself as an observer. Initially I found the task of observation very difficult in terms of the guidelines set by the tutor... I tended to focus on individual aspects of the performance instead; of the bigger picture...

- I learnt that interpreting is a more complex skill than I initially perceived it to be...

– Some of them [the interpreter students] had good techniques which I have
  tried to adopt; e.g. trying to be as invisible as possible while interpreting...

This selection of evaluations demonstrates clearly how students have influenced
one another and how peer observation has helped students to monitor themselves.

Student-devised assessment criteria

Students entering for the Diploma in Public Service Interpreting examination
have to pass two short written translation examinations as well as two interpreting
tasks. When students are learning to write their own assessment criteria, translation tasks can be used as a starting point. Students were asked to devise their own
criteria and apply them to their own and to others' translations.

In the first instance, trainee interpreters were set the task of examining a
poor translation. In the translation there were examples of inappropriate style,
false cognates, poor expression and inappropriate choice of vocabulary as well as
grammatical and spelling errors. Trainees were asked to identify the aspects of the
translation that were poor and consider, in groups, what criteria were needed to
achieve a "good" translation. Different groups devised criteria that differed slightly
from one another. These were then pooled and a consensus reached by the class
as to the wording of the statements and the final set of criteria. The same exercise
was carried out in two separate, but parallel, classes. Neither class had the opportunity to consult with the other, but interestingly both classes devised sets of
criteria that were highly comparable, and, in some cases, almost identical. Once
the criteria were devised, the next stage was for the students to apply them to each
other's translated texts.

Here are some examples of the student-devised criteria:

– The target language text (TLT) respects the order and coherence of the source
  language text
– The TLT can be easily understood by a native speaker
– The TLT is grammatically correct and free of punctuation errors
– The TLT carries the same intended meaning as the SL text
– The TLT uses the correct technical terms, using explanations where appropri-
  ate
– The TLT respects the layout of the SL text
– The TLT is culture friendly
– The TLT has a similar style to the SL text

When they began to apply the criteria, students soon began to realize the limitations. In some cases the descriptors appeared to be too vague, so that some students might judge a peer to have reached the criteria, whereas others might have judged that the same student failed to achieve them. They also learnt that merely stating that their peer had achieved the criteria was not enough; that concrete evidence had to be sought to back up their statements. This had the effect of forcing them to examine the source text more minutely and to identify the need to change the criteria. There were perceptive suggestions about the criteria and for amending them (the student-devised criteria are in italics):

- There are too many similarities in the assessment criteria... I found that I made the same responses to some of the questions I had to ask myself...

- *Easily understood by a native speaker*... It depends on whether the reader is from mainland France or the former colonies and on his/her level of education or familiarity with legal language or procedures...

- I do not think that simply *respecting the coherence of the source language text* is a good idea if the original is incoherent. I think we should revise the criteria to include something about *making assumptions about the source text's intended meaning if it is unclear*....

- The concept of *culture-friendliness* is too vague. This could be split into *the target language text takes into account the reader's assumed level of knowledge and education* and *it does not cause offence to the person the translation is intended for*...

- Clear criteria like *order, layout and accuracy of grammar, spelling and punctuation* are much easier to apply than vaguer or more subjective comments like *coherence* and *culture friendly*.

Students demonstrate in their evaluations that they have developed the confidence to criticise and amend their own criteria in the light of their attempts to assess each other's work. The evaluations also show how assessing others' work has led to a reflection upon the process of translation itself, rather than the final product.

When asked to evaluate this procedure, students varied in their assessment of how useful the task had been, but most had found it valuable:

- I have learnt from this exercise that there is more than one way of saying something with the same meaning...

– This exercise made me go back to the source text to really work out what it means...

– I have learnt that we think differently and that we go about solving problems differently. It is difficult to get inside someone's head and know why they chose one expression rather than another.

– Sometimes it is very hard to assess someone...an expression may not sound or feel quite right, and yet it is difficult to pinpoint what the problem is.

– It is as though one is questioning one's own translation techniques, uses of terminology, register, style, etc. I found myself using my own translation as a guide, not because I thought my own translation was necessarily better, but to give myself an alternative to what I had to correct. Assessing one's peers also makes one more aware of the shortcomings in one's own work, and so this task acts as a learning instrument for the assessor. It is just as challenging a task as doing the translation...

Conclusion

Peer assessment and self-assessment are both viable and desirable for the developing professional interpreter. The first step towards being able to assess oneself as an interpreter is to demonstrate the ability to assess fellow students' interpreting performances. In order to do this trainees must be sufficiently sensitive to the learning needs of peers and sufficiently knowledgeable about the theoretical aspects of interpreting to be able to provide useful feedback to the trainees being assessed. By doing this, the trainees develop reflective skills and raise their self-awareness of their own interpreting performance. Trainee interpreters are also perfectly capable of devising their own assessment criteria and of applying them to each other and to themselves, but where tutors devise the assessment criteria, students are greatly empowered by having these criteria made explicit to them. In devising and applying their own assessment criteria, trainees are mirroring the role of the tutor and thus become vigorously engaged in their own professional development.

References

Bostock, S. 2000. *Student Peer Assessment.* www.keele.ac.uk/depts/cs/Stephen_Bostock/docs/bostock_peer_assessment.htm

Brown, S, Rust, C., Gibbs, G. 1995. Involving students in the assessment process. In Strategies for Diversifying Assessment in Higher Education. Oxford: Oxford Centre for Staff Development, and at DeLiberations. http:/www.lgu.ac.uk/deliberations/ocsd-pubs/div-ass5.html

Black, P. & Wiliam, D. 1996. Meanings and Consequences: a basis for distinguishing formative and summative assessment? *British Education Research Journal,* 22 (5) 537–548.

Black, P. & Wiliam, D. 1998. Inside the black box: raising standards through classroom assessment. *Phi Beta Kappan* 80 (2).

Bruner, J. 1966. *Toward a Theory of Instruction.* The Belknap Press of Harvard University Press. Cambridge, Massachussetts.

Niska, H. 1998. Testing community interpreters: a theory, a model and a plea for research. (cited 200X-xx-xx). http://tisa.toIk.su.se/OOTEST.HTM

Ramaprasad, A. 1983. On the definition of feedback. *Behavioural Science* 28, 4–13.

Sadler, D R.1989. Formative assessment and the design of instructional systems. *Instructional Science* 18,145–165.

Interpreter internship program

Forging employer-community partnerships

Sheila Johnston
Canadian Hearing Society, Canada

This paper discusses the need for employer internship opportunities that are based on employer-community partnerships. Interpreter graduates lack the experience necessary to allow them to successfully make the transition between interpreting student and working community interpreter. The failure to make this transition impedes the professionalisation of the field as interpreters with widely varying skills are providing service in the community. The Canadian Hearing Society (CHS), an organization serving Deaf, deafened and hard of hearing consumers, has developed and piloted an Interpreter Internship Program. Unlike a placement opportunity, interns are graduates from interpreter training programs hired by the agency. The process of establishing such a program, developing curriculum and blending formal training with hands on experience is highlighted. Discussion will focus on initial outcomes and lessons learned.

Introduction

In Canada there are two major sign languages used – American Sign Language (ASL) used by the majority of Deaf people, and Langue des Signes Quebecoise (LSQ) used mainly in the province of Quebec by French Canadian Deaf people. There is evidence of Maritime Sign Language on the east coast of the country as well as Inuit Sign Language in the north. American Sign Language is common to both the United States and Canada. There are regional variations but the over all structure and syntax is the same. This paper deals with the provision of ASL-English interpreters only.

The Association of Visual Language Interpreters of Canada (AVLIC) is the professional association that certifies ASL-English interpreters. At present there is no national certification for LSQ-French interpreters. The AVLIC certification process is not meant to measure entry-level skills but to be an indication of a high national standard. The number of nationally certified interpreters is relatively small. AVLIC certification is not required to use the title of ASL Interpreter nor is membership in AVLIC a prerequisite for employment. Many individuals with varying qualifications continue to function in the role of interpreter.

The Canadian Hearing Society (CHS) is a non-profit community agency serving Deaf, deafened and hard of hearing consumers in the province of Ontario. ASL-English interpreters are provided for appointments that fall into the following categories – medical, mental health, employment, and personal business. CHS recognizes and supports AVLIC certification; however they also recognize the need for an entry-level standard to ensure a minimal level of service. In order to do this Ontario Interpreter Services (OIS), the interpreting department within The Candian Hearing Society, developed an employer-screening tool that has evolved as the field has developed. Interpreters registered with Ontario Interpreter Services must successfully complete a Videotape Skills Screening and a Knowledge and Attitude Interview. In the absence of required certification, OIS Registration has become a recognized benchmark for employers and consumers alike.

The demand for interpreters in community settings far exceeds the supply of OIS registered interpreters. While interpreter training programs exist in the province, approximately 95% of recent graduates are unsuccessful on their first attempt at the OIS Videotape Skills Screening. This is not a reflection of the programs but more an indication of the need for a formal process to assist in the transition between interpreting student and professional, community interpreter. Mentorships exist with varying degrees of success but tend to be informal relationships that are not automatically available to all new graduates. It is clear that a more formalized induction into the profession is necessary.

In 1997 the Supreme Court of Canada ruled that British Columbia was required to pay for sign language interpreters when Deaf people access health care (Eldridge v. British Columbia (Attorney General) 1997). In 2001 the Ontario government and the Ministry of Health offered funding to The Canadian Hearing Society to provide after-hours emergency interpreting services. Unable to meet the demand for daytime assignments it was clear that this increase in service would not be possible with the current pool of interpreters. The logical solution was to find a means of increasing the resources available by assisting newer interpreters to reach entry-level standards. The Ministry of Health agreed to provide additional funding for a pilot internship program. The goal of this program was to bring new interpreters to a level of skill that would allow them to pass the OIS Registration Process.

Identifying key stakeholders

The field of ASL-English interpreting in both Canada and the United States is supportive of the concept of formal and informal mentoring. It is clear that, as with many professions, a formal means of induction would assist new interpreters in transitioning into the working world. While educational programs offer real-life experience through placement or co-op opportunities, these placements have their limitations. It is often difficult to get meaningful community interpreting experience as freelance interpreters may find it difficult to obtain consumer permission to bring a student to an assignment. After researching the field it was obvious that a unique model of interning was required to meet the needs of new interpreters as well as the agency's need to increase resources. It was critical to identify partnerships in the community to ensure that the program met with the maximum level of success.

Interpreter education programs were obvious partners: they were familiar with their students and would be able to identify skill areas needing additional growth. It was imperative that the internship program not be seen as a criticism of current training programs. In no way is the internship program a replacement to formal education; instead it is an opportunity to enhance skills acquired through interpreter training programs.

The second set of key stakeholders was community interpreters who had either taught in programs in the past or had extensive experience in working with students during placement. The interpreters invited to be part of the community consultation were also registered with OIS as freelance interpreters and several of them had their AVLIC certification. These groups of stakeholders were asked to assist in becoming the architects of the program.

Analysis of the results of candidates on the OIS Videotape Skills Screening indicated common areas of weakness. This data was considered when looking at curriculum development. Two working groups were also established to further identify areas for skill and knowledge development. One group consisted of ASL trainers from the three provincial interpreter education programs. The second group was made up of five working interpreters, four of which held national certification and all of whom had training background. The ASL trainers identified key ASL skill and knowledge areas and rated interpreters' ability to demonstrate these features from novice to expert. The interpreter group identified skills and knowledge lacking in newer interpreters but essential to the task of community interpreters. The overlap between English and ASL proficiency and knowledge of settings and interpreter challenges was clearly noted.

In 2003 the groups met over a period of six months and included information being shared between meetings via ASL video and text format. Collaboratively the groups were able to establish learning outcomes that reflected daily work. A working curriculum was developed which addressed common themes. Each learning module was broken down into the following areas: (1) Content Specific Knowledge, (2) Interpreting Challenges (3) Context, (4) Protocol (5) Ethics. A stand-alone module on Ethics was also developed but the importance of ethical decision-making and the fact that ethical challenges underpin all assignments meant it was an essential part of each module. Modules included clear outcomes to guide lesson planning.

Program structure

The program initially was an eight-month program, seven months in Toronto and a one-month placement in a regional office. Due to the need to generate a higher number of graduates and to increase the pool of registered interpreters the program was shortened to seven months in length, six of which are in Toronto and one month in the region. This was found to be too short a length and the program has returned to an eight-month period. The program consists of a part-time coordinator/trainer, a full time ASL trainer, a digital-video technician and an administrative assistant. Freelance interpreters are hired to complement this staff make up and work one day a week each as mentor/trainers. Additional trainers or workshop presenters are hired to discuss specialized areas.

The interpreter mentors do in-class teaching as well as accompanying interns on community assignments. OIS is the largest employer of community interpreters in Ontario and is therefore able to access consumers at time of booking and seek consent to bring an intern to the assignment. Due to the amount of public relations that has been done there is tremendous acceptance and support for the program. Following community assignments the senior interpreter provides one-to-one feedback to the intern on their individual skill needs. The feedback includes discussion on the broader aspects of interpreting such as analysis of setting, speaker's goals, interpersonal dynamics and discourse analysis. These seem to be areas that are unfamiliar to new interpreters who often lack world knowledge and are reticent to make judgments about the world around them. Coming from a framework of theory they are unable or unwilling to transfer knowledge from one setting to another and tend to be quite concrete, struggling with their belief that to be objective means they are blank slates in each assignment and are not able to anticipate possible outcomes. The program attempts to assist interns to become critical thinkers aware of the dynamics of each situation.

The program accepts four interns per session. The high trainer to intern ratio allows for the development of individual goals. Often classes are team taught so that a two-to-four ratio may occur in class. Interns are expected to complete assignments that reflect community work. Feedback is given on assignments and in class work by both the ASL trainer and the senior interpreters. When on assignment with senior interpreters interns either team interpret or interpret alone, but with the senior interpreter present in order to provide feedback and support. Consumers are aware that the intern has not passed the OIS registration process but that they will be accompanied by a senior interpreter, several of whom are also nationally certified. Guidelines have been developed for the booking co-coordinators so that only assignments that are appropriate for newer interpreters are accepted. Post-assignment feedback incorporates the learning goals outlined in the curriculum and the feedback forms used reflect these goals.

Throughout the seven months in Toronto individual intern plans are monitored. At two-month intervals the trainers meet for a full day session to discuss progress and red-flag concerns. As the senior interpreters are freelancers this meeting allows them to stay connected with each other. The coordinator acts as the central contact throughout the program and ensures trainers are aware of any concerns regarding interns. The measurable exit outcome is successful completion of the OIS Videotape Skills Screening. At the two-month, four-month and six-month point each intern takes a mini-screening to benchmark progress and highlight areas that continue to be problematic. Individual plans incorporate these results.

To apply for the internship program candidates must first take the OIS Videotape Skills Screening in order to assess relative skill and potential to pass the screening following the eight-month training. Consideration is given to candidates applying from under serviced regions as OIS has a mandate to provide interpreting service throughout the province including rural and northern Ontario. If a candidate is from an under serviced area they may be offered additional time in the program in order to ensure that resources are expanded throughout the province. Interns are all graduates of accredited interpreter training programs: some are very recent graduates while others have been working in the field for one to five years.

Those candidates chosen for interviews are seen by two panels. One panel is conducted in ASL and is made up of Deaf interviewers, including the ASL trainer. The coordinator is present at this interview but does not actively conduct the interview. The second interview is made up of interpreter mentor/trainers and is conducted in English. The separate interviews allow candidates to interact in both their L1 and L2 without language interference. It is interesting to note that candidates may display different characteristics depending on the language being used; this may be a result of lack of fluency in their L2 or knowledge and comfort with discourse norms in that language. Successful candidates are asked to make a commitment to working for OIS as either staff or freelance interpreters.

Program emphasis

New interpreters lack the ability to analyze their work. Lacking real fluency in ASL they miss the interplay of related features that affect meaning. Although they may be able to identify these features separately, they have not developed an internal mirror that allows them to see themselves as the listener sees them. An example of where disagreement of features may influence meaning is with the marking of subject and object. Although they may be aware of features such as eye gaze, indexing, role shift and spatial set up as means to mark subject, they often do not have agreement between these features. They may, for example, index to the right but their eye gaze remains central. Attempts to role shift are influenced by inability to return to neutral space. Many of these features are complex and all are inter-related. Newer interpreters, believing that what they *signed* is in fact what was *said* are unable to notice that meaning is dramatically influenced by subtle mistakes. The program places emphasis on self-analysis. Recognizing that one must first have sufficient language knowledge to identify errors, and noting that peer analysis has limitations when both peers exhibit similar errors, trainers spend time, either one-to-one or one-to-four being the interns' "mirror", so that they can begin to notice deceptive interpretation. Too often peer analysis has led to affirmation of incorrect language use. We cannot expect novice interpreters to take on the role of language experts given this lack of language knowledge. The program focuses on developing an internal monitoring system that, if unable to correct the error, at least allows the interpreter to recognize they are unclear and to attempt to seek clarification and assistance.

Along with further language analysis, much emphasis is on discourse analysis and how language changes depending on the goal of the discourse. As mentioned earlier new interpreters often approach the task of interpreting as if they were "blank slates" unable to anticipate speaker's goals, relationships between players, type of discourse and the influence of setting on language use. Throughout the program, and with every assignment worked, the staff guide the interns to become critical thinkers capable of making educated assumptions, testing hypothesis, and being more active in the interpretation process. As affect is one of the features most lacking in a new interpreter's performance – novice interpreters concentrate on what is said not how it is said or how it is intended – much work is done on this area also.

Innovative software was developed for the program that allows for trainer feedback and independent study. The intern views a source movie and interprets the text either from ASL to English or English to ASL. At completion of the interpretation the intern saves the source movie and interpreted movie in one movie file. This blends the two works allowing one to then view a new movie that has both the source language, for example a Deaf role model, with the interns voice perfectly synced. The trainer, when viewing the work, can then stop the movie when a miscue occurs, videotape themselves giving feedback and a link is made between the intern's work and the trainer's feedback. The intern can later view his or her own work that has been saved to the computer. When a link appears another window is shown on the computer with the trainer's feedback. The two windows are linked and shown side by side so that the intern can view their rendition of the interpretation, see the trainer's response, back up and analyze their work again. This unique software allows for independent study and increases the intern's ability to compare and analyze language use. The intern can also add links so that they can compare their original work to a second version.

In addition to this software the program has developed Canadian materials that are setting specific and reflect regional language use. It is often difficult to find materials that reflect the Canadian experience, are authentic and incorporate consumer diversity. For this reason we hired Deaf and hearing role models and developed materials that reflect the diversity of larger cities, including new Canadians, as well as rural communities. Consumers range in age, gender, and educational background. These materials are also used on a broader level with staff and freelance interpreters when workshops are provided to all OIS registered interpreters.

Discussion – Initial outcomes and lessons learned

As of August 2004 the program can report an 87.5% success rate. The first session ended with all interns successfully completing the OIS Videotape Skills Screening and beginning work in various regions of the province. The second session had one intern unsuccessful on the screening. It should be noted however that their outcome results were significantly higher than their original scores on the screening and they will continue to be offered support and use of resources on an unpaid basis to assist in weaker areas. It is anticipated that they will be successful on their next attempt. This continued support is an indication of the commitment of the program to interns, but also the commitment of the interns to the ultimate goal of transitioning into community interpreters. The other three interns from the second session have successfully completed the screening. The successful interns from both sessions have accepted positions ranging from full time staff to freelance interpreters. More than success on the exit criteria – the OIS Videotape Skills Screening – the real success of the program can be measured in the increase in the integrity of the interns' interpreting performance. At the outset of the program the screening results indicated interpreters who were often unable to seek clarification or to monitor their own work. Although candidates are allowed to pause or rewind the videotape screening a maximum of three times per scenario, new interpreters rarely do this. In ASL to English sections they are more aware of their errors, but rarely do they stop the tape to re-construct the interpretation when working from English to ASL. This is again an indication of their lack of fluency in ASL and an inability to analyze their work for accuracy. At the end of the program all of the screenings showed interns who were stopping the tape to seek clarification or to change their original interpretation. This is perhaps the most dramatic outcome as it has implications on how they will conduct themselves in actual assignments. If an interpreter appears confident in their interpretation, even if the work is deceptive, it is often difficult for the consumer, either Deaf or hearing, to question the message. When an interpreter is aware that they are unclear, even if they are not accurately able to correct themselves, they open up the possibility of dialogue with the participants. A consumer, seeing the interpreter stop and re-attempt the interpretation, is aware that there are difficulties and may suggest alternative choices or assist in clarifying misunderstandings. This allows participants to become actively involved in the process and means the interpreter is more likely to accept responsibility for the interpretation. These skills are much more important than the simple passing of a measurable outcome such as a screening tool. Changes in interpretation strategies will carry the learning process far beyond the original formal induction and into everyday practice.

The fact that the OIS Interpreter Internship Program was developed with community partners meant that the community felt a degree of ownership and a vested interest in seeing the program succeed. Had the agency developed and implemented the program in isolation it would be seen as agency-owned and would not have the same support from the college programs and working interpreters. Due to this "community ownership" and the success of the program we have been able to develop a larger pool of interpreter/trainers, both Deaf and hearing. There is excitement in the community and an interest in being part of the program as it provides a learning experience for both senior interpreters and interns. The curriculum is fully developed and lesson plans exist for each module. The interpreters who were part of the original think-tank group mentor new trainers that come into the program. The heavy emphasis on community assignments, and the rich experience this offers to new interpreters, has created loyalty to the process of community interpreting. This is noted among senior interpreters, many of whom had moved from the grassroots assignments such as medical appointments to business setting, as well as with new interns who are given a chance to understand the community at a different level.

The original outcomes, both statistically and in terms of community perspective, are strong indicators that a formalized induction process is one of the ways to successfully transition from interpreter student to community interpreter. It seems clear that providing structure and intense feedback allows new interpreters to balance practice with theory and to navigate the slippery road from novice to working interpreter. It would seem likely that such programs would be beneficial in other settings as well. The professionalisation of the field can only be assisted by internship opportunities for new interpreters.

Acknowledgements

OIS gratefully acknowledges the Ministry of Health and the Ontario Government in funding this innovative project. We also would like to recognize the members of the original think tank groups – the ASL trainers from the three Ontario interpreter programs and the senior interpreters who worked as partners with us to develop this program.

Additional note

At time of writing the statistic for success has changed to 100% success on the OIS Videotape Skills Screening as of six months post-program. The program continues to offer bi-yearly intake.

On-line and between the lines

The internet and glossary production for public service interpreters

Jane Straker
City University, London, United Kingdom

The present paper aims to share some know-how and sources of information found useful for glossary production courses, addressing teachers and students alike. Drawing on my experience from systematic, professional "terminology" work and from teaching glossary production classes, I argue that developing small-scale glossaries in fields relevant to the interpreter's work is both practically and personally rewarding. The paper also reflects experiences from workshop settings, such as the one organised for an international group of tutors and practising public service interpreters at the Stockholm Critical Link 4.

Background

Over the last ten years in teaching public service interpreting in the United Kingdom, one particular aspect of language study has become more manageable. More data is being made available on-line in the areas of health, law and local government and access to the information via the Internet is increasing in homes, cafés and public libraries as well as colleges and universities. Whilst much information is available in many languages, glossary production and terminology management continue to challenge interpreting students at City University and at City College, Birmingham. Comparing my experience of teaching glossary production to these students and to students on a postgraduate translation diploma course I noted that the translators found the exercise, though difficult, more easily realisable than many of my UK interpreting students.

Graduates of the Escuela de Traductores in Buenos Aires have for some years been studying translation diploma courses under an agreement with City University in London. Nearly all of the modules were structured using a distance-learning programme, although some students came to London and attended face-to-face classes. From 1999 to 2004 I taught these translators Spanish/English glossary production (science or technology fields only), in London on 10-hour short courses, and, via the Internet, for those in Argentina.

In all groups of translation students competence levels in both English and mother tongue were extremely high. The imperative to meet draft deadlines was strictly observed. Some of the finished 200-word glossaries would merit publication, notably three separate student pieces of work, one on genetically modified organisms, another on bridge construction and one on pacemakers. The last two were refereed by notable experts in the fields of civil engineering and cardiology.

This contrasted with the groups of Spanish-speaking and other interpreting students who live permanently in London, who had lost flexibility and fluency in their mother tongue and whose command of formal written English was unpractised and unpolished. For trainee interpreters who have been away from formal study for many years, or those new to the dedicated study of L^1 rather than L^2 the challenges have also been formidable. Speakers of languages such as Bengali, Cantonese, Farsi, Italian, Kurdish, Portuguese, Russian and Somali, have started glossary production without a background of translator training, writing not talking, and using unfamiliar compilation, archival and retrieval methods from written texts.

Praxis Language Unit in East London, in association with City University and SOAS (School of Oriental and African Studies, University of London) offered a 40-hour 'pre-glossary' Introduction to Terminology course to practising interpreters as well as dedicated, single language Glossary Production courses. With funding from the local government authority and a charitable foundation, courses were made available, at no cost to the individual, to selected students who were already working as interpreters in the public sector. The interpreter groups and the translator groups had been given similar descriptors before their glossary courses began. Differences between the groups could be classified as follows:

(a) attitudes to speed of response: interpreters must be ready 'on the spot' with instant solutions, whilst translators can take time to reflect and consult.

(b) varied accessibility to and familiarity with various types of reference sources, including bi-/ and monolingual dictionaries and specialist source/target texts.

(c) a 'listening and speaking' culture rather than one of 'reading and writing'.

(d) very often the interpreters lacked, but the translators had, background education and training in linguistics, and most specifically, socio-linguistics, morphology, syntax, semantics, lexicology and dialectology.

(e) relatively poor keyboard skills of many interpreters compared with translators.

(f) in the case of certain languages, e.g. Somali, and also Kurdish, a dearth of written materials or corpora from which to start extracting terms for glossary development.

If glossary production is demonstrably difficult for trainee public service interpreters, is there a useful purpose to its inclusion on an interpreting course? I think so. Both of the student cohorts, the graduate translators and the experienced interpreters, had in common a frenetic enthusiasm for acquisition of specialist terms. Many students also had a deep personal interest in their chosen glossary topic. Debates about social and geographic variants for terms, together with normative and descriptivist battles were never far from the surface in class. Argentinian distance learners were not entirely deprived of this interactivity as there was a chat room available on-line, but were perhaps more anxious to get their tasks completed within tight schedules than to spend time sharing opinions with colleagues.

Glossary production for public-service interpreters is not very different from the work of terminologists. Many years ago, as a trainee terminologist at the European Parliament in Luxembourg, I conducted a small survey of Parliament translators, hoping to discover what they thought of the Bureau de Terminologie, where I worked. Translators then told me that if they found out, through their own reading and research, how to translate a 'new' term, they kept it to themselves; they did not have time to ease the workload of terminologists by letting us know about it. While we compiled specialist, paper-based, multilingual glossaries all day, they were too busy translating their daily quota of pages to contact us. Nowadays, using search engines and e-mail, translators and interpreters can consult colleagues, friends and the great storehouse of information on the Internet in seconds rather than waiting days or weeks. In *Terminologie et Traduction 3*, Baudouin and Swalef have made comparisons between 'hits' of various search engines. "Google is the most wide-used by EU Commission translators", they assert (2001: 12). In a recent UNESCO publication, David Block discusses his research on the "Internet as a means of disseminating information, a medium for exchange and a market place" (2004: 35). He concludes that languages other than English (the examples refer to Catalan, Hawaiian, and Tamil) can gain considerably as distant speakers link up via the Net.

Drawing on my later experience I will summarise what I have found to be valuable information for both tutors and students in glossary production classes.

Terms and terminology

What is a term, the starting point for glossary production? The short answer is that it is a word used in specialist context. But a term is not always a word. Pearson (1998) elaborates on the differences between words and terms in the first chapter of *Terms in Context*. In *Entre signe et concept*, an illuminating book on the relation between terms and concept, Loïc Depecker (2002) gives the essential base for students of terms, terminology and glossary production. One way of grasping what terms are and their function is to look at a thing such as 'lawn seed', a condition such as 'painful', or a relationship such as '=' and then consider who wants or needs to define these concepts precisely and unequivocally. If the answer is a specialist in a particular domain such as botany or medicine or mathematics, then the word, combination of words or symbol is likely to be a term. That term will represent a fundamental concept and will have an internationally agreed definition.

Various organisations, national, international and supranational have been established to deal with terminology, i.e. concepts and their representations created by domain experts, as well as terminological methods, data and tools. Many of them are in Europe, but not all.

Infoterm, the international information centre for terminology, founded in 1971 by UNESCO, is in Vienna. As a clearing-house and referral centre for terminology, it deals with 50 million records of terminological data, increasing at a rate of 10% per year.

The International Standards Organisation (ISO) convenes technical committees of numerous experts (TCs) to negotiate definitions of concepts. ISO/TC37 is the terminology technical committee; established in 1951, it deals with principles of terminology management. TC1, established in 1908, now has 21 participating member states and both standardises and co-ordinates terms and definitions and gives equivalent terms in different languages. There are international standards on the presentation of translation and on terminology, on documentation and on graphic symbols as well as on products. There is an ISO recommendation on definitions and on terms.

The *International Institute for Terminology Research* (IITF), established in Austria in 1989, promotes teacher exchanges and develops terminology summer schools. Other bodies deal with specific languages. The *Réseau international de terminologie et néologie* (Rint) is concerned mostly with French language. The *Red iberoamericana de terminología* (RITerm) is primarily for Latin American Spanish. The *Hellenic Organisation for Standardisation* (ELOT) deals with Greek terminology. The *European Association for Terminology* (EAT), founded in 1996, is not exclusively concerned with European Union languages as evidenced in their

1999 conference, which included a paper on terminology in African languages. Within the EU there are a number of initiatives such as the *European Terminology Information Server* (ETIS), the Commission's programme for the *Multilingual Information Society* (MLIS).

Terminology, which is both the study of terms and the activity of terminologists, has progressed speedily in the last twenty years with the development of computational linguistics and corpus linguistics. And the terminology octopus has quite a few arms wiggling in different directions. One arm is computing, another philosophy, another linguistics, and another is national politics. Not all interpreters will wish to study terminology in depth, but an understanding of its scope is essential for glossary writing.

Glossaries

The gloss, according the Oxford Advanced Learner's Dictionary of Current English, is "a note or comment added to a piece of writing to explain a difficult word or phrase" (1971: 366). The practice of adding interlinear comments ('between the lines') was used at very early dates to clarify obscure meanings in religious texts. A collection of such explanations is a glossary, very often found as an appendix in a book, article or leaflet which has been written by a specialist, but then edited by a non-specialist who has a view to increasing the readership by making very explicit those terms which the author took for granted as clear and unambiguous.

In *Working with Specialized Language*, Bowker and Pearson describe one type of glossary as containing "lists of terms and their equivalents in one or more foreign languages" (2002: 137). Far removed from these simplified word-for-word term lists are "glossaries which every translation student and language student dreams of having" (ibid: 138). In this treasure house of a glossary, terms are defined, shown in context with synonyms and variants in different registers, and eventually translated. It is this very useful type of glossary which interpreters are encouraged to produce. By glossing (explaining) given specialist terms, interpreters can take charge of terms instead of fearing them. Even Bowker and Pearson (2002), whose book *Working with Specialised Language* is subtitled "practical guide to using corpora for translators, technical writers and subject specialists", include a glossary of over fifty terms.

A type of glossing known as 'jargon-busting' is sometimes used to describe the unravelling of texts such as local government documents, instructions or directives which need to reach a wider audience than a small in-house team. In a comprehensive discussion of the term 'jargon', included in: *Terminology: an Introduction*, Picht and Draskau (1985) list ten definitions by various authors. They offer a taxonomy reflecting these definitions of jargon and its relationship to slang, cant, colloquial language, regional language, dialect, standard language, and language for special purposes (LSP) (ibid.: 12).

A printed or Internet glossary of terms compiled by someone else, maybe by a professional terminologist, in an attractive and portable format, can tempt an interpreter into buying or downloading. A handy work tool, giving us clear explanations of difficult or specialist terms so as to make them understandable to the layperson is a joy and delight. My favourites usually have pictures or diagrams, are sometimes called 'Understanding X' or are written for children.

A trawl of glossaries available on the Internet, some for sale, but often free, can produce a wide range of publications varying hugely in price, reliability and authenticity. Multilingual terminology databases have been in existence since the 1950's, according to Gerhard Budin and Alan Melby (2000) who analyse the problems of accessibility of multilingual terminological resources, but the compilation, printing and publication of even monolingual small circulation glossaries is very expensive. Some dictionaries are published on CD-ROM discs; by regularly updating discs readers keep up with linguistic changes. Glossaries on disc are easy to update and students should be encouraged to store their work electronically.

Domains and definitions

A glossary starts with a need to explore an area of activity where specialists are using LSP, containing terminology that a non-specialist, such as an interpreter, finds difficult to understand. The first challenge for a glossary writer is to limit an area of study from very broad to very narrow. In my experience, students find this particularly difficult and want to choose enormously broad domains such as 'health', 'law', or 'sport', unmanageable by any one individual with limited time. The construction of a Spanish-English microthesaurus in the field of doping control is not recommendable as a project for one student alone, but a task for many Spanish-English experts. Even the frequently chosen domains of 'immigration' or 'breast cancer' have proven too broad. Some students would choose a glossary topic because they thought there was a ready-made version in the Internet, which they could use. Small and very precise topics, e.g. 'local rubbish collection services', 'the language of schoolteachers when discussing pupils' progress at parents' evenings', 'khat' or 'photographic paper' have proved achievable. When students take the opportunity to gloss terms with which they are unfamiliar, it can turn out to be an enjoyable exercise. One Birmingham student wrote in a self-evaluation following the completion of a 10 term glossary assignment: "It was a golden opportunity for me to spend time on researching a lot of terms and meet new websites [...]

the best thing I learnt is how to gain as much information as possible from (the) corpus".

It is not always easy to decide whether any given element in a body of text (corpus) is a term or part of language for general purposes (LGP). In order to make a decision whether or not to include a term in a glossary, it may be necessary to find a definition of the term. Does defining require special training or do we all know how to define from quite a young age? In an article on children's language, Bonnie Litowitz (1977) suggests five stages of learning to define, starting at where level 1, where the child makes a simple gesture in answer to an adult's question: 'What's a snap?' At level 2 the child gives an ambiguous, telegraphic response to the adult's question: 'What's a bicycle?': 'A man, a lady'. The level 3 answer to the same question is 'You ride and you fall off or you could use it to ride to Bruce's not always in the street'. This idiosyncratic reply comes from the child's own experience. At level 4 the child is aware that word meanings are shared by others. Adult: 'What's a knife?' Child: 'A knife is when you cut with it'. By the age of 9 children are clearly able to define; level 5 shows children defining X as a kind of Y which has the features of Z. Examples given are 'What's a shoe?' – 'A thing you put on your foot' and 'What's an apple?' – 'It's a sort of fruit and it's round and green or red and it grows on trees and we eat it' (Litowitz 1977: 294–296).

A gap certainly exists between the child's informal definition of an apple and the description that might be given by a botanist. The level of precision of definition for any given term in a glossary must be decided by the requirements of the interpreter (or translator). If the answer is too simple an answer, as, for instance, Q: 'What is a car?' A: either 'that' + pointing gesture or 'It's a machine', and the interpreter is not much further forward. Too complex a definition of a disease such as schizophrenia will leave an interpreter more confused than when they started. Helpful examples are quoted by Heidi Suonuuti in a Nordterm *Guide to Terminology* (1997: 17–24). This booklet also contains a summary of ISO standards used in terminology. Once a transparent, accurate and unambiguous definition of a term has been located, it will be easier to gloss since there will be an indication both of the semantic field and of register. If a context showing usage is given, then the job is further simplified. Thus the English term 'case' may belong to the field of medicine, law, packaging or linguistics, but only its surrounding context will help us to choose which one.

The crucial stage in glossary development is when an interpreter can let go of the formal definition and take charge of a term by explaining it in layperson's language. 'Putting it in your own words', paraphrasing, maybe simplifying, or possibly expanding are all valid strategies when glossing a term. As interpreting demands accurate transmission of an oral message, in similar fashion, a gloss should explain but not distort the intended meaning of a term.

Corpus linguistics, computing and terminology

Corpora are bodies of language; when stored in a computer memory, they can be used as an electronic library, consulted by students and analysts of language. Using electronic tagging programmes, studies of term frequency, concordance, classification and retrieval all become feasible short-term exercises. Pearson defines corpus studies and corpus linguistics fully in *Terms in Context* (1998). Interpreters and translators, who need dictionaries as basic tools for work, are already benefiting from progress in corpus-based dictionaries and parallel corpora studies. Over the last two decades monolingual and bi-/multilingual lexicography has changed in speed and range. With the use of corpora, dictionary entries can be compiled using written texts and transcribed discourse collected from a multitude of sources provided by these huge samples of 'real' language.

If corpora can be used for dictionaries, are they useful for glossary production? Quite clearly, large bodies of written text can offer useful samples from which to choose terms, but for interpreters the terms that need glossing may well be part of untranscribed discourse. When considering the relevance of corpora for glossary translation, we see a vast amount of material already collected in English, French, Spanish, German and some other indo-European languages, but no great electronic storage chests in other languages used by UK public service interpreters.

Some further computing tools are available for both interpreters and translators and commercial software packages such as MultiTerm® and Translator's Workbench® can help the organisation of term storage and retrieval. Terminology products can be useful for specific languages. The Quebec Government in Canada funds the *Office de la langue française* (OLF), which produces the *Grand Dictionnaire de Terminologie* with 3 million terms in English and French in 200 domains. SYSTRAN is an 18 language combination translation programme with over 3.2 M dictionary entries and is used by the Brussels-based translation company EUROLOGOS. However many shortcuts we may find to term management, the end of the glossary production trail nearly always leads to hard work for experienced and inexperienced interpreter alike, learning to define and categorise, to probe and enquire, and eventually to interpret more competently.

Benefits of public service interpreters' glossary productions

There are professional and personal gains which students of public service interpreting can make, even at an early stage, by studying glossary production and producing their own small-scale, bi-lingual glossaries. Glossary production is an activity that should help move trainee interpreters away from concentrating on 'the word' into developing an automatic sense of the primacy of 'the idea' as the building block for any interpreting practice. Similar to the oral exercise of re-formulation, which many of us use to train students in simultaneous interpreting, glossary production demands considerable personal effort on the student's part. However, this written exercise can be achieved without the pressures involved when an instantaneous oral response is required.

Suggested benefits of learning and practising glossary production when training public service interpreters can be listed as follows:

(a) Students can achieve a finished glossary that is of *practical use* in their everyday interpreting for public service assignment in health, legal, or local government settings.

(b) Students can *maximise effort* in a class by sharing the fruits of their work with colleagues; swapping glossaries with other who have the same L^1 is possible, but exchanging with students who only share L^2 (e.g. English) is also useful.

(c) Glossary production leads students into areas with which they are unfamiliar, *de-mystifying terms* which may have been "no-go" areas, and lowers those thresholds of fear and panic easily spring up, especially when dealing with personal, disturbing, intimate or taboo topics.

(d) Practising the philosophy of 'I don't know the answer, but I'll find somebody who does', students can learn to diffuse the pain of linguistic, and especially semantic challenges, at their own pace, clarifying and *preparing their minds to be more enquiring,* leaving to the experts the task of specialist definitions.

(e) Glossary production *empowers students* as they capture the meaning and essence of a term; self-esteem rises when an interpreter can use that specialist term in an appropriate and accurate manner, or, at least, understands it in context.

(f) Current students can use the Internet for *potential links to specialists* in public service domains, to interpreter and translator colleagues, national and international term-banks, terminology enquiry services and to huge reference sources such as the million-word British National Corpus collection of English language or the Google bank of 88 million images.

(g) Students can become adept at glossary production, especially using commercial mono-/ or multilingual terminology software packages; many public service institutions as well as commercial firms now use glossaries in their outreach publicity and to improve a communications strategy. A skilled bi-/ multilingual glossary writer could therefore find this new professional expertise as *marketable* as interpreting.

References

Baudouin, S. & Swalef, H. 2001. Search Engines, in *Terminologie et Traduction 3*.

Block, D. 2004. Globalization, Transnational Communication and the Internet, in *International Journal of Multicultural Societies* 6:1, UNESCO (22–37), available on the internet at www.unesco.org/shs/ijms/vol6/issue1

Bowker, L. & Pearson, J. 2002. *Working with specialized language – a practical guide to using corpora*. London: Routledge.

Budin, G. & Melby, A. 2000. Accessibility of Multilingual Resources – Current Problems and Prospects for the Future, SALT Project EU Commission IST 5th Framework Programme.

Clarke, P. 1994. *French Glossary of Car and Driving Terms*. London: Impact Books.

Depecker, L. 2002. *Entre signe et concept*. Paris: Presses de la Sorbonne nouvelle.

Litowitz, B. 1977. Learning to make defintions, in *Journal of Child Language, 4*.

Oxford Advanced Learners' Dictionary of Current English, 3rd Edition 1971, Oxford University Press: Oxford.

Pearson, J. 1998. *Terms in Context*. Amsterdam/Philadelphia: John Benjamins.

Picht, H. & Draskau, J. 1985. *Terminology: an introduction*, Guildford: University of Surrey.

Stein, S. 1999. *Learning, Teaching and Researching on the Internet*. Harlow: Pearson Education Limited.

Suonuuti, H. 1997. *Guide to Terminology*. Helsinki: Teniikan Sanastokeskus.

Interpreter training from scratch

Beppie van den Bogaerde
Hogeschool Utrecht, the Netherlands

In this paper a brief overview is given of an interpreter-training programme in Utrecht, the Netherlands, which admits students who have no or very little prior knowledge of Sign Language of the Netherlands, *Nederlandse Gebarentaal* (henceforth: NGT). The paper will focus on the NGT and interpreting modules and on the assessment procedures developed within this programme. Special attention is paid to a description of the practice periods (in-service training) of the students in the final year of the study, and an example is given of the assessment lists that are used to observe students and their performance on a linguistic, a technical (interpreting skills) and a professional level.

Introduction

In the Netherlands, as in many countries, interpreting between a spoken language and a sign language has long been the field of Children of Deaf Adults (codas): hearing children who are raised by deaf parents using a sign language in the home and who thus become native signers. Inherent to the emancipation of deaf communities in many western countries in the last quarter of the last century (Woll & Ladd 2003) the demand for professional, qualified interpreters has sharply increased. There are insufficient numbers of codas with the desire to train as interpreters and thus meet the needs of the Deaf community. As a consequence, many hearing people, who are not native signers, are being trained to become interpreters in NGT and Dutch.

In this paper I will give an outline of how we took up the challenge to develop a Bachelor's degree curriculum for interpreter NGT-Dutch. In 1997 the sign language of the Netherlands was only partially described (and even now this is still the case). It has been taught as a second language from the 1990s onward and hardly any teaching material on a higher vocational level was available when we started interpreter training; no didactics existed, as far as we knew, to train interpreters from scratch within a four years period. In the next sections I will give some information on the teaching of NGT as a foreign language, and focus on how we assess our students during the practice periods in community interpreting.

The four year Bachelor programme[1]

In contrast to languages like English, French and German, which are taught as foreign languages in secondary schools, NGT is not part of the curriculum. As a result most students have no or hardly any knowledge of NGT when they enter our programme. The focus in the first two years of study is thus on their acquisition and learning of NGT. Furthermore the students are offered subjects like general linguistics, communication, Dutch, interpreting skills and techniques, transliteration, ethics and psychology. In the third and fourth year, while language teaching continues, the focus shifts to interpreting skills, which the students practise in the field, with continuous feedback from a mentor in the field and from teachers in the school. A mentor is a fully qualified interpreter, actively working in the field, who has followed a course in student coaching, with the ability to follow the student's performance and progress, and who can assess the student on the three levels and give feedback.

We base our curriculum on three major competences: a) NGT skills (and Dutch, but this will not be described here) (lexicon, grammar, fluency), b) interpreting skills (memory, voicing, lag time, interruption etc.) and c) professional skills (attitude, knowledge of Deaf culture (Van den Bogaerde & Stuifzand 2003), ethics etc.).

We offer a modular system, where the weight of each module is measured in credits (ec: European credit transfer system). Each ec is worth 28 hours of study for the student, roughly consisting of 7 hours of class and 21 hours of self-study, exams and such. The total BA programme is 240 ec (= 6720 hours). The students are expected to show initiative in what they want to learn themselves in the form of portfolios and by keeping a personal learning plan (PLP) in which they monitor their own progress.

---

1.   In January 2005 we started a MA programme for teachers of NGT (first degree) and a Deaf Studies MA.

Figure 1. 'to sign' in NGT on the Effatha website (www.effathaguyot.nl)

NGT skills

Over the four years, with decreasing frequency, the students have to study NGT for 60 ec, which is 1932 hours (28% of the programme). This includes pragmatics and syntax, with emphasis on the lexicon and fluency. At the moment there are some 10.000 signs available on CD-ROMs (www.gebarencentrum.nl), on the internet (www.effathaguyot.nl) (see Figure 1) and on video.

The students are offered more signs in class and in interaction with deaf people, as not all signs can be found in dictionaries.

Besides being integrated in the NGT classes, special attention is paid to NGT syntax in separate modules, as well as to language use and fluency.

Interpreting skills

The modules of interpreting skills comprise 52 ec (1428 hours, 21% of total programme) and are offered from the first year onward with increasing frequency up to year four. Besides transliteration, and interpreting from NGT to Dutch and vice versa, the students are also taught to interpret in Sign Supported Dutch (NmG) for clients with late onset of deafness and they have to follow an introductory course in communicating with deaf-blind people (which they can follow up with a minor, see below). From year one, special attention is paid to voicing (interpreting from NGT to spoken Dutch).

Professional skills

Professional skills are practised in several modules, in total 36 ec (1008 hours, 15% of total programme) which comprise Deaf culture, deaf-blindness, psychology, multicultural society, intercultural conflicts, ethics, second language acquisition, social and communication skills and what we have called "intervision". This last module is designed for ethical training that supports our students to be independent, considerate and trustworthy interpreters, who take into account their role in the communication process and take responsibility for this (Turner & Harrington 2001). We teach them to reflect critically on their own and colleagues' professional performance and to give feedback in a supportive and motivating manner.

Minors

In the Bachelor/master structure that was introduced in 2002, students have a major of 210 ec, and a minor of at least 30 ec. We offer our interpreting students the following minors:

– Speech-to-text interpreting (note-takers). The students learn to type on a special keyboard (Vey-board), which enables them to type at speech rate (goal: 500–700 letters per minute), and to transliterate spoken and written Dutch consecutively and simultaneously.
– Interpreting for young children, and for people with minimal language skills. The focus is on adapting the level of interpreting to the cognitive level of the children/adults, mainly in educational settings.
– Interpreting for people with late onset of deafness, deaf blind people and in (Mental) Health services. There are three separate courses that focus on a particular group of deaf people. Students become aware of the special needs of each group, and acquire the appropriate vocabulary, communication form and professional attitude.

Description of practice periods

During the four years of training the students are sent out into the deaf world, not only to learn about Deaf culture, but also to set up a network within the community, consisting of deaf people, hearing and deaf parents of deaf children, and professionals working in the field of deafness. In total they have to do 34 credits (925 hours, or 14% of the total programme) on practice training, which can either be integrated in the various modules in the form of assignments, or are full periods spent outside the school in the second, third and fourth year. We have formulated three goals for the practice periods:

Table 1. Description of the practice periods in the 4-year programme

Year	Form	Brief description	Ec's
1	Integrated in modules of Deaf Culture	8 assignments in the Deaf community, to be discussed in class	2
2	1 Integrated in modules of Deaf Culture 2 Free choice work 3 Observation	1 a family with deaf member(s) is visited, or a workplace with deaf employees, with a PPT presentation as exam 2 the student does voluntary work in a Deaf organisation, or visits a similar training institution abroad, or does preparing work for a minor in the third year (written paper) 3 each student observes his/her mentor in 10 assignments, and observes other interpreters in four settings of his/her own choice (written and oral discussion)	5
3	With mentor and co-students	The students work in couples, observe their mentor, and start to interpret with mentor present + feedback afterwards (portfolio, PLP and personal assessment)	8
4	Independent, with visits from mentor and teacher	The students work in couples or alone, and on the basis of written reports, portfolio and PLP and observations in school and on the job are continuously assessed by mentor, teacher and themselves.	21

– NGT practice, interacting with deaf people and hearing people of different language background
– Interpreting practice, feedback from mentor and clients on performance
– Contact with Deaf culture, practice of professional skills.

Table 1 shows a more detailed description of the contents of the practice periods.

During all periods the students are assessed on a linguistic, interpreting and professional level. This is done by teachers of the school, and in the later periods also by a mentor. The students also have to assess themselves, formulate learning goals and track their own progress. There is always intensive communication between the mentor, the student and the school, so that the student will have optimal feedback during his or her training.

In all years the student, the mentor and the teacher at school fill in assessment lists[2] (see Section 4) on the performance of the student. If a student is not up to the level required for a particular assignment or practice goal, the student is given

---

2. The assessment lists are the result of a joined effort of many teachers. Thanks to Lida Blokker, Pieter Bodbijl, Irma Bosman, Ester Bot, Belinda Dolman, Martie Emmerzaal, Susanne Heuff, Corline Koolhof, Greetje Kreulen, Nicoline de Pater, Mariska van Scheijndel, Maartje

a chance to do extra work in the field or in the school and assessed a second time before given permission to move on to the next stage.

Assessment in school and 'on the job'

Throughout their training, the students need to be assessed on a linguistic, interpreting and professional level, by themselves, the mentors and the teachers in the school. We have developed assessment lists, which are used from year one to four. These lists do not change very much over the years, although understandably the focus of attention may shift, according to the level of NGT fluency, interpreting skills and professional experience. In Appendix I an English translation is given of one of the assessment lists, used in the fourth year. Not only is it used within the practice assignments of that year, but also in the NGT classes and the Interpreting modules. Because (parts of) the same list are used in these three different contexts during the whole year, we gain a thorough insight into the performance of the student and his/her progress on the three levels NGT fluency, interpreting skills and professionalism. In the Appendix also a short explanation of terms and content is supplied.

The list consists of two parts: an Assessment of Linguistic and Interpreting skills (ALIS) and an Assessment of Interaction skills (AIS).

The ALIS list has 7 items: 1. Introduction to deaf and hearing clients, 2. Interruption, 3. Quality of translation which is subdivided into a) course of conversation, b) NGT to Dutch content, c) NGT to Dutch use of language, d) Dutch to NGT content and e) Dutch to NGT use of language. For each item a certain number of points can be obtained, which are specified on the list. The score per item is then assigned a certain weight, for instance, 2. Interruption is weighted once (X1) but 3b NGT to Dutch content has X4, which means that the score is multiplied by four, because at this point in the study (fourth year) the content of the message is still subject to many mistakes, while we expect students to make few errors in the way they interrupt (since this has been practised already extensively in the third year).

The AIS list is specified for interpreting in a conversation between several people, for example in a community setting. There are 6 items on this list: 1. Manner of introduction, 2. Decision on position, 3. Neutrality of interpreter, 4. Way of interruption, 5. Dealings with clients, 6. Attitude. As in the ALIS list, the various

Sleiffer, Willem Terpstra, Nicolette de Wandeler, Tineke Williams, Erica Zeegers and many others.

items can differ in weight. The weight can change over the years, depending on the focus of the assignment or the level of the module.

Final remarks

In this paper a very brief description has been given of the sign language and interpreting modules used in our training programme. We find that the intensive training of our students on the job, in the form of practice periods, gives the students enough experience to be able to function as independent, professional interpreters in sign language and Dutch, for different deaf and hearing clients. The close monitoring of the student's progress by means of assessment lists, which are used by the students, their mentors and the teachers in the schools alike, makes it possible to discern patterns in their performance on a linguistic (NGT and Dutch), a technical (interpreting skills) and a professional (attitude and performance) level. Even though most students have no prior knowledge of NGT, and we have only four years to teach them the language *and* train them as professional interpreters, we are confident that when they graduate, they can start as professional interpreters in the Deaf community of the Netherlands.

References

Leary, T. F. 1957. *Interpersonal diagnosis of personality*. New York: Ronald Press.
Turner, G. H. & Harrington, F. 2001. *Interpreting interpreting: studies and reflections on sign language interpreting*. Coleford: Douglas McLean.
Van den Bogaerde, B. & Stuifzand, M. 2003. Sign Language of the Netherlands and Deaf Culture. *Academic Exchange Quarterly*, Summer 2003, volume 7, issue 2. http://rapidintellect. com/AEQweb.
Woll, B. & Ladd, P. 2003. "Deaf Communities." In *Oxford Handbook of Deaf studies, language and education*, M. Marschark & P.E. Spencer (eds), 151–163. Oxford: Oxford University Press.
www.effathaguyot.nl
www.gebarencentrum.nl
http://ngt.feo.hvu.nl/

Appendix

a)   Assessment of linguistic and interpreting skills (4th year, also module TV11)

General: if you cannot score, don't count. Fill in: not applicable and adapt score. Items marked
* are explained in section c) Explanation of terms.

Assignment 1 Interpreting a meeting				
	F/P	Points	Weight	Total
Introduction to deaf and hearing clients		0-1-2-3	X 1	
1. Uses correct modality *		**Scores:**		
2. If needed, explain function *		0-2 items 0 point		
3. Decides on method (with deaf client)		3-4 items 1 point		
4. Decides on voicing (with deaf client)		5 items 2 points		
5. Consult with chairperson *		6 items 3 points		
6. Correct position *				
Interruption		0-1-2-3	X 1	
7. At the right moment		**Scores:**		
8. In the correct modality *		0 items 0 points		
9. Give justification		1-2 items 1 point		
10. Indicates until when has been interpreted		3 items 2 points		
		4 items 3 points		
Quality of translation				
Course of conversation		0-1-2-3	X 2	
11. All participants can contribute sufficiently *		**Scores:**		
12. Interruption at necessary moments *		0-1 item 0 points		
13. Makes adjacent pairs		2 items 1 point		
14. Frequency of interruption: not irritating.		3 items 2 points		
		4 items 3 points		
NGT to Dutch: Content		0-1-2-3	X 4	
15. Quality of omissions *		**Scores:**		
16. Quality of replacements *		0 items 0 points		
17. Quality of additions *		1-2 items 1 point		
18. Correct relations *		3-4 items 2 points		
19. Correct summary *		5 items 3 points		
NGT to Dutch: Use of language		0 1 2 3	X 1	
20. No supporting signs		**Scores:**		
21. Register		0 items 0 points		
22. Grammatically correct sentences *		1-3 items 1 point		
23. Fluent utterances		4 items 2 points		
24. Volume of voice		5 items 3 points		

Assignment 1 Interpreting a meeting			
Dutch to NGT: Content		*0-1-2-3* |*X 4*	
25. Quality of omissions *		**Scores:**	
26. Quality of replacements *		0 items 0 points	
27. Quality of additions *		1-2 items 1 point	
28. Correct relations *		3-4 items 2 points	
29. Correct surmise *		5 items 3 points	
Dutch to NGT: Use of language		*0-1-2-3* |*X 1*	
30. No whispering or voice		Scores:	
31. Register		0 items 0 points	
32. Grammatically correct utterances *		1-2 items 1 point	
33. Fluent utterances.		3-4 items 2 points	
34. Signing space		5 items 3 points	
Pass at 65 % of total 69 points = 45 points			*F/P*

b) Assessment of Interaction skills

Assignment 1 Interpreting a conversation				
	F/P	*Points*	*Weight*	*Total*
Manner of introduction		*0-1-2-3*	*X 2*	
35. Friendly		Scores:		
36. Calm		½ point per item		
37. With both clients				
38. Considering the situation				
39. Correct positioning (Leary)				
Decide on position		*0-1-2-3*	*X 1*	
40. With hearing client		Scores:		
41. With deaf client		0 items 0 points		
42. Assertive		1 items 1 point		
		2 items 2 points		
		3 items 3 points		
Neutrality of interpreter		*0-1-2-3*	*X 2*	
43. Own norms and values are not noticeable		Scores:		
44. Suitable clothes		0 items 0 points		
45. Appropriate behaviour		1 items 1 point		
		2 items 2 points		
		3 items 3 points		

Assignment 1 Interpreting a conversation				
Way of interruption		*0-1-2-3*	*X 2*	
46. By means of an 'I-message'		**Scores:**		
47. Appropriate intonation		0 items 0 points		
48. Assertive		1 items 1 point		
		2 items 2 points		
		3 items 3 points		
Dealings with clients		*0-1-2-3*	*X 3*	
49. Appropriate distance (dependent on situation)		*Scores:*		
50. Equal approach of deaf and hearing clients		0 items 0 points		
51. Friendly and functionally appropriate dealings with personal question(s)		1 items 1 point		
		2 items 2 points		
		3 items 3 points		
Attitude		*0-1-2-3*	*X 2*	
52. Interpreter shows confidence		*Scores:*		
53. Active listening posture / attitude		0 items 0 points		
54. Interpreter is alert and concentrated		1 items 1 point		
		2 items 2 points		
		3 items 3 points		
Pass at 36 points				

c) Explanation of terms

Main assessment: did the student attain the purpose of the assignment?

The items to be assessed are clustered. Each cluster is scored on a scale of 0 to 3. The *scores* are given according to the *points* and are dependent on the number of items that can be scored Failed (F) or Passed (P).

Each cluster has been given a certain weight. Together the *scores* and **the weight** prevent the student from passing, if *less essential parts* are added up together, for example the introduction.

Four out of 5 items need to be passed if 2 points are to be scored and 5 items for the full 3 points. Together with weight (X1) this prevents this part (introduction) to be measured too heavy in the total score. Compare this to cluster *NGT to Dutch: content* which has weight X4.

Justification: in the end a good communication is what counts. Therefore translating the content is more important than the introduction.

Most items are self-explanatory. A few items are discussed below. The numbers correspond with the numbers of the items.

1 (Modality during introduction.)
Look at items 2 – 5. Score Modality once (1x). If one modality is being used consistently, mark P. If you notice inconsistent use, mark F.

2 (Explanation of function)
a) If the introduction is not fully executed initially, but corrected during the course of the situation, mark P.

b) The function needs to be explained when one (or both) of the client(s) has no experience with an interpreter. The explanation needs not always be extensive. During the situation explanations may appear to be necessary. The student needs to show understanding of this, and act upon it.

Checklist Introduction interpreting in a meeting

Introduction to the deaf client(s)
–   Name and function
–   Decide on position, with arguments
–   Ask about experience with interpreter NGT
–   If yes, no further introduction
–   If no, tell client about your function as interpreter
–   Interpret everything during setting
–   Not a participant in conversation
–   Interruption may be needed
–   Sworn to secrecy
–   If more than one deaf client, make clear what modality is chosen.

Introduction to hearing client(s)
–   Name and function
–   Decide on position, with arguments
–   Ask about experience with interpreter NGT
–   If yes, no further introduction
–   If no, tell client about your function as interpreter
–   Interpret everything during setting
–   Not a participant in conversation
–   Sworn to secrecy
–   No eye-contact with hearing client
–   Interruption may be needed (make rules clear, e.g. with chairperson if appropriate within this setting)

5 (Consult with chairperson)
–   Check whether or not it is necessary to explain function to other participants. (If yes: who does this, chairperson or interpreter).
–   Clearly indicate that participants cannot talk at the same time.
–   Ask for the agenda/proceedings of the meeting.

6 (Correct position)
Assessment: For P, dependent on the influence of the position on the situation as a whole.

11 (All participants can contribute sufficiently) [BvdB: by this we mean that the interpreter pays attention to all participants in the same manner and interprets for all]
Score positive, even when student is lagging much, but makes clear who is talking through correct interpretation.

12 (Interruption when necessary)
When the student has such a high level of interpretation, that no interruption is necessary, also score P.

15 and 25 (Omissions)
The severity of the omission(s) and the consequences thereof for the situation is decisive for P or F. Notice the style! and correct tense.

16 and 26 (Replacements)
The severity of the replacement(s) and the consequences thereof for the situation is decisive for P or F. Notice the style! and correct tense.

17 and 27 (Additions)
The severity of the addition(s) and the consequences thereof for the situation is decisive for P or F. Notice the style! and correct tense.

18 and 28 (Relations)
Make correct relations. This refers to the relation between persons, things, actions, times etc.

19–29 (Summary)
Used as a strategy. The summary must contain the major points.

22 and 31 (Grammatically correct sentences)
If one sentence is wrong, both grammatically and in meaning, score 1x as omission, replacement or addition.

Interaction skills

Manner of introduction:
35. Friendly: both verbally and non-verbally.
36. Calm: both verbally and non-verbally.
39. Correct positioning: by this we mean that the behaviour of the interpreter must resemble, both verbally and non-verbally, that of the other partners, according to Leary (1957). This means that, starting from the equality of the interpreter, there is a changing position during the introduction, the interpreter must show evidence that he/she wants to *cooperate*.

Decide on position:
42. Assertive: this means considering the interpreter's own conditions as well as those of the other partners. At least in such a way, that the interpreter mentions the correct conditions for the position so that efficient and professional work is made possible.

Way of interruption:
46, 47 and 48: interruption (I-message) is important because the interpreter takes responsibility. Example: "sorry" (with appropriate intonation, don't be too humble). Be clear with a smile and remain friendly.

Dealings with clients:

49. Appropriate distance: Both literally and metaphorically. E.g., while interpreting during a job-application distance and a business-like attitude is asked for. When interpreting for children, closeness is better to enhance communication.

50. Equal approach: the interpreter should give equal space to the deaf and to the hearing client. Don't interrupt or stop the hearing person to accommodate the deaf client, or vice versa. Or, when you know the deaf client, don't let this show by acting in a familiar way, because this can exclude the hearing client.

Attitude:

52, 53 and 55: the interpreter shows confidence, alertness and concentration, but without losing sight of the function/role of interpreter.

From helpers to professionals

Training of community interpreters in Sweden

Helge Niska
Stockholm University, Sweden

In this presentation I will first briefly describe the Swedish community interpreting scene and its historical background. Secondly, I will outline the various currently existing training opportunities for interpreters. Interpreter training, both at university level and in vocational courses, has been instrumental in developing professionalism and creating standards for quality interpreter services. The third and last part of the paper describes initiatives in promoting professionalism not only among interpreters but also among trainers of interpreters.[1]

Interpreter service – a right

Community interpreting

The point of departure of the interpreter services for immigrants is the aims of Swedish immigrant policy unanimously adopted by the Swedish Parliament thirty years ago: *equality, freedom of choice* and *co-operation*.

In 1997 the Parliament further defined the goals of Swedish integration policy:

– Equal rights, obligations and opportunities for all, regardless of ethnic and cultural background
– A societal unity grounded on social pluralism
– A social development which is characterised by mutual respect and tolerance and which everyone, regardless of background, will take part in and will feel responsible for.

---

1. I am grateful to Anna-Lena Nilsson and Birgitta Englund Dimitrova for allowing me to quote from their articles concerning sign language interpreting and training of trainers, respectively.

Integration policy aims at enabling individuals to support themselves and take part in society. It is also intended to safeguard basic democratic values, work for equal rights and opportunities for men and women, and prevent and counteract discrimination, xenophobia and racism.

There are an estimated 5000 community interpreters in Sweden, most of them working part-time as free-lancers, in over 100 working languages (SOU 2004). To provide interpreters in situations of acute need, an on-call service has been set up in the largest municipalities. There is also a number of agencies that offer remote interpreting by telephone or video.

Every day, 3000 hours of interpreting are provided, mainly in medical care and social welfare services. The yearly cost of interpreting services amounts to more than 400 million SEK (45 million EUR), mainly financed by public funds.

A statutory right

Anybody who does not speak Swedish or who is severely impaired in speech and hearing enjoys a statutory right to an interpreter under the Code of Judicial Procedure (*rättegångsbalken*), the Administrative Court Procedure Act (*förvaltningsprocesslagen*) and the Administrative Procedure Act (*förvaltningslagen*). The first two laws deal with interpretation in a judicial context, and the Administrative Procedure Act regulates the way cases are handled by the administrative authorities and is thus of great importance for the entire field of interpretation.

Section 8 of the Administrative Procedure Act provides that a public authority should use an interpreter 'if necessary', when dealing with a person who does not speak Swedish.

The Nordic Language Convention

Citizens of the five Nordic countries (Denmark, Finland, Iceland, Norway and Sweden) have specific rights with respect to interpreting and translation services in other Nordic countries. These rights are specified in the Nordic Language Convention (Nordiska språkkonventionen, in effect since 1987). The Nordic Language Convention guarantees all Nordic citizens the right to use their native language when dealing with the authorities or public offices of another Nordic country. These include health care, social, tax, education, and employment authorities, the police and courts.

National minorities in Sweden

The policy on national minorities was adopted by the Swedish parliament in December 1999, and the Government subsequently ratified the Council of Europe's Framework Convention for the Protection of National Minorities and the European Charter for Regional or Minority Languages.

The policy decision on minorities recognises five national minorities in Sweden. These are the Sami – an indigenous people –, the Swedish Finns, the Tornedalers (on the Finnish border in the north), the Roma and the Jews. All of these groups have existed in Sweden for a very long time and are therefore part of Sweden's cultural heritage. Since the Sami are an indigenous population, Sweden also has a specific Sami policy. The recognised minority languages in Sweden are all forms of Sami, Finnish, Meänkieli (Tornedal Finnish) and all forms of Romany and Yiddish.

Providing support for minority languages with a view to keeping them alive is an important part of the Swedish policy on national minorities. There are special laws entitling individuals to use Sami, Finnish and Meänkieli in dealings with administrative authorities and courts of law in the geographical areas in which these languages have traditionally flourished. This legislation comprises a number of municipalities in the Northern Swedish county of Norrbotten, which are known as the administrative districts for Sami, Finnish and Meänkieli.[2]

Two district courts in Norrbotten employ "public interpreters" (*allmän tolk*) for the Finnish and Meänkieli-speaking population. Interpreting provision in Finnish and Romany is part of the regular community interpreting service all over the country.

Interpreting service for deaf, deaf-blind and deafened adults[3]

The first mention of deaf people's right to an interpreter, and legislation regarding their right to an interpreter during legal proceedings, dates back to 1947. In 1968 the Swedish Parliament provided money for interpreting services on an experimental basis, and in 1969 one full-time interpreter was employed. As of 1976, there have been full-time interpreters employed throughout the country, financed by public funds as part of the health budget.

In 1981, deaf people in Sweden were acknowledged as bilingual with a right to be "fluent in their visual/gestual sign language and in the language society sur-

---

2. Government of Sweden, Ministry of Justice 2003: National minorities.

3. Based on Nilsson (1997).

rounds them with – Swedish." (Swedish Parliament, 14 May 1981.) This recognition has led to an increased awareness of the importance of the language for deaf people, and hence a greater interest on the part of the public.

Under the Health and Medical Services Act (1994), all of Sweden's 20 county councils and one local authority (Gotland) are responsible for organising, financing and providing interpreting services for deaf, deaf-blind and hearing impaired persons. These services include interpreting in daily activities like health care, contacts with authorities, important purchases, information and meetings at the workplace, weddings, and funerals. They also include interpreting in leisure-time activities and working life. The law specifically states that interpreting services should not be restricted to those situations listed in the law itself. There is no upper limit to the number of hours of interpreting a person is entitled to.

A look in the mirror: The birth of a profession

Interpreter service in Sweden is nowadays to a large extent a well-organised activity and a recognised part of public service, provided by a large number of well-trained professional interpreters. But professionalism did not happen overnight. As in other countries, it took a long time for society to wake up to the need to communicate with a growing number of immigrants, and the growing demands of the deaf community for competent interpreter services. After all, interpreting *per se* is a normal activity in the daily lives of most of the world's population and a perfectly trivial affair in everyday communication in bilingual or multilingual societies, i.e. the greatest part of the world. Linguistic assistance in communication with people from other ethnic communities has been around for thousands of years, very often without any remuneration. This historical combination of trivial, everyday activity and giving humanitarian linguistic help to fellow community members has most probably been an obstacle in the contemporary efforts of professionalizing community interpreting.

Interpreter training has been instrumental in developing professionalism and creating standards for quality interpreter services. When interpreting service agencies started their work in the late 1960s, one of their goals was to get rid of self-acclaimed "interpreters", lacking the proper linguistic and interpreting skills, who were involved in "helping" their fellow countrymen, often for a substantial fee. The deaf community also abounded with helpful Samaritans, sometimes with a second agenda such as combining interpreting with taking care of the client's spiritual needs.

The changing role of the interpreter

In the 1960s and -70s, the Swedish trade unions were very active in promoting interpretation at workplaces. This was natural because of the enormous influx of immigrant labour to Sweden especially during the 60s as a result of the massive recruitment campaigns by Swedish companies in Southern European countries, the Balkan and Turkey. Care for the immigrant workers' health, and information needs, for example concerning safety at work, were the reasons for the unions to promote obligatory interpreting services at workplaces. In fact, the first interpreter training courses in Sweden were geared towards interpreting at workplaces, and the students were employees who had been appointed by the union as workplace interpreters. The workplace interpreter as an elected official was entitled to interpret during working hours without a reduction of salary.

Needless to say, this policy was not always very popular with the employers. They felt that the unions were using interpreters as an instrument for the empowerment of the labour force, and not as mere translators. A great deal of time and effort was spent on futile discussions between union and employers' representatives about the possibility or impossibility of combining the role of shop steward with the one of a neutral interpreter.

In the beginning of the 1970s interpreter training, and consequently interpreting services, took a new turn. The government started to arrange interpreter-training courses with professional interpreters as teachers and course developers. After only a few years, in the middle of the 1970s, the first code of ethics, *God tolksed* (Good interpreting practice) was published by the government agency which had just started to authorise interpreters. This publication was in fact a codification and part modification of the prevailing rules and conventions within the interpreter community, for example organisations like AIIC, the international association of conference interpreters. The leading principle in this code is that the interpreter is neutral and impartial. The latest and more or less identical edition of this document was published in 2004 (Kammarkollegiet 2004).

The first professional organisation of interpreters to appear in Sweden was *Sveriges Teckenspråkstolkars Förening* (STTF), The Swedish National Association of Sign Language Interpreters, which was founded in 1969. Six years later, in 1975, the first organisation of community interpreters, *Sveriges Tolkförbund* (STOF), The Swedish Association of Interpreters) was established. One of its aims was to promote high quality interpreting and interpreter training. Members of that association also took an active part in the development of the code of ethics. These standards constitute a minimal common platform for the approximately 5000 professional community interpreters active in Sweden today. The code of ethics is frequently discussed, questioned and eventually shared, basically in and through training courses for interpreters.

Interpreter training

The number of immigrant languages in Sweden is at least 150. In the last 10 years, more than 140 languages have been represented at interpreter training courses; however, it has been possible to arrange bilingual instruction in only 38 languages. The remaining language groups have had instruction in Swedish only.

Institutions responsible for training

Training of interpreters for immigrants has been organised in Sweden since 1968. Since its inauguration in 1986, *Tolk- och översättarinstitutet* (TÖI) (The Institute for Interpretation and Translation Studies), Stockholm University, has the over-riding responsibility for all interpreter training in Sweden. There are two types of interpreter training programmes, academic courses at Swedish universities, and vocational training courses at adult education centres and voluntary educational associations.

The Institute regularly organises academic training at different universities in Sweden, mostly Stockholm, but the greater part of the training of community interpreters is given at adult education centres and voluntary educational associations. Non-academic level courses for community interpreters and sign language interpreters are not organised directly by the Institute, but its task is to distribute government grants and to supervise and evaluate the training.

Community interpreter training – scope and organisation

The areas of instruction in community interpreter training are social welfare, medical services, labour market and legal interpreting. The basic training can then be supplemented with special courses and further education in, for example, psychology, dental care, women's diseases, tropical diseases, and interpreting for special categories of clients, e.g. children and victims of torture.

University training of community interpreters currently consists of a 1 year basic course plus 1 + 1 semester specialisation (medical or/and legal interpreting). About 50 per cent of the tuition consists of practical exercises in interpreting and terminology. Continuous tests are carried out during the academic year at the end of sub-courses. There is a final examination in interpreting, leading to government authorisation. Those who pass the university examination do not have to sit for the government authorisation test, but the authorisation itself is given by the government (cf. Leena Idh in this volume).

University programmes in community interpreting involve courses in the Swedish language (including grammar, language norms, language for special purposes (LSP)), the foreign language (grammar, language norms, LSP), terminology, factual knowledge in the social, labour market, legal and medical fields, ethics of interpreting, interpretation technique, and interpretation exercises.

University training of community interpreters is planned to be rearranged as of the academic year 2007/2008. It will start with a one semester-long Basic course in interpreting and translation, common for both interpreter and translator training students. During this semester, students can choose if they want to specialise in translation or interpreting. For those who choose interpreting, the interpreter training "proper" will be given during semesters 2 and 3. Optionally, instead of going on with interpreting during the third semester, the students may take a separate Bachelor's course in interpreting, which will entitle them to apply for a BA in interpreting (providing that all other requirements for a BA are fulfilled). Prerequisites for enrolment in the interpreter training programme is at least one year of university studies of the language in which interpreter training is given.

Interpreter training in non-university courses

Up until now, more than 3,000 participants per year have attended some two hundred different courses at adult education colleges and educational associations, with a total of about 7,000 hours of instruction. More than 140 languages have been represented at interpreter training courses; however, it has been possible to arrange bilingual instruction in only about 40 languages. The remaining language groups have had instruction in Swedish only. From 2007, a new one year training programme will be offered at six colleges and educational associations in the country; one of them will be organised as Internet-based distance education. The programme starts with a short introductory course where the participants are introduced to the interpreting profession and its technical and ethical demands. This is followed by six sub-courses covering the most common working areas for community interpreters: social welfare and security, labour market, medical, and legal interpreting (encompassing the basics of law, police and court interpreting and interpreting in asylum cases.) Participants are selected through an entrance test, and each sub-course ends with a test which equals the state authorisation test in that subject area. To become an authorised interpreter, the students will nevertheless have to sit in the state authorisation test.

Objectives of training

The overall aim of interpreter training at adult education colleges and voluntary educational associations (adopted by the Board of TÖI, 2003-09-23) is to help fulfil the need of adequate interpreting service in society between a person who does not master the Swedish language and authorities, service institutions and organisations.

Instruction is given in the following main areas: Social and security interpreting, medical interpreting, labour market interpreting, basics of law and court interpreting. In addition, introductory courses and advanced and special courses can be organised, as well as training of interpreting teachers/instructors.

The objectives are:

- to develop the community interpreters' language proficiency and knowledge of terminology in Swedish and in their other interpreted language in a contrastive perspective;
- to provide training in interpretation technique as well as knowledge of the ethical and psychological demands of interpreting;
- to provide factual knowledge in relevant fields, and to provide a good understanding of social, political, cultural and labour affairs in Sweden and the other language areas.

The instruction should furthermore:

- be organised to allow the interpreters themselves the opportunity to expand their knowledge independently, both during the instruction period and afterwards,
- provide information on the channels available to them in this respect in the various fields.

Guidelines and syllabuses for community interpreter courses in Sweden are laid down by TÖI.

Career prospects

Most of the students at vocational, non-university, community interpreter training courses are persons who are either working as interpreters or have just enrolled for a job as community interpreter. However, because of the uncertainty in the labour market, many interpreters combine interpreting with other careers, e.g. teaching, social work and health care.

This applies also to university training courses, although students in these courses are more often people who do not have any connection with Interpreting agencies. Contrary to conference interpreting students, who usually get a job at the EU immediately upon graduation, most students at the community interpreting courses at university do not end up as full-time, or even part-time interpreters, but in other professions, mostly within teaching or administration. Surveys have shown that many former students think that the education has given them mastery in active language skills which they could not have acquired elsewhere, and which is highly rated by employers.

Sign language interpreter training[4]

Training programmes for sign language interpreters have been developed constantly over the years. The first courses were organised in the late 1960s, and the courses lasted one to six weeks. The first courses in interpreting for the deaf-blind were organised in 1975 and for the deafened in 1981. The training programmes have since then been expanded in parallel with the development of interpreting services and the rise in awareness of the needs of the groups concerned.

The responsibility for training interpreters for deaf, deaf-blind and deafened adults rests with the adult education colleges, under the supervision of TÖI. The organisation and content of the programmes have evolved as a result of the interaction between the Swedish disability organisations, the adult education colleges and the state authorities concerned.

Two types of training

Today there are two types of interpreter training in this area: a) one that prepares for the profession of sign language interpreter and interpreter for the deaf-blind; and b) one that prepares professional interpreters for the deafened.

Sign language/deaf-blind interpreters

A full training programme for sign language/deaf blind interpreters takes (at least) four years and is offered by a small number of adult education colleges. Prerequisites are completion of secondary school, very good skills in Swedish, and the passing of an admittance test. In this programme, the greatest part of the training during the first two years consists of sign-language education, and during the last

---

4. Based on Nilsson (1997).

two years the emphasis is on intensive interpreter training. In some schools, there is a separate test between the two levels. The four-year programme is divided into modules, which means that students who have already acquired the necessary skills in sign language or other subjects, can start their training at an appropriate level. The interpreter training programme is recognised as a highly qualified tertiary educational programme at university level, albeit delivered trough adult education colleges.

Besides sign language and sign language interpreting, subjects taught in this programme are Swedish, deaf-blind interpreting, and factual knowledge subjects like deaf society and culture, social psychology and social studies. A substantial emphasis in the training programme is given to personal and professional development. Here, work placements play an important role. In the course of the studies, the students are given 8–16 weeks of practical experience as an interpreter at an interpreting service agency.

Interpreters for deafened adults
The training of interpreters for deafened adults is a three-year programme which is given at irregular intervals at one adult education college. It is a full-time training programme, and the prerequisites are secondary school with a good grade in Swedish and the passing of an entrance test.

A total of some 30 students can attend this programme. A great deal of time is devoted to learning how to use the Veyboard, a special keyboard for fast on-screen translation. Several other special interpreting methods for deafened and hearing-impaired adults are also presented.

Career prospects
There are about 8,000–12,000 deaf persons in Sweden, and the need for interpreters is far from satisfied. Only an estimated 30 interpreters can be trained every year. This volume would need to be increased 10-fold to cover the need. However, interpreter agencies have been slow in creating the necessary number of positions for interpreters. This leads to uncertainty among interpreters and prospective interpreter students.

Training of trainers

Training the trainers of translators and interpreters is necessary both in view of promoting professionalisation in the field and for establishing translation and interpreting as an academic discipline.

The majority of those who train community interpreters are immigrants to Sweden. Their educational and professional backgrounds vary considerably, but few of them have had any specific interpreter training or professional experience in that field before coming to Sweden. They usually teach at evening or week-end courses. Short methodological seminars ranging from two week-ends up to two weeks have been organized regularly for this category of interpreter trainers since the beginning of the 1980s. These seminars usually cover the methodology of teaching adults, methods for training interpreting technique, interpreting ethics, testing and evaluating interpreters, and factual knowledge within one or several subject areas. The total number of community interpreter trainers is currently about 200.

Trainers of sign language interpreters, interpreters for deaf-blind and interpreters for deafened adults are generally Swedes, and their background includes a formal interpreter training of various length, from just a few weeks or months up to two years. Many of those teachers have substantial teaching experience. As a group, these teachers are often better prepared, both in linguistic matters and in methodology, than are the community interpreter trainers. In Sweden, the total number of this type of interpreter trainer stands at around 20, but demand outstrips this provision, resulting in a shortage in this area.

An academic course for interpreter trainers

As a national institute for interpreter training, TÖI has a responsibility for all of the three main areas of interpreting which are usually distinguished – sign language interpreting (including various techniques for interpreting for deaf-blind and deafened adults), conference interpreting, and community interpreting (including court interpreting). Initiating and organising various kinds of interpreter training, the institute has been able to see quite clearly which skills, taught and trained in interpreter programmes, are common to all or several kinds of interpreting. These include interpreting techniques, memory skills, skills of analysis of speeches and of turn-taking in conversation, terminology management in potentially new areas of expertise, interpersonal "skills", language competence in more than one language, rhetorical skills, etc. All this enhances the likelihood that experiences from one area of interpreter training will be of interest and value to other areas as well.

It was therefore decided to launch a special course for interpreter trainers where one of the main goals was to give impetus to "cross-disciplinary" development and cooperation in the training of interpreters.[5]

The programme

The programme is delivered at Stockholm University, formally at undergraduate level. A prerequisite for enrolment is documented experience as an interpreter trainer or as an interpreter. The whole course consists of 20 credits, which equals 20 weeks or half an academic year; one credit is equal to one week of full-time study.

Syllabus
The course is divided into five modules:

1.   Language, communication and interpretation, 4 credits.
2.   Language for specific purposes, terminology and lexicography, 3 credits.
3.   Teaching the techniques and ethics of interpretation, 5 credits.
4.   Assessment of interpretation, 4 credits.
5.   Course paper, 4 credits.

Working forms
The course is offered half-time during one academic year. The group meets in Stockholm for two days roughly once a month, from September to May. The meetings are devoted to lectures, seminars, discussions, group work, etc. Students read general literature on language and linguistics, as well as specialized literature on conversation analysis, on interaction, and naturally, on interpreting and on how to teach it. In choosing literature dealing more specifically with interpreting, great care has been taken to include books and articles from all areas of interpreting, and as much as possible in equal proportions.

Examination
Each module also contains an independent project, which simultaneously constitutes the examination for that module. The topic for this project work is selected by the respective student, and should preferably have a close relation to their own daily teaching or interpreting practice.

For instance, the project in the terminological module consists of conducting a terminological investigation in a restricted subject area according to termi-

---

5.   The following account is based largely on Englund Dimitrova (2001).

nological principles. The project in the module on didactics consists of detailed planning of a training lesson.

The concluding course paper can for example be devoted to developing the syllabus of a completely new course, improving the syllabus of an existing one, planning one semester of a course, etc. It can also consist of developing new teaching and learning materials.

The project format allows the students to specialize individually in their respective areas. Cooperation between students is encouraged. An interesting, innovative project "across boundaries" was the design of a course aimed at training community interpreters in interpreting for deafened immigrant adults.

Opening up new horizons

During the last couple of years, a new development has emerged. Many interpreter trainers are beginning to feel a need for cooperation with colleagues, not only from their own area of interpreting, but other areas as well. Sign language interpreters and community interpreters have realised that they have many areas of common ground – and that there are lots of interesting differences as well. International conference interpreters meet new colleagues who have started their careers as community interpreters in languages which were once concerned to be "exotic". Interpreter trainers start to reassess their own training programmes when they begin to learn how training is organised elsewhere and for other categories of interpreters.

A special Interpreting methods project (TMU) was set up in 2003 to work with these issues. The project has arranged a number of seminars for interpreter trainers in several locations throughout the country, and one national conference per year. Besides giving participants the possibility to listen to presentations by experts and researchers on various aspects of interpreting, the idea is to enable people to get to know each other and learn about each others' work. This will then hopefully initiate a process leading to more cooperation and pedagogical development in the area of interpreter training. An example of this has already occurred within this project, with the discovery of a new area of interpreting: audio description.

Members of the coordinating group of the project represent training institutions within spoken as well as signed language interpreting. The group also has representatives from users of interpreting services, thereby giving all participants a hands-on experience of the various interpreter needs in society. The project is an endeavour to promote professionalism not only among interpreters, but also among trainers of interpreters.

Obviously, the Critical Link Conference in Stockholm in 2004 had a tremendous impact on the work within this project, providing much inspiration and new ideas.

References

Englund Dimitrova, B. 2001. Training the interpreter trainers – the Swedish experience. Presentation at the 3rd Critical Link conference in Montreal, Canada 2001. Manuscript.

Government of Sweden, Ministry of Justice 2003. National minorities and minority languages. A summary of the Swedish Government's policy on national minorities. Fact sheet Ju 03.10e. http://www.sweden.gov.se/content/1/c6/01/62/46/4cf4b38c.pdf

Kammarkollegiet (The Swedish Legal, Financial and Administrative Services Agency) 2004. *God tolksed – Vägledning för auktoriserade tolkar* [Good interpreting practice – guidelines for authorised interpreters]. http://www.kammarkollegiet.se/tolktrans/godtolk04.pdf

Nilsson, A.-L. 1997. Sign Language Interpreting in Sweden. *Meta*, XLII, 3, 1997.

SOU 2004:15 Statens offentliga utredningar [Public State Commissions of Inquiry No. 2004:15]. *Tolkförmedling – kvalitet, registrering, tillsyn.* [Interpreter service – quality, registration, supervision.]

Index

A

accreditation 126, 129
accreditation for agencies 129
accuracy 84
ad hoc solutions 84
admittance test 305
adult education 302
advocacy 127, 173
    see also advocacy role 208
advocates 13
Agger-Gupta 175
Agis projects 151, 164
Allies conferences 200
altruism 182
Alvir 220
American Sign Language 263
American Translators Associations 122
Anderson 15, 182
Angelelli 95, 169, 170, 172, 173, 175, 243
Apfelbaum 54, 227, 238
Argyris 168
Aristotle 242
ASL 263
ATA 122
Atherton 182
audio description 309
AUSIT 168, 205
Australia 121, 126
authorisation 303
authorisation test 303
awareness 54, 62, 82

B

BiBi movement 200

BA in interpreting 303
Baker-Shenk 182
Barik 16
Barsky 41, 46
Baudouin 275
Beauchamp 169
Beaugrande 17, 20
Bell 108, 115, 206, 207
Bercher 216
Berger 169
Berk-Seligson 182
Bisgaard 155
Black 255
Block 275
Blommaert 40
Bostock 253, 255
Bot 95, 217
Bowen 8
Bowker 277
Brennan 79
Brien 182
Brown 41, 182, 253
Brown and Levinson 40, 43
Bruner 255
Budin 278
business skills 122
Bélanger 15, 184

C

caller hegemony 72
Canadian Hearing Society 264
Carbaugh 196
Carr 17
Checkland 111, 112
Chesters 207
Childress 169
Chun 168, 171, 172
co-construction 189

co-operation 189
co-operative 183, 188
co-participants 186, 187
co-participation 183, 189
co-production 188, 189
code of conduct 139, 141, 145, 147, 201
code of ethics 14, 124, 125, 301
codes of industry practice 125
cognitive linguistics 20
    processing 15, 17, 20
    science 16, 17
Cohen 65
Cokely 190
Colin 205, 229
collaboration 188, 189
collusion 195
communication management 86
community-based interpreting 13
community agencies 170
computational linguistics 277
conduit model 172
confabulation 183
conference interpreter 14, 15, 16, 19, 301, 309
    interpreting 103, 307
consecutive interpreting 12, 16
consumers 181
contract interpreters 123, 125, 128
conversational axis 27
    dynamics 54, 61
    initiatives 34

conversation analysis   17
corpus-based dictionaries
    280
corpus linguistics   277
    studies   280
Corsellis   141, 153
court interpreter   19, 213
    see also legal interpreting
    and translation   151, 156
courtroom   19
cultural mediators   41
cultural responsiveness   171
cycle of empowerment   188

D
Davidson   3, 28
Deaf   182, 188
deaf-blind   300, 305
deaf-blind interpreting   306
deaf society and culture   306
de Jonckheere   216
Denmark   152, 155, 156
Depecker   276
de Pury   216
descriptive approaches   54
descriptivist   275
dialogue interpreting   12, 19
disciplinary procedures   141
discourse   17, 20
    analysis   39
    management   19, 20
    studies   20
Dodds   16
Downing   122
Draskau   277
Dressler   20
Drucker   116
Dubslaff   95
Duncan   75
dyadic-triadic shifts   71

E
ECHR   152
Edwards   229
Ehlich   44
Elghezouani   203
emotion   197, 199
empirical philosophy   242
entrance test   303, 306

equivalence   16
Erickson   40
error correction   54, 61, 62
ethical dilemmas   89
ethics   96, 184
    see also code of ethics
    14, 124, 125, 301
European Commission   152
    Parliament   159
    Union   151
evidence   80
examination   308
explanation   55, 58, 61

F
Fabbro   17
face   41
face-threatening acts   41
face work   50
Fairclough   39
FIT   230
Flores et al.   169
focus-group study   169
Fogazzaro   27
footing   50, 55, 61, 198
Fortier   122
Fowler   79
free-lancers   121

G
Garber   124
García-Landa   15
gate-keeping   40
Gavioli   27
Gerver   14, 16, 17, 19
Gibbs   253
Gile   16, 234
Gilliard   222
Goffman   27, 41, 42, 198,
    218, 235
González   205, 229
Gran   16
Grice   41
Grossen   217
Grotius projects   151, 155,
    156, 158
Gumperz   20
Gustavsson   242

H
Haga   242
Hale   207, 227, 229, 230, 236,
    237
Harrington   182, 189, 286
Harris   123
Hatim   20
Hauswirth   222
health beliefs   169, 173
hearing-impaired   300, 306
Heh   126, 127
Hertog   79, 153, 155
Hewitt   183
Hofmann   242, 248
Hopper   67, 72
human activity system   110
Hymes   20

I
Ibrahim   108, 206, 207, 210
immigrant policy   297
impartiality   199, 202, 203,
    230, 239
Infoterm   276
Inghilleri   227, 238
instructional resource   55
integration policy   297
intentionality   169
interaction   15, 16, 17, 20
interactional patterns   54, 55
interactionist approach   238
interaction models   15
intercultural agents   41
interdependence   188, 189
International Federation of
    Translators (FIT)   230
International Institute for
    Terminology Research
    276
International Standards
    Organisation   276
interpreter associations   123
    intuition   171
interpreting studies   11,
    15, 21
interpretive theory   16
interviews   206, 208
invisibility   185, 243

J

Jacobs   169
jargon   277
Jefferson   28, 232
job preparation   96
   satisfaction   96, 99
Jonsen   248

K

Katan   218, 243
Kaufert   172, 219
Keith   54, 57
Kent   196
key symbol   196
Kierzkowska   102
Knapp   41, 43
Ko   54
Kontrimas   173
Koolage   172, 219
Krouglov   79, 227, 237
Kuhn   15, 20

L

Ladd   283
Lang   54
language for general
   purposes   279
Language Line Services   126
Langue des Signes
   Quebecoise   263
Laplace   15
legal interpreting and
   translation   151, 156
   see also court interpreter
   19, 213
legislation   13
Le Page   183
Levinson   41
Linell   238
linguistics   16, 17
Litowitz   279
Little   186
logistics   84
Longley   14
Luckman   169

M

Mackintosh   16

Malaysian Association of
   translators   116
Malaysia National Institute of
   Translation   108
Martinsen   95, 155
Mason   18, 20, 41, 184
McDermott   110
McIntire   14, 182
mediation   19
Melby   278
mentor   284
meta-dialogue   195
Metzger   173, 182, 237, 243
Mikkelson   18, 66, 229, 230,
   231
Mindess   182
Mink   174
minority languages   138
Mintz   65
Mintzberg   173
modelling of roles   182
Mol   241
Monnier   40
Morris   41, 205, 229
Moser-Mercer   16, 55
Métraux   220

N

narratives   183
national minorities   299
natural interpreters   43
Nederlandse
   Gebarentaal   283
negative face   41
negotiator   184
neuropsychology   17
neutrality   230, 239
Nguyen   174
Niska   65, 67, 96, 121, 254
non-renditions   28, 34, 71
Nordic Language Convention
   298
norms   96, 103
note-taking   16

O

O'Connor   110
Okahara   126, 174
on-call service   298

Oviatt   65
Ozolins   107, 121, 129

P

paradigm   15, 17, 20, 21
Parnell   54
Parson   2
Pearce   169
Pearson   276, 277
Perez   79
Peräkylä   228, 237
Phelan   229
Philip   182
Picht   277
Piret   220
poiesis   245
politeness theory   41
Pollard   168
Pollitt   129, 181, 182, 184,
   186, 190
positive face   41
power   12, 14, 244
praxis   245
prescribed role   182
procedural fairness   80
processing models   15
professional association   123,
   124
   ethics   13, 227
   register   141, 149
   skills   285
professionalism   300, 309
psychology   17
punctuality   123, 125
Putsch   169, 172, 219
Pöchhacker   3, 17, 96, 181
Pöllabauer   39

Q

quantum interpreting   189
questioning techniques   92
questionnaire   83, 96

R

Ramaprasad   254
Reddy   172
relevance theory   20
repair activities   55, 57, 61, 62
resistance   201, 202

responsibilities   182, 183
Roat   122
Roberts   2, 14, 66, 96
Robinson   32
role   14, 86, 103, 195, 196,
    199, 201, 203, 227, 234
    see also advocacy role
    208
    deviation   86
    ideology   239
    prescribed role   182
role-play   55, 137
Rosenberg   71
Roy   17, 27, 172, 182, 184, 185,
    199, 217, 221, 238
Rudvin   193, 203, 238
Rust   253

S
Sacks   28, 232
Sadler   253, 255
Samuels   209
Sanderson   182
Sarangi   2
Sarfatti-Larsson   2
Sauvêtre   122
Scheffer   40, 47
Schegloff   28, 232
Scholes   111
Schultz   40
Schumacher   40
Schäffner   11, 54
Schön   168
Scotland   80
Scott Gibson   181, 182
Seleskovitch   15
sense   16
setting   12, 19
Setton   20
Shlesinger   17
sign language interpretation
    194, 200
sign language interpreting
    14, 17, 203, 305
simultaneous interpreting
    12, 15

Sinaiko   14
Sironi   216
situational context   16
skopos theory   17
Skutnabb-Kangas   195, 202
slang   86
Snell-Hornby   3
social psychology   17
sociolinguistics   17
Softic   126
soft systems
    methodology   109
Speech-to-text
    interpreting   286
speech act theory   20
standards   123, 125, 129, 151
Stansfield   110
Stenzl   16
Stewart   41
Straniero Sergio   27, 243
Stuifzand   284
Suonuuti   279
supervision   126, 128
Swalef   275
Sweden   121
Swedish sign language   138
systems thinking   109

T
Tabouret-Keller   183
talk projects   183
Tampere   157
Tate   182
technical interpreting   55
telephone interpreting   81
Teo   208, 211
terminology   277, 302, 307
    databases   278
    management   273
    search   57, 62
term lists   277
test   136
testing and evaluating   307
text linguistics   17, 20
    production   17

The National Association of
    the Deaf (NAD)   200
think-aloud protocols   68
Toury   3, 17
training the trainers   306
transparency   173
trust   85, 243, 247
Tryuk   96
Turner   182, 188, 286

U
Union of Court
    interpreters   116
United Kingdom   129
university training   303

V
Van den Bogaerde   284
Van der Vlis   155
Vehviläinen   228, 237
Venuti   243
Vermeer   17, 20
veyboard   306
Vidal   65
videophony   67
video recording   54, 62
VITS LanguageLink   126
vocational training   302

W
Wadensjö   17, 19, 20, 27, 28,
    41, 42, 55, 65, 71, 99, 173,
    182, 184, 217, 218, 224, 227,
    232, 237, 238
Watters   219
Weber   244
Weine   221
Wiliam   255
Wilson   79
Woll   283
workplace interpreters   301
written test   136

Z
zero rendition   28, 30, 38, 71
Zimann   96

Benjamins Translation Library

A complete list of titles in this series can be found on *www.benjamins.com*

73 **GOUADEC, Daniel:** Translation as a Profession. xv, 387 pp. + index. *Expected June 2007*

72 **GAMBIER, Yves, Miriam SHLESINGER and Radegundis STOLZE (eds.):** Doubts and Directions in Translation Studies. Selected contributions from the EST Congress, Lisbon 2004. xii, 356 pp. + index. **[EST Subseries 4]** *Expected July 2007*

71 **ST-PIERRE, Paul and Prafulla C. KAR (eds.):** In Translation – Reflections, Refractions, Transformations. 2007. xv, 313 pp.

70 **WADENSJÖ, Cecilia, Birgitta ENGLUND DIMITROVA and Anna-Lena NILSSON (eds.):** The Critical Link 4. Professionalisation of interpreting in the community. Selected papers from the 4th International Conference on Interpreting in Legal, Health and Social Service Settings, Stockholm, Sweden, 20-23 May 2004. 2007. x, 314 pp.

69 **DELABASTITA, Dirk, Lieven D'HULST and Reine MEYLAERTS (eds.):** Functional Approaches to Culture and Translation. Selected papers by José Lambert. 2006. xxviii, 226 pp.

68 **DUARTE, João Ferreira, Alexandra ASSIS ROSA and Teresa SERUYA (eds.):** Translation Studies at the Interface of Disciplines. 2006. vi, 207 pp.

67 **PYM, Anthony, Miriam SHLESINGER and Zuzana JETTMAROVÁ (eds.):** Sociocultural Aspects of Translating and Interpreting. 2006. viii, 255 pp.

66 **SNELL-HORNBY, Mary:** The Turns of Translation Studies. New paradigms or shifting viewpoints? 2006. xi, 205 pp.

65 **DOHERTY, Monika:** Structural Propensities. Translating nominal word groups from English into German. 2006. xxii, 196 pp.

64 **ENGLUND DIMITROVA, Birgitta:** Expertise and Explicitation in the Translation Process. 2005. xx, 295 pp.

63 **JANZEN, Terry (ed.):** Topics in Signed Language Interpreting. Theory and practice. 2005. xii, 362 pp.

62 **POKORN, Nike K.:** Challenging the Traditional Axioms. Translation into a non-mother tongue. 2005. xii, 166 pp. **[EST Subseries 3]**

61 **HUNG, Eva (ed.):** Translation and Cultural Change. Studies in history, norms and image-projection. 2005. xvi, 195 pp.

60 **TENNENT, Martha (ed.):** Training for the New Millennium. Pedagogies for translation and interpreting. 2005. xxvi, 276 pp.

59 **MALMKJÆR, Kirsten (ed.):** Translation in Undergraduate Degree Programmes. 2004. vi, 202 pp.

58 **BRANCHADELL, Albert and Lovell Margaret WEST (eds.):** Less Translated Languages. 2005. viii, 416 pp.

57 **CHERNOV, Ghelly V.:** Inference and Anticipation in Simultaneous Interpreting. A probability-prediction model. Edited with a critical foreword by Robin Setton and Adelina Hild. 2004. xxx, 268 pp. **[EST Subseries 2]**

56 **ORERO, Pilar (ed.):** Topics in Audiovisual Translation. 2004. xiv, 227 pp.

55 **ANGELELLI, Claudia V.:** Revisiting the Interpreter's Role. A study of conference, court, and medical interpreters in Canada, Mexico, and the United States. 2004. xvi, 127 pp.

54 **GONZÁLEZ DAVIES, Maria:** Multiple Voices in the Translation Classroom. Activities, tasks and projects. 2004. x, 262 pp.

53 **DIRIKER, Ebru:** De-/Re-Contextualizing Conference Interpreting. Interpreters in the Ivory Tower? 2004. x, 223 pp.

52 **HALE, Sandra:** The Discourse of Court Interpreting. Discourse practices of the law, the witness and the interpreter. 2004. xviii, 267 pp.

51 **CHAN, Leo Tak-hung:** Twentieth-Century Chinese Translation Theory. Modes, issues and debates. 2004. xvi, 277 pp.

50 **HANSEN, Gyde, Kirsten MALMKJÆR and Daniel GILE (eds.):** Claims, Changes and Challenges in Translation Studies. Selected contributions from the EST Congress, Copenhagen 2001. 2004. xiv, 320 pp. **[EST Subseries 1]**

49 **PYM, Anthony:** The Moving Text. Localization, translation, and distribution. 2004. xviii, 223 pp.

48 **MAURANEN, Anna and Pekka KUJAMÄKI (eds.):** Translation Universals. Do they exist? 2004. vi, 224 pp.

47 **SAWYER, David B.:** Fundamental Aspects of Interpreter Education. Curriculum and Assessment. 2004. xviii, 312 pp.

46   **BRUNETTE, Louise, Georges BASTIN, Isabelle HEMLIN and Heather CLARKE (eds.):** The Critical Link 3. Interpreters in the Community. Selected papers from the Third International Conference on Interpreting in Legal, Health and Social Service Settings, Montréal, Quebec, Canada 22–26 May 2001. 2003. xii, 359 pp.

45   **ALVES, Fabio (ed.):** Triangulating Translation. Perspectives in process oriented research. 2003. x, 165 pp.

44   **SINGERMAN, Robert:** Jewish Translation History. A bibliography of bibliographies and studies. With an introductory essay by Gideon Toury. 2002. xxxvi, 420 pp.

43   **GARZONE, Giuliana and Maurizio VIEZZI (eds.):** Interpreting in the 21st Century. Challenges and opportunities. 2002. x, 337 pp.

42   **HUNG, Eva (ed.):** Teaching Translation and Interpreting 4. Building bridges. 2002. xii, 243 pp.

41   **NIDA, Eugene A.:** Contexts in Translating. 2002. x, 127 pp.

40   **ENGLUND DIMITROVA, Birgitta and Kenneth HYLTENSTAM (eds.):** Language Processing and Simultaneous Interpreting. Interdisciplinary perspectives. 2000. xvi, 164 pp.

39   **CHESTERMAN, Andrew, Natividad GALLARDO SAN SALVADOR and Yves GAMBIER (eds.):** Translation in Context. Selected papers from the EST Congress, Granada 1998. 2000. x, 393 pp.

38   **SCHÄFFNER, Christina and Beverly ADAB (eds.):** Developing Translation Competence. 2000. xvi, 244 pp.

37   **TIRKKONEN-CONDIT, Sonja and Riitta JÄÄSKELÄINEN (eds.):** Tapping and Mapping the Processes of Translation and Interpreting. Outlooks on empirical research. 2000. x, 176 pp.

36   **SCHMID, Monika S.:** Translating the Elusive. Marked word order and subjectivity in English-German translation. 1999. xii, 174 pp.

35   **SOMERS, Harold (ed.):** Computers and Translation. A translator's guide. 2003. xvi, 351 pp.

34   **GAMBIER, Yves and Henrik GOTTLIEB (eds.):** (Multi) Media Translation. Concepts, practices, and research. 2001. xx, 300 pp.

33   **GILE, Daniel, Helle V. DAM, Friedel DUBSLAFF, Bodil MARTINSEN and Anne SCHJOLDAGER (eds.):** Getting Started in Interpreting Research. Methodological reflections, personal accounts and advice for beginners. 2001. xiv, 255 pp.

32   **BEEBY, Allison, Doris ENSINGER and Marisa PRESAS (eds.):** Investigating Translation. Selected papers from the 4th International Congress on Translation, Barcelona, 1998. 2000. xiv, 296 pp.

31   **ROBERTS, Roda P., Silvana E. CARR, Diana ABRAHAM and Aideen DUFOUR (eds.):** The Critical Link 2: Interpreters in the Community. Selected papers from the Second International Conference on Interpreting in legal, health and social service settings, Vancouver, BC, Canada, 19–23 May 1998. 2000. vii, 316 pp.

30   **DOLLERUP, Cay:** Tales and Translation. The Grimm Tales from Pan-Germanic narratives to shared international fairytales. 1999. xiv, 384 pp.

29   **WILSS, Wolfram:** Translation and Interpreting in the 20th Century. Focus on German. 1999. xiii, 256 pp.

28   **SETTON, Robin:** Simultaneous Interpretation. A cognitive-pragmatic analysis. 1999. xvi, 397 pp.

27   **BEYLARD-OZEROFF, Ann, Jana KRÁLOVÁ and Barbara MOSER-MERCER (eds.):** Translators' Strategies and Creativity. Selected Papers from the 9th International Conference on Translation and Interpreting, Prague, September 1995. In honor of Jiří Levý and Anton Popovič. 1998. xiv, 230 pp.

26   **TROSBORG, Anna (ed.):** Text Typology and Translation. 1997. xvi, 342 pp.

25   **POLLARD, David E. (ed.):** Translation and Creation. Readings of Western Literature in Early Modern China, 1840–1918. 1998. vi, 336 pp.

24   **ORERO, Pilar and Juan C. SAGER (eds.):** The Translator's Dialogue. Giovanni Pontiero. 1997. xiv, 252 pp.

23   **GAMBIER, Yves, Daniel GILE and Christopher TAYLOR (eds.):** Conference Interpreting: Current Trends in Research. Proceedings of the International Conference on Interpreting: What do we know and how? 1997. iv, 246 pp.

22   **CHESTERMAN, Andrew:** Memes of Translation. The spread of ideas in translation theory. 1997. vii, 219 pp.

21   **BUSH, Peter and Kirsten MALMKJÆR (eds.):** Rimbaud's Rainbow. Literary translation in higher education. 1998. x, 200 pp.

20   **SNELL-HORNBY, Mary, Zuzana JETTMAROVÁ and Klaus KAINDL (eds.):** Translation as Intercultural Communication. Selected papers from the EST Congress, Prague 1995. 1997. x, 354 pp.

19   **CARR, Silvana E., Roda P. ROBERTS, Aideen DUFOUR and Dini STEYN (eds.):** The Critical Link: Interpreters in the Community. Papers from the 1st international conference on interpreting in legal, health and social service settings, Geneva Park, Canada, 1–4 June 1995. 1997. viii, 322 pp.

18 **SOMERS, Harold (ed.):** Terminology, LSP and Translation. Studies in language engineering in honour of Juan C. Sager. 1996. xii, 250 pp.

17 **POYATOS, Fernando (ed.):** Nonverbal Communication and Translation. New perspectives and challenges in literature, interpretation and the media. 1997. xii, 361 pp.

16 **DOLLERUP, Cay and Vibeke APPEL (eds.):** Teaching Translation and Interpreting 3. New Horizons. Papers from the Third Language International Conference, Elsinore, Denmark, 1995. 1996. viii, 338 pp.

15 **WILSS, Wolfram:** Knowledge and Skills in Translator Behavior. 1996. xiii, 259 pp.

14 **MELBY, Alan K. and Terry WARNER:** The Possibility of Language. A discussion of the nature of language, with implications for human and machine translation. 1995. xxvi, 276 pp.

13 **DELISLE, Jean and Judith WOODSWORTH (eds.):** Translators through History. 1995. xvi, 346 pp.

12 **BERGENHOLTZ, Henning and Sven TARP (eds.):** Manual of Specialised Lexicography. The preparation of specialised dictionaries. 1995. 256 pp.

11 **VINAY, Jean-Paul and Jean DARBELNET:** Comparative Stylistics of French and English. A methodology for translation. Translated and edited by Juan C. Sager, M.-J. Hamel. 1995. xx, 359 pp.

10 **KUSSMAUL, Paul:** Training the Translator. 1995. x, 178 pp.

9   **REY, Alain:** Essays on Terminology. Translated by Juan C. Sager. With an introduction by Bruno de Bessé. 1995. xiv, 223 pp.

8   **GILE, Daniel:** Basic Concepts and Models for Interpreter and Translator Training. 1995. xvi, 278 pp.

7   **BEAUGRANDE, Robert de, Abdullah SHUNNAQ and Mohamed Helmy HELIEL (eds.):** Language, Discourse and Translation in the West and Middle East. 1994. xii, 256 pp.

6   **EDWARDS, Alicia B.:** The Practice of Court Interpreting. 1995. xiii, 192 pp.

5   **DOLLERUP, Cay and Annette LINDEGAARD (eds.):** Teaching Translation and Interpreting 2. Insights, aims and visions. Papers from the Second Language International Conference Elsinore, 1993. 1994. viii, 358 pp.

4   **TOURY, Gideon:** Descriptive Translation Studies – and beyond. 1995. viii, 312 pp.

3   **LAMBERT, Sylvie and Barbara MOSER-MERCER (eds.):** Bridging the Gap. Empirical research in simultaneous interpretation. 1994. 362 pp.

2   **SNELL-HORNBY, Mary, Franz PÖCHHACKER and Klaus KAINDL (eds.):** Translation Studies: An Interdiscipline. Selected papers from the Translation Studies Congress, Vienna, 1992. 1994. xii, 438 pp.

1   **SAGER, Juan C.:** Language Engineering and Translation. Consequences of automation. 1994. xx, 345 pp.